Out of My Mind
A Decade of Faith and Humour
2010 - 2020

Terrie Todd

©2020 Terrie Todd
All Rights Reserved

No part of this book may be reproduced, or stored in a retrieval system, or transmitted in any form or by any means, electronic, mechanical, photocopying, recording, or otherwise, without express written permission of the author.

Scripture taken from the Holy Bible, New International Version. Copyright ©1973, 1978, 1984 International Bible Society. Used by permission of Zondervan Bible Publishers.

Grateful acknowledgment is made to reprint the following public domain hymns:

Brumley, Albert E., 1905-1977, "This World is Not My Home"
Buell, Hattie E., 1834-1910, "A Child of the King"
Crosby, Fanny, 1820-1915, and Lowry, Robert, 1826-1899 "All the Way My Savior Leads Me"
DeArmond, Lizzie, 1847-1936, "My Mother's Prayers Have Followed Me"
Dwight, John Sullivan, 1813-1893, "O Holy Night"
Hoffman, Elisha, 1839-1929, "Leaning on the Everlasting Arms"
Longfellow, Henry Wadsworth, 1807-1882, "I Heard the Bells on Christmas Day"
Martin, W. C. (William Clark), 1864-1914, "My Anchor Holds"
Oatman, Johnson Jr., 1856-1922, "Count Your Blessings"
Simpson, Albert B., 1843-1919, "What Will You Do with Jesus?"
Wesley, Charles, 1707-1788, "Hark the Herald Angels Sing"

Cover photo and Author photo: G. Loewen Photography
ISBN: 9781708216702

To Jon

Thanks for letting me tell our stories,
the flattering and mortifying alike.

CONTENTS

Introduction ix

Section 1: Faith
Where Do You Lean? 3
Driving Miss Terrie 5
Auffahrtsumritt: Say What? 7
Three Lessons from Mama Robin 9
Child of the King 11
Lessons from a Foggy Day 13
Grandma Currier's Quilt 15
Of Life, Death and Road Trips 17
Honey, I'm Home! 19
She Stuck in Her Thumb 21
A Disarming Anniversary 23
Happy Tonsillectomy to Me 25
Music Lessons, Life Lessons 27
Mirror, Mirror on the Wall 29
Glimpsing through the Gap 31
Love in Any Language 33
Battle of the Senses 35
The Kindness of a Stranger 37
New Furniture, Same Old Heart 39
The Day I Stepped Out of Line 41
Remembering Shane 43
How to be Your Own Selfish Pig 45
How Do You Solve a Problem Like Latin? 49
Chess with Keegan 51
Changing the Atmosphere 53
Everybody's Doing It 55
Why the Cross Does Not Have the Final Word   57
Will You Come to My Funeral if I Go to Yours?   59
I Can Only Imagine 61
The Fine Art of Name-Calling 63
The Racist in Us All 65
Stewing to Beat Sixty 67
Florida in February 69
No Such Thing as Unplanned 71
It Tolls for Thee 73
How About Those *Thoughs?* 75

Rickety Bridges	77
What If?	79
Section 2: Marriage & Family	
A Rat Tale	83
Hats Off to Romance	85
On Becoming a Grandmother	87
How to Live with Me for Thirty-Five Years...	89
Pennies (stolen) from Heaven	91
Braver than We Knew	93
One Rascally Long Day	95
My Big Hairy First World Problem	99
Parents, You Really Do Have a Clue	101
Confessions of a Party Pooper	103
Why I'll Never Win Mother of the Year	107
Of Love and Undershorts	109
A Lesson from Winter on Love, Sex & Marriage	111
Filling My Shoes	113
Section 3: The Writing Life	
Hey, Haven't I Seen You Somewhere?	117
Columnist Bids a Fond Farewell	119
She's Baa-aack!	121
Three Facts I Didn't Know I Didn't Know	123
Great Minds	125
Yes or No, the Struggle is Real	127
The Good, Good Father	129
To Plant an Oke	131
A Letter from the Palace	135
From "As If" to "What If"	137
Acrostic Stories	
Ziggy 'Fesses Up	143
Save the Last Dance	145
Quintessa Takes Flight	147
Payday for Stacey	149
A Kitty's Tale	151
Section 4: Health, Fitness, and Life in General	
Diary of a Mad Yogi	155
Out of My Guardian Angel's Mind	157
Living with Chronic Nocturnal Positional Paroxysmal Bechesthesis	159
The Theatrical Side of the Lung Saga	161

A Souper-Dooper Adventure............................	163
Getting Rusty..	165
Just Me and My Man-Flu................................	167
How My Daughter-in-Law Drove Me to Drink	169
I'm Pickin' Up Good Vibrations......................	171
In Which I Discover the Fountain of Youth..	173
Practically a Spa Day.......................................	175
It was a Dark and Spooky Night.....................	177
Strange Doin's are A-Brewin'...........................	179
When God Surprises You.................................	181
Falling Down on Escalators.............................	183
Explaining Social Media to My 15-Year-Old Self...	185
The China Cabinet..	189

Section 5: Special Days & Seasons
Easter

Why My Grandsons Won't Be Getting a Clucking Bunny...	195
The Real Hero...	197
Outrageous Grace..	199
The Value of a Good Question.......................	201
Hands I've Held Dear......................................	203
What's on Your Key Ring?...............................	205
Waiting for the Reunion..................................	207

Mother's Day

Heartstrings...	211
Don't Look Now, But Your Mother's Prayers May Be Following You.................................	213
A Mother's Legacy of Faith and Perseverance	215
Never Too Old to Need Mama.......................	217

Father's Day

God's Got a Great Big Fridge.........................	221
Remembering Dad..	223
A Father's Patience Remembered....................	225
Nine Things I'd Do with Dad.........................	227
Ahead by a Century..	229

Thanksgiving

A Thanksgiving Lesson from Alfalfa...............	233
Five Ways to Be Grateful, even when You Don't Feel Like It..................................	235

Five Things I Don't Have that I Don't Want ... 237
Remembrance Day
  Why I Wear a Poppy ... 241
  Glorious and Free ... 243
  A Bone to Pick ... 245
  Never Been to War ... 247
Christmas
  Heartbreak Hotel ... 251
  Over My Dead Body ... 253
  Our Finest Gifts We Bring ... 255
  And Heaven and Nature Sing ... 257
  The Dawn of Redeeming Grace ... 259
  A Thrill of Hope in an Evil World ... 261
  Their Old Familiar Carols Play ... 263
  The Annual Christmas Newsletter:
    Jots from Joseph ... 265
    Notes from Nessa ... 269
    Greetings from Gavish ... 273
    Musings from Melchior ... 277
  Christmas Presents I Remember
    The Mix Master ... 279
    The Charm Bracelet ... 281
    The Typewriter ... 283
    The Doll House ... 285
    The Radio & Cassette Tape Recorder ... 287
  Christmas Ornaments I Love
    The Glass Nativity Ball ... 289
    The Pageant Bears ... 291
    The Ugliest Little Stocking ... 293
    The Little Wooden Ornaments ... 295
  Christmas Concerts to Remember
    The Marvelous Human Christmas Tree ... 297
    That Time I Played Scrooge ... 299
  Christmas Movies Worth Revisiting
    You'll Shoot Your Eye Out! ... 301
    How the Grinch (Almost) Stole Christmas ... 303
    Elf: A Longing to Belong ... 305
    A Charlie Brown Christmas ... 307
    The Nativity Story ... 309
    New and Glorious Morn ... 311

INTRODUCTION

In September of 2010, my local newspaper in Portage la Prairie, Manitoba (then known as *The Central Plains Herald-Leader*) was advertising for freelance writers. In one of my boldest acts of reckless abandon, I called and requested an appointment with then-editor, Elisha Dacey. Seated in her office and trying not to reveal my nerves, I told her I wanted to write a weekly column. It would be a "slice of life," I said. Some humour, some faith. Hopefully a little of both sprinkled into each. I gave her three samples of the sort of stories I had in mind.

She hired me. I'm forever grateful that she did, and I want to acknowledge all the editors I've worked with over the years. Special thanks to Clarise Klassen who helped me edit this book. Many thanks also go out to the people who have allowed me to tell their stories, and to the readers who have made it all worthwhile.

One of the funniest stories occurred about a year into my column-writing. It was Election day, and when I showed up at the polling station to cast my ballot, I gave the lady my name.

"Are you the Terrie Todd who writes for the Graphic?" she asked.

"Yes, I am."

She frowned a bit. "Huh. I thought you'd be shorter."

I assured her I would try to sound taller from then on.

These ten years have taught me much about the relentlessness of deadlines, the ups and downs of the publishing world, and the challenges of finding something new to say. But they have also revealed the loyalty of readers, the faithfulness of the God I serve, and the utter joy of bringing a smile or a tear or a new thought to someone else's day through the words I write.

Selecting which columns to include in this collection — about a third of the total — was not the quick and easy task I expected. Within these pages, I hope you'll find stories to read aloud at themed events, words to give you a lift in a quiet moment at home, or perhaps a bit of nostalgia because you recall the column as it originally appeared. Most of all, as always, I pray my work draws you just one baby step closer to your Creator.

Terrie Todd
July 2020

P.S. to my American friends, especially the writers and editors among you: I've intentionally chosen to adhere to Canadian spellings and the Canadian Press Style Guide. I trust you can deal with it and hang onto all your hair and teeth.

And finally, if you enjoy this book, I hope you'll check out my novels as well. You can do that from my author page on Amazon by from my blog at www.terrietodd.blogspot.com.

Section 1: Faith

Now faith is confidence in what we hope for and assurance about what we do not see.

Hebrews 11:1

TERRIE TODD

Where Do You Lean?
(Appeared April 9, 2011)

The soundtrack from the 2010 movie *True Grit* includes a song called *Leaning on the Everlasting Arms*. I haven't seen the movie yet, and haven't heard the song much since childhood, but evidently its message is ingrained as deeply as the blood vessels carrying the gift of life through my veins.

I found this out while attending a writers' conference recently. Because it is a Christian conference, they incorporate times of worship singing and prayer. Because they are writers, they choose the wordy old hymns, sung to an upbeat tempo. A good choice for people who love words and who are coming from many varied locales and backgrounds. I happily joined in.

When *Leaning on the Everlasting Arms* was sung, I was immediately transported back to age seven.

It's 1966 and I'm sitting with the other kids in the front row at the Amaranth Sunday School Mission. My big brother has been hospitalized due to a serious accident with a horse, resulting in a head injury. He lies in a coma at Winnipeg Children's Hospital two hours away. Friends and family are praying for him and for us. At seven, I am far from understanding the seriousness of the situation. I have been spending a lot of time at my cousins' house and that makes me happy. Mom and Dad are pretty preoccupied, and that makes me sad. But what happens next will take forty years to fully penetrate my heart with its implications.

My father and mother stand up in front of the congregation and sing a duet. They do not know whether their twelve-year old son will live or die, but in sweet harmony they sing *Leaning on the Everlasting Arms*. And they mean it.

Fast forward to 1995. My husband has been in a horrible farm accident and is about to have his right arm amputated. My friend Melanie tells the story of greeting me in the emergency waiting room that day with a hug. She says I looked her in the eyes and said, "for this, we have Jesus."

Although it didn't appear to faze me as a seven-year-old, it would seem my parents taught their children, by example and by song, where one leans when one is hurting and afraid. A lesson to be treasured.

Where do *you* lean?

What have I to dread, what have I to fear?
Leaning on the everlasting arms;
I have blessed peace with my Lord so near,
Leaning on the everlasting arms.

— Elisha Albright Hoffman, 1887

Driving Miss Terrie
(Appeared August 13, 2011)

Recently, one of my seatbelt buckles broke. Not a big deal if it's just one person driving around, but while still waiting on parts, my husband and I needed to make a trip to Winnipeg. I had two options: travel illegally and unsafely; or, ride in the back seat like Miss Daisy. I opted for the latter.

Normally, no one rides in the back seat unless the front seat is occupied. It causes others to stare — hoping for a glimpse of royalty or celebrity. And me without my tiara.

"Don't worry," my chauffeur/husband said as I waved to my adoring public. "If the lack of a tiara doesn't give you away, the missing hubcap, cracked windshield, and desperate need of a wash job will."

At that point I nicknamed my chauffeur *Killjoy*.

Once I relaxed, I noticed something. With the front passenger seat empty, the view from the back is actually superior to the view from the front, because you not only see out the windshield, you see a lot more along both sides. It was a beautiful summer morning, and I relished the panoramic scenes of yellow canola fields, ripening flax fields, and ... um ... crumbling rows of aging straw bales along the Number One Highway. (Okay, so maybe we don't live in the most picturesque corner of the country.)

My new exalted position got me thinking. If such a slight change, just three feet further back, could make that much difference in my outlook, how much more could be accomplished with a slight shift in other areas?

The next day, our kids from Alberta arrived for a 10-day stay which I'd been gleefully anticipating for months. When the kids from Winnipeg joined us, we were all together for the first time since Christmas 2008. I was one happy mama!

Then the inevitable moment came when they were all gone again and I went through what every mama does ... sniffling my way through the day, wondering whether the joy of reunion was worth the pain of separation.

The following day in church, my perspective changed in an instant. I left my seat to embrace a woman who was commemorating the one-year anniversary of the death of her teenage son. Even with a year of firsts under their belts, this family's heartache had only begun.

I cannot imagine their pain. But by changing my field of vision, I went home flooded with gratitude for all that is still mine. My thoughts shifted from "poor lonely me" to prayers of compassion for those who have real losses to grieve.

Need a new view? Try a different seat.

Auffahrtsumritt: Say What?
(Appeared May 17, 2012)

Ten years ago this week, I woke up to the clanging of church bells from a 900-year-old Catholic church just across the narrow, cobblestone street outside my shuttered window. The four-storey house in which I awoke was half that age. Once the residence for priests of the church, the house belonged to a young family who provided bed and breakfast to guests like us. Descending its solid wooden staircase, I felt awed to feel the polished grooves of centuries of feet under my own. I was in Beromünster, Switzerland, where our daughter Mindy worked as an au pair.

We arrived the day before Ascension Day. The only thing I knew about Ascension Day was that it marks the day Jesus Christ ascended to Heaven, 40 days after his resurrection. But in Beromünster, the day includes an unparalleled custom called "Auffahrtsumritt" in Swiss German.

In the early morning, a colourful group of local clergy and other religious figures leaves the town on horseback, along with some 200 believers. Large crowds follow on foot, praying blessings on the fields within the boundary line. The local priest leads the way, escorted by mounted soldiers, a brass band, church choir, and numerous crosses and flags. Stops are made at specific places, where readings are given.

In the early afternoon, the group completes the circle and enters the town to more ringing of bells. A benediction pronounced in front of the church brings the pageantry to a close.

I agreed to participate with Mindy in the prayer walk. Starting at 5:00 a.m. (relatively easy to my jet-lagged body), we walked from village to village. It was a gorgeous day and those around us prayed through their rosaries as they walked. Mindy and I, however, having been separated 10 long months, were less inclined to pray. Our constant chatter earned us at least one impatient shushing from one of the faithful.

Ignorant foreigners that we were, I felt embarrassed and chastised but far too happy to let it bother me for long. Who could feel anything but euphoric – reunited with my daughter, surrounded by fragrant, rolling meadows, the constant ringing of sheep bells, and gorgeous mountains in every direction? The breath-taking beauty around us left me longing for more.

And so it should. Though my outward behaviour may have appeared disrespectful, I celebrated Ascension Day embracing Jesus' promise that where he was going, I could one day follow.

Happy Ascension Day!

Three Lessons from Momma Robin
(Appeared May 31, 2012)

When a pair of robins began construction in the cedar shrub outside our kitchen window, I figured the only decent thing to do was stay out of the kitchen for a couple of months and give them their space. My husband, however, decided closing the venetian blind between us and the nest would grant them all the privacy required. Bummer.

This process is providing a delightful education. Here are three lessons I have observed so far.

Number One: Do the thing that lies within you to do. With fascination, I watched the robins create the nest, placing the twigs just so, then tamping them into place with their little feet. I couldn't build a nest like that without a kit of supplies, written instructions, and a whole lot of super glue. Even then, it would be shaped all wrong and probably fall apart in the first wind.

Robins, however, can't not build a nest. It's what they are hard-wired to do.

I believe God has placed within each of us at least one thing we "can't not" do. Be it music, teaching, building, growing flowers — you name it — we know deep down we are hard-wired to do that thing. The difference between robins and humans is, we have a choice. We can abandon our one thing, and in the face of opposition, we often do.

But it's never too late to start again. The world needs your one thing, even when you're tired or discouraged and would rather let it lie. A half-built nest is worthless.

Number Two: Defend what you've been given to defend. Over the course of three days, Momma Robin laid three beautiful blue eggs and began the tenacious process of incubation. I knew there would be no more opening the window to snap photos unless I wanted a close-up of a bird attack. Just coming near the window earned me an instant open beak of warning. I wondered if she feels inclined to fly away instead, never to return.

What have you been called to protect and fight for? Family? The poor? The abused? Your own gifts and talents? Guaranteed, your thing to protect will be threatened and attacked. The enemy of your soul wants your one thing destroyed, not blessing the world like it was intended. You'll be tempted to let him win, to step aside and surrender because it's easier. Please don't stop fighting when fighting is right.

Number Three: Hang on tight through the storms. When the May 14th windstorm hit Portage la Prairie, we watched from the safety of our house while the cedar bush by the kitchen window swayed and swirled. What would Momma Robin do? Could she hang on? Would she find a safer place? Would the nest come apart, dropping the eggs to the ground?

Though I can't imagine how fast her tiny heart must have been beating, she held firm. This chick knows her priorities.

I want to hang tough through the storms of life, too. And they do come, to all of us. Some bring more damage than others, but their threats seldom equal our fears. Morning eventually comes, bringing calm and sunshine and hope.

That's a lot of education from such a small creature — and all before the eggs hatched. Somehow, I suspect there is more to come.

Child of the King
(Appeared October 11, 2012)

So apparently, I am related to Elvis Presley. At a family wedding recently, my siblings informed me our dad's sister's husband's first cousin was Elvis Presley's mother. Guess that explains my hunka-hunka burnin' personality.

"Well, anybody could say that," I argued. But they insisted, giving me a look that says, "You ain't nuthin' but a hound dog." How had I remained ignorant of this important piece of trivia when they'd all known it forever?

"Don't be cruel," I said.

We all wondered the same thing: when would a piece of the Graceland pie come our way? The cheques must be in the mail.

Pondering what I'll do with my share when it arrives, it occurred to me that Elvis's daughter was married to the late Michael Jackson for a couple of years. Imagine the loot accompanying THAT union! When I was 13 years old and plastering my bedroom walls with pages torn from *Tiger Beat* magazine and ruining the fake woodgrain wallpaper by taping up pictures of the Jackson Five (right between Donny Osmond and David Cassidy), it never occurred to me that little Michael and I would one day be kin. But it does explain the remarkable resemblance.

Checking out the branches of Elvis's family tree online, I never did find myself — or even his mom's cousin who married Dad's sister. But I did learn some things I didn't know, probably common knowledge to hard-core Elvis fans. Did you know his maternal great-great-great-grandmother, Morning White Dove, was a full-blooded Cherokee Indian? His paternal great-grandmother, Rosella, bore nine children out of wedlock and never once revealed to her children who their fathers were.

His maternal grandparents were first cousins (the inspiration for "Kissin' Cousins?") He had an identical twin who was stillborn, named Jesse Garon. Imagine if there had been two of them. Methinks somebody's blue suede shoes might have been stepped on after all.

Isn't it interesting how we feel self-important in unearthing a connection to the rich and famous, regardless how all-shook-up their lineage? The truth is, go back far enough and you'll eventually discover we are all connected. Humbling, ain't it?

I confess, I've never taken much interest in genealogy. I figure it doesn't really matter when you've been adopted by the most famous King of all. The documentation goes back much farther than the internet, too. The Bible tells me things like:

"But to all who believed him and accepted him, he gave the right to become children of God." (John 1:12)

"For you are all the children of God by faith in Christ Jesus." (Galatians 3:26); and

"See how very much our Father loves us, for he calls us his children, and that is what we are!" (I John 3).

I could go on.

In her hymn, *Child of the King*, Harriett Buell wrote:

I once was an outcast stranger on earth,
a sinner by choice and an alien by birth.
But I've been adopted, my name's written down;
an heir to a mansion, a robe, and a crown.

Now that's an inheritance worth waiting for.

Lessons from a Foggy Day
(Appeared November 22, 2012)

I confess I'm a wimp when it comes to winter driving, especially at night. Being married to a professional driver has me spoiled. Last weekend, my chauffeur down with a cold, I missed out on seeing our son's girlfriend in one of her final university-level dance recitals because I was too chicken to make the trip alone. I felt disappointed in myself for being such an old granny, but it didn't seem worth the risk.

The next day, however, I ventured out on my own so as not to miss our grandson's third birthday party while Grandpa remained home in bed. It's only a half-hour down the highway, but the intense fog made me determined to return home before dark.

It turned into an insightful trip when I discovered how much fog is like life. In fog and in life:

#1. You can see only far enough to take the next step.

The fog hung so thick, I was nearly on top of road signs before I saw them. Though I desperately wished to see further down the road, I could not. Still, enough pavement always remained visible to keep me moving forward.

In life, I often think I'd love to know how things are going to turn out. What will happen next year? Where will I be in five? When will I die and how?

But I don't need to know those things today. I know what I need to know for the next tentative step of my journey, and that's okay.

#2. Just because conditions aren't ideal doesn't mean beauty cannot live there.

So intent was I on the road ahead, so concerned about my decreased visibility, I almost missed it. The fog had turned the trees into a glorious hoarfrost wonderland. Beauty surrounded me if only I took the time to notice.

Life is never so dark or dreary that beauty is not nearby, waiting quietly. Grief and splendour can co-exist. Trouble and loveliness can walk hand-in-hand. Life will never be perfect. In fact, it is pretty much always difficult. But it will never be without some measure of beauty, either. Take time to look for it.

#3. Sometimes getting ahead means slowing down.
Cars passed me in the fog, even though I drove the maximum speed limit. What was their big hurry? If surprised by a deer or a stopped vehicle ahead, they'd have no chance. I held steady to my slower pace and arrived at my destination just fine.

We pack so much pressure and urgency into our days. Our Creator instructed us to rest one day in every seven because he knows what our bodies, minds and spirits need. But even those of us who claim to follow him often fill our Sabbath day with activities not necessarily restful. Then we wonder why we're weary, why our wheels only spin.

In life, sometimes getting ahead means not only slowing down, but sitting still.

Are you in a foggy time of life right now? Wish you could see more? Can't find the beauty in it? Slow down. Look around. Be still.

You'll get there.

Grandma Currier's Quilt
(Appeared April 11, 2013)

All of four feet-nine inches tall and hard of hearing, Grandma Currier was as full of vim and vinegar as anyone I know. She wasn't really my grandmother. We weren't even related. But, 500 miles from home and attending a Christian high school with her real granddaughter, I was privileged to be included in many a weekend in her home. You wouldn't think such a tiny woman could intimidate me. But this was not a lady I wanted to tangle with, and she had my full respect. I was treated as one of her own, with the same rights and responsibilities: midnight curfew; do the dishes; sleep as late as you want on Saturday; church on Sunday.

Grandma Currier was famous for her homemade quilts. I especially admired the denim patch quilts she created for each of her grandkids, every square embroidered with a unique picture. I was delighted when, on the birth of my firstborn, I received an appliquéd baby quilt. I quickly declared it too beautiful for anything except hanging on the wall. There it hung through my second and third babies and was all too soon folded and relegated to a closet shelf. That is, until the year the Romanian orphans were in the media on a daily basis. News clips showing neglected children huddled together without the basics of survival prompted me to put together a care package to send over with a local adoptive parent. It seemed the least I could do. In an uncharacteristic act of generous abandon, I included the beautiful baby quilt, imagining how special it might become to a needy child.

On occasion, I thought of the little quilt and regretted parting with it, especially the day I learned Grandma Currier had died. It would have been nice to have something to remember her by, but I chastised myself for being so self-centered and chose to believe she would have approved of my gift.

Then, the unexpected happened.

I didn't know my in-laws were the owners of one of Grandma Currier's quilts — a full-size one, big enough to serve as a bedspread on a double bed. On a visit to our home, they left the quilt with us, with instructions to return it to Donna — Grandma Currier's daughter. Perhaps she'd like to have it in memory.

Before we had a chance to do so, however, I received a call from Donna. "I hear you're holding one of my mom's quilts for me," she said. "But since I already have several, I wondered if you might like to keep it."

It still graces our guestroom bed.

They say you can't out-give God. What do you suppose might happen if we ever really tried?

Of Life, Death and Road Trips
(Appeared May 2, 2013)

I may be the only person in the history of the world to have made a round trip from Portage la Prairie to Three Hills, Alberta, as the lone female in a 1992 Cadillac with three generations of Todd boys.

My husband, our elder son, and two of his sons escorted me, the two little ones travelling in pajamas since we pulled them straight from their beds at 5:00 a.m. I didn't have to drive, but took my turn entertaining the five- and three-year-old boys in the back seat. Lucky for us, their mother had brilliantly packed enough books, toys and snacks to make this relatively easy.

A snowstorm and engine failure contributed richly to our adventure, especially when you take into account we'd already been cooped up in the car for 12 hours by that point. Sketchy cell service, CAA, a tow truck and eventual rescue by yet another Todd boy — my brother-in-law — entered into the story as well. Not to mention (okay, I'm mentioning it) a certain writer's full bladder. Ladies, have you ever tried to "relax" on the side of the highway, in broad daylight, with nothing to hide behind but your car, while being pelted with snow and sleet? Enough said.

For the ride home four days later, our younger son joined us too. This time, we made it without incident except for the extra sardine can-esque squishiness. As always, I felt overjoyed to see Portage and my own bed.

The purpose of this multi-generational trip was to say our goodbyes (I won't say "final" because we'll see him again) to my father-in-law, and to hopefully bring a little joy into the heart of Mom/Grandma/Great-grandma Todd. Tears and laughter both played parts in our time together. Our grief mingled with relief to know Dad is free at last from the insidious thievery of Alzheimer's disease.

Hubby and I spent a day sorting through piles of family albums, selecting and scanning photos, and creating a

PowerPoint show to play at the memorial service. Combined with some powerful music, it provided a deeply meaningful tribute to Dad's life.

I saw bits of my father-in-law's life I'd never witnessed. Snapshots of his childhood, teen years and early adulthood served to remind us, not only of the brevity of life, but of all the elements that combine to make us who we are. We were reminded of the many children he and Mom invested in, besides their own, as they foster-parented for 20 years. Something sobering happens when you watch 80 years go by in a 10-minute slide show, like those time-lapse videos of a flower budding, coming into full bloom, then shrivelling back to nothing in mere seconds.

We celebrated Dad's life with sadness, yes, but also with joyful anticipation. We know he is reunited with his parents, siblings and son, and we will share in that reunion in less time than we imagine. Our faith in Jesus assures us we don't need to grieve "as those who have no hope."

The parallels between life and road trips have not gone unnoticed. While we're in the thick of it, the way seems long and the trials hard to bear. But when it's done and we've made it home, those trials dwindle into whimsical stories to tell and mere circumstances that shaped us into stronger people. The only truly crucial things, in both life and road trips, are the precious people with whom we share the journey, and reaching our desired destination.

Happy trails.

Honey, I'm Home!
(Appeared July 25, 2013)

I'm writing this, my first column from our new house, surrounded by packed boxes still stacked high and rain pouring out the window. But the electric fireplace blazes, tea is on, and I am home.

Call us late bloomers. After 36 years of marriage, for the first time ever, Hubby and I own both the house we live in and the property on which it sits. Having raised three terrific people to adulthood in a mobile home, I understand a "real house" is not essential to a good life. But I still gotta say, it feels great to call it ours.

Our previous move was a temporary arrangement. Two years grew to four. The place before that was supposed to be temporary, but "a year or two" morphed into seven. We leased the place before that a year at a time, always hoping to buy "maybe next year," as soon as the owner agreed to sell. After 15 years, we gave up and moved.

The temporary nature of our homes has felt unsettling, unmotivating, and sometimes, disheartening. Now, as long as we pay our mortgage and property taxes, we can stay. We can paint our walls periwinkle blue and Persian melon. We can let the weeds grow, and so far we've done a superb job of that.

If you've ever purchased a home, you already know every house comes with its quirks and things that go bump in the night. Some of these you find quickly, like discovering your basement landing has only one light switch, and it's upstairs. Other secrets will reveal themselves over time. It's the nature of home ownership, or, as some call it, the money pit.

And even if you could create the perfect house filled with impeccable furnishings and fixtures, it's only a matter of time before the law of entropy rears its ugly head – everything tends toward disorder. (Which shoots a massive hole in the theory of evolution, but that's a topic for another day.) Chances are, you'll ding up the new paint or scuff the floor just moving in furniture. If it's perfection you need, don't look for it on this planet. And if you find it, it won't last.

For whether you live in a mortgage-free mansion or a one-room apartment, the truth is, it's all temporary. The day approaches when we will move on, some of us straight to a pine box and some of us via the scenic route of assisted living, nursing home and hospital. There's no getting around it.

But I, for one, possess no desire to "get around it."

On the contrary. I can relax about the quirks of my house, the repairs that will inevitably become necessary, and the impermanence of it all. You see, the most talented carpenter who ever walked the planet is preparing a home for me. The same designer who paints the sunset is choosing the colours. It's going to be flawlessly and completely custom-designed especially for me by the One who created me and knows me better than I know myself. And it will never wear out. How do I know? One of the last things Jesus told his disciples before he went back to his Father was: "I am going to prepare a place for you, so that where I am, there you may be also."

An old spiritual by Mary Reeves Davis says:
This world is not my home, I'm just a-passin' through.
My treasures are laid up somewhere beyond the blue.
The angels beckon me from Heaven's open door,
and I can't feel at home in this world anymore.

She Stuck in Her Thumb ...
(Appeared September 12, 2013)

Last May, when we first viewed our new home, the one and only tree on the property was exploding with gorgeous white blossoms and sashaying in the breeze like Amy Adams at the Oscars. It looked and smelled wonderful! Still, I suspected it might bear those sour, tiny plums that create a major mess in the yard and wondered how long it would take us to hate the tree. A taste of its fruit in late July confirmed my notion.

But I was wrong.

I needed a little more patience. When our friend Noel Smith saw the tree, he immediately identified it as a Pembina Plum and assured us it was healthy and would produce edible fruit. By late August, we were picking the loveliest, juiciest, sweetest plums and eating them simply for the pleasure of it. My daughter-in-law used a bunch for smoothies, crepe sauce, and plain-ol' feeding her brood of boys. I finally tossed the last handful into my juicer to keep our kitchen's fruit fly population under control. And yes, the wasps and compost site accepted their share of the windfall.

I've since learned from Linda Szumilak that her dad, Roman Lebedynski, planted the tree for his neighbour more than 40 years ago. I never met Roman, nor the neighbor who built our house. I just get to enjoy the results of their labour.

In Joshua 24, God tells his people, "I gave you land you had not worked on, and I gave you towns you did not build — the towns where you are now living. I gave you vineyards and olive groves for food, though you did not plant them."

When you think about it, we each inherited things we held no control over. If you're like me, it's easy to grumble about the stuff we'd just as soon trade, like your mother's nose or your dad's legs. Maybe you were blessed with a genetic disease or the famous family temper. Perhaps your parents handed down a legacy of poverty or alcohol abuse and you struggle with the same through no fault of your own.

But we forget the many good things that come our way through no fault of our own, every day. Think about your town, your school, your church. Others cleared the land, raised the funds, constructed the buildings, invoked God's assistance, paved the streets, planted the crops, wrote the books, and invented the conveniences that enrich our lives. Others sacrificed so you could have. If you think about it enough, you can see this through every moment of your day, from the time your feet hit the floor in the morning. We are the beneficiaries of those who have gone before.

The twelfth century theologian and author John of Salisbury said, "We are like dwarfs sitting on the shoulders of giants. We see more, and things that are more distant, than they did, not because our sight is superior or because we are taller than they, but because they raise us up, and by their great stature add to ours."

What are you planting today that future generations will reap?

A Disarming Anniversary
(Appeared September 26, 2013)

As of next week, I have been married for 36 years, half of them to a right-handed man and half to a left-handed one. I suppose you could argue it's the same man. Like greatness, some people are born left-handed and others have left-handedness thrust upon them.

Many families can name a day that slashed a giant mark across their life's timeline, forever dividing "before" from "after." For us, it was September 29, 1995: the day Hubby lost an argument with a piece of farm machinery and subsequently, his right arm.

Once, after we described this before-and-after concept in a group setting, a friend nodded knowingly, then embarrassed herself by calling the event "The Great Cut-Off." We all laughed wildly and learned laughter really can help.

To prove it, Hubby's been known to accuse long-winded people of talking his arm off.

I once told my husband he'd make a great magician because he has nothing up his sleeve.

And when he took too long in Polo Park one day, I threatened to leave him behind, reasoning he could hitchhike home since he still had a thumb.

I know. Be quiet.

Did you know there are actually advantages to being left-handed?

Everyone knows you can't sit left of a lefty at the dinner table, or you'll bump elbows. Smart southpaws use this to their advantage to gain a spot with more space.

Apparently, many more words can be typed solely with the left hand than with the right.

And southpaws also have an easier time writing in Hebrew because it's written from right to left. How handy is that?

However, finding advantages to being one-handed proved a greater challenge. But if he ever visits Belarus, where clapping is outlawed because dissidents use applause as a form of protest, it is unlikely Hubby will be arrested. Good to know.

Two days after his accident, we celebrated our 18th wedding anniversary in the hospital. I remember falling asleep that night with the words of our marriage vows running through my head: "For better or for worse, for richer or for poorer, in sickness and in health, 'til death do us part." I particularly focused on the "for worse ... for poorer ... in sickness" sections. In the following weeks and months, all three would surface, but death had not parted us yet and for that, I was grateful. Neither of us knew there would be ugly days ahead when we would wish it had. I won't lie to you — it sucks.

But the God who promises to walk with us through the dark valleys keeps his word. In those early days, a peace settled over our home that can only be the result of hundreds of prayers raised on our behalf. We gained a new reverence for life, more gratitude for community, and a deeper perspective on what matters. We grew closer as a family and felt ourselves carried along by a sweet spirit. Supportive friends and strangers blessed us in countless practical ways. I like to think our kids are more kindhearted people because this happened to us.

Would we get Hubby's arm back if we could? In a heartbeat.

But it's been my bittersweet privilege to observe a man grow in his faith when he might have scorned it forever. Where he could display bitterness, I've seen him instead demonstrate compassion toward fellow strugglers because everyone carries their burden of seen and unseen pain. I've watched him tackle the daily challenges of one-handedness in a two-handed world with patience, determination, courage and grace. I am certain I would not have done as well, and I am proud of my lefty.

Happy Anniversaries, Jon. And safe harvest, everyone.

Happy Tonsillectomy to Me
(Appeared March 6, 2014)

It was probably *Marcus Welby, MD*, or a similar type of show. Age eight or nine when I watched it, the memory is fuzzy. All I recall about the story is some kid stuck in the hospital for their birthday. The child's family, along with a dozen hospital staff, surrounded the bed, presenting the birthday kid with helium balloons while singing "Happy Birthday." Everyone was smiling, including the not-very-sick-looking centre of attention.

So when told I would be getting my tonsils removed the day before my 10th birthday, it was not a difficult sell. My inner drama queen welcomed the adventure, the attention, the sympathy, the break from school, and the helium balloons I was sure to receive. Maybe I'd even get Dr. Welby's autograph.

The day before my surgery, my parents drove the 60 miles from Amaranth and checked me into the Portage Hospital where I spent a rather enjoyable evening reading in bed. A nice young lady came around to give me a back rub. (Things were much different in 1969!)

The next morning, Dr. Collier yanked out my tonsils. I remember the surprise of waking in more pain than I'd ever experienced and wishing they'd let me go back to sleep. The rest of that day remains a blur, except for the frequent offerings of ice cream, sherbet and Jell-O — all of which I stubbornly refused in order to avoid the pain of swallowing.

The following morning, I felt alert enough to know it was my birthday. I tried to share this information with the first adult who came around, but I could only whisper. My voice was gone and I couldn't make her understand me. I was still in pain, I couldn't talk, and I hadn't seen my family since they left me there. What a relief when Dad arrived mid-afternoon to take me home! I'm sure some acknowledgement of my birthday awaited me there, but all I remember is I didn't speak or eat for a week.

Forty-five years and several surgeries later, this memory came back with my recent birthday and made me cry for that disappointed 10-year-old. Why it chose to surface now, I'm not certain. But something about elaborate children's birthday parties has always bugged me — a fact which, in itself, bugged me. Why did I hold such a miserly attitude? Why couldn't I fully engage and celebrate a child's life with joy, instead of begrudgingly feeling kids don't "deserve" showers of toys and attention merely for staying alive one more year? Could my mature, 55-year-old self seriously feel jealous of little kids?

Yep, I think she could. More precisely, the little girl inside her could.

Ignoring the hurts of childhood, big or small, does not make us better adults. But exploring them can. You may need help with the tougher ones, but don't sweep them under the rug. It pays to take heed when you experience strong emotions over events that seem trivial or when memories emerge. Time does not heal all wounds. God does. In time. When we invite him into the middle of them.

I think even Dr. Welby might agree.

Music Lessons, Life Lessons
(Appeared March 20, 2014)

It's been 17 months since I first picked up a saxophone. I may not play well, but I play loud. I cannot, in fact, seem to get the hang of playing anything other than loud. My new motto is the first verse of the 100th Psalm. Look it up.

As a kid suffering my way through the interminable torment of piano practices, I didn't detect the more subtle life lessons I'm discovering from my saxophone. I like to pretend that's because I'm mature and insightful now. Maybe it's only because I write a column now and need to churn out something mature and insightful-sounding every week. Here, for your own interminable torment, are some of my insights:

#1. Practice pays.

This may seem obvious, but by the time we're in our fifties, most of us figure we've mastered whatever skills we're going to master and everything else remains status-quo. When I first attempted the saxophone, practice times were torture because I was puffing, sweating and squawking. But the worst of it was my lips. They just couldn't hold up through an entire song.

But I'm tightfisted enough that if I'm going to cough up money for lessons, I'm going to make sure I get the most bang for my buck — which means a half hour every day with my sax. Lately I've noticed I can hit the high and low notes I couldn't hit before, I'm not panting, and my lips don't give out. How did that happen? Practice. What was true when we were kids still holds.

Think what might happen if we practiced relational skills with the same diligence.

#2. Everybody has their unique style.

It took a year for my teacher, Ritchard, and I to notice the uniqueness of our hands. He couldn't understand why I had so much trouble "rolling" my thumb from the thumb rest onto the octave key and back, like he does. When I watched him do it, I pointed out that my thumbs don't curl backwards the way a lot of thumbs do. Mine are the "one-way only" kind, and no amount of practice will change their tree-stumpiness.

"Would you look at that," Ritchard said. "I've never seen that before."

It was a relief to know I'm a freak of nature. It provides a great excuse to develop my own way of compensating.

Think what might happen if we let others do things their way instead of insisting ours is the only one.

#3. Harmony makes everything better.

My favourite times in this journey are the last 10 minutes of every lesson, when Ritchard tunes his sax to mine and we play duets. Oh, there are still plenty of errors. One of us tends to get the giggles, I won't say who. But there's something about playing in harmony with another that improves everything by more than the sum of its parts. Just like life.

Think what might happen if we could learn to live in harmony and in tune with each other.

#4. A deeper purpose means everything.

I spent the first several weeks playing ditties like *Hot Cross Buns* and *Jingle Bells*, and I was having fun. But when Ritchard set a book of worship songs on the stand and I heard myself playing the melody of *I Love You, Lord*, something shifted. Though no one sang along, the familiar words rang in my head and suddenly I felt so moved, I could hardly read the page for tears.

How this can be true, I don't fully understand, but the God of creation heard my frail but heartfelt attempts and took joy in them.

Think what might happen if we applied this to every action, every moment of our lives.

Mirror, Mirror on the Wall
(Appeared March 27, 2014)

Have you seen the Facebook challenge where one woman nominates another to post a photo of herself devoid of makeup and hairstyling? The purpose of this exercise, if I understand it, is to celebrate the natural beauty of all women and to recognize that what's on the inside is what makes a woman truly beautiful.

I started wearing makeup when I was two, the time I resourcefully pulled out Mom's dresser drawers to form a ladder to its surface, where her Avon awaited. After a 12-year hiatus, I began using makeup again as a sophisticated eighth grader and never looked back.

This puts me at a disadvantage on those rare occasions when I venture out in public without my Maybelline. People tend to look at me with concern. "Are you feeling all right? You look tired."

I never know whether to milk it for the sympathy or to admit I'm fine, this is just my face. It makes me regret ever starting with the cosmetics.

On the flip side, women who don't wear makeup daily look especially awesome on those special occasions when they do. My beautiful daughter-in-law, Dara, is one of these smart ladies. My advice to young girls? Don't start! The best cosmetic you can ever wear is a genuine smile.

Here's the beauty challenge I'd like to propose, if I could have my wish: for every woman to hear the words "you're beautiful" from someone she loves every day for one month and watch what happens. We'd see a lot more healthy women. Healthy women are happier women. Happy women make for happy homes. Happy homes make for happy communities, and happy communities make for a happy world.

Too simple? Of course. But what could it hurt to try?

The January 2014 cover of *People* magazine featured Christy Brinkley, at 60, modeling a swimsuit. Someone left a copy in our coffee room at work and the conversation among my female co-workers and myself sounded like:

"Well, she's obviously had a lot of work done."

"Maybe if I had a personal trainer ..."

"The picture's obviously air-brushed ..."

"Maybe if I had her money ..."

"She doesn't have to work; she can exercise all day ..."

"Maybe if I had my own private chef ..."

"Maybe if I had my own private hair and makeup professional ..."

It felt as if we were trying to convince ourselves that, given enough money, we'd all look just as good as Brinkley. I hate to break it to you, girls, but all the money in the world isn't going to make any of us look that gorgeous. If seen next to Christie Brinkley, I would get asked if I were her mother, even though she's five years my senior. I'd reply, "Actually, I'm her grandmother. Lookin' pretty good for 105, eh?"

The magazine's cover promised to reveal Brinkley's diet and fitness tips. It didn't mention her four divorces.

In her book, *Do You Think I'm Beautiful?* Angela Thomas maintains this is the question attached to the soul of every woman; that inside each of us lives a skirt-twirling little girl who secretly aches for a fairy godmother to wave a wand and transform her into the princess she has always longed to be. To make her beautiful. Captivating. Adored.

I believe beauty and the appreciation of it were placed in us by our maker, that true beauty is an essence given to every woman at her creation. But, like so many gifts, this fallen world has distorted beauty into something so twisted people are willing to mutilate themselves in its pursuit. Meanwhile, our hearts cry out for a love that comes only from the one who made us, the one who first saw us as beautiful, and the one who always will.

Glimpsing Through the Gap
(Appeared June 19, 2014)

My backyard neighbours have temporarily removed a portion of the privacy fence between our properties in order to put up a new garage. The gap in the fence enables me to see directly into their yard from my kitchen window. Not that I'm a snoop or anything. I'm just sayin.'

As long as the fence stood uninterrupted, all I could see over the top was a clothesline, a few bird feeders, and the squirrels who use them. I had no idea the yard was actually a gorgeous, park-like work of art! We are clearly getting the better end of this deal.

Now, while I'm washing dishes, instead of feasting my eyes on my own pathetic attempt at a garden and a boring white fence, I can pretend the other man's greener grass is an extension of our own. By focusing just a little further away, my whole perspective changes. Since the gap, I've also spoken more to the neighbours and met a sweet, 17-year-old cat I never knew lived there.

I think I'll miss the gap when the work is completed. Maybe privacy is overrated.

What lovely views do we miss because we allow fences to block our vision? Fences come in many forms. Anxiety, illness, grudges, loss and strained relationships can create a fence between what we're looking at and what we could be looking at. We're so focused on the problem it becomes a barrier to our vision. For example, if you are stressed out over money troubles and you learned you were going to inherit a million dollars next month, your focus would change, even though your bills remained unpaid in the moment. Am I right?

For me, struggling with daily physical pain shortens my sight incredibly. Sometimes all I can see is the here and now. This highly unattractive fence makes me think negative thoughts. *This hurts. I don't like it. I don't want to live like this. It's hopeless. I can't cope.*

But when I choose to focus on something better, even if it's farther away and all I have to peer through is a tiny knothole, the fence blurs and begins to diminish. I realize a greater truth exists on the other side of the fence. A future worthy of joyful anticipation awaits. I possess reasons to remain thankful and glad.

You can find one of these knothole promises in the first chapter of Peter's first epistle:

"Now we live with great expectation, and we have a priceless inheritance — an inheritance that is kept in heaven for you, pure and undefiled, beyond the reach of change and decay. And through your faith, God is protecting you by his power until you receive this salvation, which is ready to be revealed on the last day for all to see.

"So be truly glad. There is wonderful joy ahead, even though you have to endure many trials for a little while. These trials will show that your faith is genuine. It is being tested as fire tests and purifies gold — though your faith is far more precious than mere gold. So when your faith remains strong through many trials, it will bring you much praise and glory and honour on the day when Jesus Christ is revealed to the whole world."

By focusing just a little further away, your whole perspective changes.

Love in Any Language
(Appeared July 31, 2014)

In 2002, we visited Switzerland and while there, attended a Sunday morning service at an upbeat church in Sursee. While we looked like most of the people in attendance, we could only smile and nod as folks greeted us warmly and shook our hands. Though we couldn't understand the sermon, we knew that family surrounded us — our spiritual family. When the worship music began, we tried to follow along with the German words on the overhead screen. As we joined in praise to God as best we could, I was struck with a brief glimpse of how it will be when we gather around the throne of God in heaven, every tribe and tongue worshipping together. The thought brought goose bumps and tears.

In 2014, Hubby and I walked the five blocks from our house to North Memorial Park where the Harvest Call First Nation Church had set up a big white tent for its nightly gospel meetings.

I won't lie. It felt out of my comfort zone. That may sound odd coming from someone who has attended church all her life. But I'm not First Nations. I'm not Pentecostal. I'm not a fan of country gospel-style music, and I'm not used to services that go on past my bedtime. Part of me just wanted a new experience. Part of me wanted to better understand my First Nations neighbours. Part of me wanted to know how the courageous handful of First Nations people who attend my church must feel. Mostly, I hoped to have my heart uplifted.

This time, we did not look like most of the other people in attendance. But this time, we could communicate easily and a saw a few familiar faces. (Plus, we knew we could be home within minutes if things got weird.)

We tapped our toes as the singers and musicians warmed up and the tent gradually filled. We listened to wonderfully encouraging stories from people whose lives changed for the better because of their faith, many of whom testify they would not even be alive today were it not for Christ.

When Pastor Bernice Catcheway officially opened the night with her powerful prayer for our city, I once again experienced what I had in Switzerland. This time, I could understand every word, and this time, it occurred in my own community. But again, I was struck with a glimpse of how it will be when we gather around the throne of God in heaven, every tribe and tongue worshipping the same God together. Again, the thought brought goose bumps and tears.

I love how Jesus makes sisters and brothers out of strangers, regardless of colour, customs or language.

When God showed the Apostle John the future, here is one of the things he described: "After this I looked, and there before me was a great multitude that no one could count, from every nation, tribe, people and language, standing before the throne and before the Lamb. They were wearing white robes and were holding palm branches in their hands." (Revelation 7:9)

When that day comes, I won't feel out of place. I'll understand every word. I'll know all the lyrics to every song. And I won't be too tired to stick around for the food.

I don't know about you, but I can hardly wait.

Battle of the Senses
(Appeared August 7, 2014)

My five senses entered into a philosophical debate about the delights of summer.

As usual, my mouth started it. "The rest of you can only hope to fathom the awesomeness of summer," it said. "You'll never sink your teeth into cool watermelon or snap into a juicy carrot fresh from the garden or dig into a buttered cob of sweet corn. You can't imagine the refreshment of a cool drink after a day of work in the sun, or the bliss of sharing a Popsicle with someone you love. And don't even get me started on ripe strawberries, new potatoes, juicy peaches or home-grown tomatoes. I'm watering just thinking about it!"

My eyes begged to differ. "You have no idea," they said. "You've never seen a little girl in a sundress or children making sandcastles on the beach. You can't see the 50 shades of green framed by the picture window, or the vivid reds, oranges and yellows of nasturtiums, the purples and pinks of pansies and petunias. You can't imagine the splendour of sailboats on the sparkling lake or the brilliance of a canola field in glorious, golden bloom, or bright pink toenails on tanned and sandaled feet. And how do I begin to explain a rainbow? Or fireworks bursting against the black sky?"

That's when my ears chimed in. "Fireworks? A racket, if you ask me. But then you can't hear what I hear. From the early morning melodies of hundreds of birds to the late-night chirping of bullfrogs and crickets, summer is kind to me. I wish you could hear the laughter and splashing around a kiddie pool, the delicate buzz of a bee pollinating the hydrangeas, the goofy chatter of squirrels, the crack of a bat against a baseball, rain tapping on the window, or the delights of an open-air concert in the park. You'll never know the joy an ice-cream truck's tinny tune offers. Even the roar of a lawn mower and the snap-snap-snapping of flip-flops on feet are music to me."

At the mention of feet, my nose couldn't stop twitching. "Are you kidding me? I knows I've got the best of it and if you'd ever smelled lilacs in full bloom, you would knows it too. Not to mention the scent of roses, lilies, or freshly cut grass. all these smells are intensified after a rain. And that's not all! You can't imagine the earthy fragrance of fresh garden beets simmering in the kitchen, the tantalizing aroma of grilling steaks, or the comforting scent of sheets dried outdoors. Why, I even like the coconutty smell of sunscreen!"

My Sense of Touch felt drawn into the discussion, too. "You all make me laugh. The rest of you are limited to one receptor, or two at most. But me! I can feel with hands, feet, everything! You haven't lived until you've felt warm sand or lush grass under bare feet. You can't possibly understand the soothing warmth of sunshine on skin or the utter relief of a gentle breeze on a hot day. You'll never experience the refreshing shock of plunging your hot body into a pool of cold water, or be rocked gently to sleep in a hammock, or embrace the heat of a campfire after dark."

My senses continued to argue, trying to outdo each other, but I tuned them out. I know it's me who is the lucky one. I'm privileged to enjoy summer using all five senses when even just one would be amazing and worthy of my gratitude. "Every good and perfect gift is from above, coming down from the Father of the heavenly lights ..." (James 1:17)

The Kindness of a Stranger
(Appeared August 14, 2014)

It happened in a gas station restroom in Dunseith, North Dakota. In August of 1978, we'd been married for 10 months and were driving from Manitoba to Texas to resume another school year. The Dunseith restroom offered those flat, dry soap leaves you may remember. The soap got caught under my wedding rings, so I took the rings off and laid them on a shelf above the sink. When I turned around to grab a towel, someone was knocking on the door, so I quickly dried my hands and left the washroom. Had no one been knocking, I'd have turned around again and seen my rings. A teenage girl went in as I left.

I returned to the car and waited for Hubby to finish filling the tank. Before he even climbed back into the car, I noticed my unadorned hand and ran back inside. The washroom was occupied, and I waited for the person to come out. But it wasn't the same person, and this one had not seen any rings. The gas station attendant hadn't either. The girl had vanished. We gave the manager (and the police) our name and address in case some honest stranger turned in the rings. Eventually, we needed to carry on our journey.

I cried for a month. I felt guilty and irresponsible, but I also believed nothing was too hard for God and begged him to convict the stranger who had my rings. I prayed they'd feel so guilty they'd turn them in.

The following Valentine's Day, Hubby bought me a small, plain wedding ring, discounted because someone else had purchased the matching engagement ring. Years later, after my father passed away, Mom divvied her rings among her daughters and I received her diamond engagement ring. I've managed to hang on to this replacement "set" ever since. I stopped praying for the return of my original rings a long time ago, but I would recognize them in an instant.

Nine years ago, Teresa Stanley lost hers as well. Of course, she and Dave searched high and low and I'm sure many tears were shed (because Dave's just that sort of a guy). They later sold their home to a family by the name of Stranger.

This year, the Strangers needed to do some plumbing work in preparation for selling the home again. And there, in the pipes, they found a wedding and engagement ring, still soldered together but black with grime.

Aimee Stranger cleaned the ring enough to discover the diamonds still intact and knew she must do something. She first contacted her realtor in order to contact Dave, who verified the ring was Teresa's. Aimee then took it to a jeweler who sent it away for cleaning. Dave and their boys kept it all a secret until the ring arrived last week.

Then, they were ready. They gave Teresa the package, videoed her priceless reaction, and uploaded the video to Facebook. Last time I checked, there were 60 comments from friends — many in tears, all celebrating with her and praising the kindness of the Strangers who were, for all practical purposes, strangers to Dave and Teresa.

Does this renew my hope that I might still be reunited with my rings? Not really. And that's okay; I've experienced enough significant losses in the intervening years to help put it into perspective. But it sure reminds me of a story Jesus told about a lost coin in Luke 15 — especially the part about friends and family celebrating over its reappearance and the trouble and expense someone else went to in order to see the rings returned as good as new. Read it for yourself to see who might be celebrating over you.

And next time you find something that's not yours, ask yourself whether you'd rather be a stranger or a Stranger.

New Furniture, Same Old Heart
(Appeared January 29, 2015)

After 37 years of marriage, Hubby and I recently bought our first new furniture. Call us late bloomers. Somehow, the items that have furnished our home until now have always landed by default. Most of them came gently used by parents, grandparents or siblings. A couple of dressers were included with our first mobile home. We've owned at least six televisions in those 37 years, but have never actually purchased one. And a couple of things I can't imagine parting with, like my solid oak World War II desk and the stuffed rocking chair I rocked my babies in, came to us free from storage warehouses.

And we've got along just fine.

Lately, though, the shortage of seating for guests and the mishmash of cast-offs in our living room (I counted nine different kinds of wood) were getting on my nerves. I began to dream of things that actually matched and spots for every bum. I decided to use the money I'd saved from my column-writing — usually reserved for writing-related expenses — on new furniture instead. So I thank you, dear readers, and the advertisers who keep the Central Plains Herald-Leader going. You've unwittingly played a role in this new acquisition at the Toddheim.

With our first furniture shopping experience, I discovered you're never too old to learn things about yourself. I didn't know what kind of furniture I liked, having never chosen for myself. I learned I don't like leather — too cold. I learned I prefer warm beiges and browns over cool greys and blues. I felt bummed to learn how much new furnishings cost. While I'd hoped to replace both seating and tables, my money ran out before we got to the tables. Guess I better keep the columns coming for a while.

But there's one thing I already knew about myself because it's true for every human on the planet. The joy provided by new possessions is temporary. The stuff we chase after will never fill our hearts. Don't misunderstand, I'm thrilled to see the new furniture in my home and hope I'll feel thankful to own it for years to come. I enjoy the satisfaction of knowing I earned it with the writing skills God gave me. But I also know a nice, new living room will not make me a nice, new person. In fact, sometimes our possessions simply begin to own us as they require maintenance, time, and vigilance to protect. We become servants of our stuff instead of the other way around.

Khaled Hosseini (author of *The Kite Runner*) wrote a dark little tale about a man who finds a magic cup and discovers that if he weeps into the cup, his tears turn into pearls. But even though he had always been poor, he was a happy man and rarely shed a tear. So he creates ways to make himself sad so his tears can make him rich. As the pearls pile up, so does his greed. The story ends with the man sitting on a mountain of pearls, knife in hand, weeping helplessly into the cup with his beloved wife's slain body in his arms.

A gruesome picture, but a vivid reminder of how greed destroys us.

Jesus understood the secret to living a contented life. In Luke chapter 12, he told his disciples, "Take care! Protect yourself against the least bit of greed. Life is not defined by what you have, even when you have a lot."

I'll reflect on that as I nap on my comfy new couch this afternoon.

The Day I Stepped Out of Line
(Appeared July 9, 2015)

I should know better than to go to a certain retail outlet on a busy Friday afternoon, but I needed to grab a birthday gift for our grandson. In spite of the crowds, it didn't take long to find the desired Lego set plus a couple of things for myself in the cosmetics department. With my purchases in hand, I made my way to the express lane where you don't know which cashier will serve you until you get to the front of the line. About 10 people waited ahead of me, but the line was moving quickly.

Just as I reached the front and stood waiting for that magical "Please proceed ..." instruction, an employee flagged me and said, "I can help you at Customer Service."

I obediently followed her, but when we got there, someone else had arrived at her counter — someone whose shopping cart bulged with groceries they were buying on credit. The clerk gave me a sheepish glance and started taking care of her customer. I looked longingly back at the express line to see if I might be able to sneak back in, but another 10 people had accumulated. I stayed put.

I'm not sure how much time went by, but I watched while the Customer Service clerk scanned the cartload of groceries, stopping intermittently to answer the phone or call for assistance. At some point she made an error and needed to start over. Three or four people now waited in line behind me. By this time, I was pretty sure the guy who'd been behind me in the original line was at home in his jammies. I started looking around for the hidden camera that would land me on *Just for Laughs*.

The waiting provided ample time for me to realize I had two choices. I could become bent out of shape, maybe even make a scene. I could call the clerk names and later rant about the store on Facebook. If I wanted to, I could probably work myself into a real dither.

Or, I could go easy on my blood pressure and remind myself of a few things, like:
1. The fact that the clerk meant well. She really did have good reason to believe she was speeding progress when she called me out of that line.
2. The fact that the clerk looked quite young. Could this be her first job? Possibly even her first week on the job? I remember those stressful, scary days.
3. The fact that I was in no real rush, and even if I had been— would an extra 10 minutes make much difference in the big picture?

I started humming a song called *Patience* that Music Machine came out with when our kids were little, sung by Herbert the Snail. Maybe you know it.

My patience was rewarded when I finally stepped to the counter and the manager said my purchases would be free.

Actually, I made that part up.

But on my way home, I came across a multi-vehicle accident in which I'd probably have died had I left the store 10 minutes earlier.

Actually, I made that part up, too.

But I did leave the store with my dignity — and the clerk's — still intact. Sometimes patience is the only reward required.

Remembering Shane
(Appeared January 7, 2016)

When I was 10 years old, my big sister and her husband presented Mom and Dad with their first grandchild and my grandparents with their first great-grandchild, a little boy named Shane. Well, maybe not so little at well over 10 pounds.

While we waited for him and his mother to be released from the hospital, Apollo 11 landed on the moon and Neil Armstrong took his famous first step on its surface. I remember gazing up at the moon, fascinated to think there were people up there taking one giant leap for mankind. Still, the news paled in comparison to the new life that had been added to our family. I couldn't wait to meet my nephew!

While all children are precious, a first grandchild holds a special place in a family's heart. I thought he was the best thing since macaroni and cheese, and visited every chance I got. When my parents took a trip to the east coast and I got to stay at my sister's to "help" care for Shane, I didn't mind missing out on the road trip one bit.

That Christmas, Shane was showered with presents as each aunt, uncle, grandparent and great-grandparent picked out something special for him. My gift was a bright orange inflatable Pluto dog — chosen no doubt because I liked it myself! All that gift-giving gradually dwindled of necessity as 13 more grandchildren eventually joined the family. Shane never knew how good he had it! But then again, he grew up to be an especially generous gift-giver himself, so who knows?

We never dreamed that 46 years later, we would find ourselves again gathering as a family around Shane — along with his wife and two sons — to express our love in a completely different way as he fought a swift and aggressive last battle this past November. You will rarely hear me swear, but I believe there are a few appropriate uses for the word "damn." One of those is cancer. With aching hearts, our family assembled to ease Shane's suffering in any way we could and to usher him from this life into the next with goodbyes and prayers and songs and hugs and tears; and then to bury his last remains, celebrate his life, and try to comfort the many broken hearts he left behind.

How is it that death is our only certainty, and yet the pain of it runs deeper than any other? If death is such an inevitable part of life, shouldn't it be easier?

Could it be because we were designed to live forever? God's original plan was not for us to die. Parents aren't supposed to bury their children. Teenagers aren't supposed to bury their dad. Grandmothers aren't supposed to suffer the multiplied pain of losing a grandchild while also seeing their own child grieving. There's really nothing "natural" about it.

And living forever would have been wonderful if this planet had retained its original design, too. Adam and Eve were created immortal. But once sin entered our world through their disobedience, immortality here would have been unbearable. Can you imagine? While there are many enjoyable things in this life to appreciate, let's face it. Does anyone really want to live forever with the inevitable aches and pains, the suffering and destruction we see around us, with no relief in sight?

God in his mercy has spared us that. In a sense, death became a blessing. It allows us to complete our journey here and move on to what we were originally created for. Why it sometimes comes "too soon" in our human opinions will remain a mystery, but in I Corinthians 15, Paul explains it far better than I ever could and I encourage you to check it out for yourself. Bottom line? "Just as everyone dies because we all belong to Adam, everyone who belongs to Christ will be given new life." (Verse 22)

Death sucks, there's no getting around it. We need to grieve, there's no getting around that either. But joy comes when we remember the final battle has already been won; the last enemy already defeated. In Revelation 3, John tells us "… God himself will be with them. He will wipe every tear from their eyes, and there will be no more death or sorrow or crying or pain. All these things are gone forever."

I can live with that. And so can you.

Forever.

TERRIE TODD

How to be Your Own Selfish Pig
(Appeared April 7, 2016)

Hubby took a road trip with our oldest grandson over spring break while I stayed home. I know some folks for whom being left home alone would feel like punishment akin to a root canal. I am not one of those folks.

Sure, I had to go to work each morning. But once I left the office, my life was mine. I could sleep when I wanted, as much as I wanted, in a blissfully quiet house. A house, I might add, that stayed clean. I could eat what I wanted, when I wanted, and IF I wanted. Truth be told, I lived on granola and salad and leftover Easter chocolate. Didn't cook even once, unless you count microwave popcorn or boiling the kettle for tea.

The shower, the phone and Netflix were always available to me exclusively. I binged on Downton Abbey. I could think my own thoughts without interruption and talk to myself with no one to eavesdrop. I rolled up the Welcome mat and exchanged it for one that said "I'm in here. You're out there. Let's keep it that way for a while."

In short, I discovered that when you're alone you can be completely selfish without inconveniencing anyone.

To be fair, not once did I need to shovel snow or mow grass. My vehicle didn't break down. The toilet didn't plug and the water heater kept heating water. Had any of those — or a dozen other possible catastrophes — happened, I'd have been only too happy to hasten Hubby's homecoming. (At our house, the distribution of tasks is pretty traditional.)

But it also confirmed what I already knew: deep down, I'm an introvert. Not everyone enjoys time alone so much. Faced with a week like mine, a more extroverted person would have been going squirrely, maybe going out to clubs or the gym or Walmart just to hang around people. Maybe even to church!

Being introverted is not to be confused with feeling shy or uncomfortable in a crowd, necessarily. It simply means we gain energy from time alone, while hanging around people drains us. It often means we're more comfortable giving a speech than mingling with our listeners afterwards. We can stand on stage and play a role in front of an audience, but making small talk with someone we don't know well is torture. Many of us love to write, but detest talking on the phone. We feel lonely at social events, but never when we're alone.

Are you more introverted or extroverted?

Neither personality holds a monopoly on self-centeredness, nor do any of us really need instructions for being our own selfish pig. It's a skill we're pretty much born with, of course. It's kindness and consideration that need to be learned. How to serve others by putting their needs first.

Here's my point. As long as I'm alone, it's easy to think I'm pretty swell. If I'd never had siblings or roommates or a spouse or kids, I might have waltzed through life believing I was a perfectly lovely person and never uncovered the ugly truth that I don't have an unselfish bone in my body.

But it's in community where we are called to live, because that's where, like the book of Proverbs says, "as iron sharpens iron, so one person sharpens another."

How Do You Solve a Problem Like Latin?
(Appeared May 10, 2016)

I know it seems a long way off, but it's a huge undertaking and rehearsals have been underway for over a month already. Next November, when the Prairie Players stage *The Sound of Music,* I will portray one of the nuns. Don't laugh. I'd make a terrific nun. If I were Catholic. And sweet and kind. And celibate. And knew Latin. It's my first musical and I have no spoken lines. I don't even have a name, so I've chosen "Sister Twisted" for myself. I'm not the greatest singer, but that only makes this feel like a greater privilege. With the talented Nita Wiebe belting the alto line into my ear, I can usually stay on key. Or close to it, although "close, but no cigar" is the rule in choral singing. If they ask me to start lip syncing, I will take it as a pretty strong indication that I'm no longer an asset to the abbey.

I auditioned because it seemed like a lark. It should have occurred to me that these particular larks do most of their singing in Latin. I can't say learning Latin ever appeared on my bucket list, even if joining the cast of *The Sound of Music* did. The language is relatively simple in that, unlike our ridiculously complicated English, it has no silent letters. And vowels are always pronounced the same way. Even so, memorizing a list of random syllables, pronouncing them correctly ("tall" vowels, not "flat," as our music director James Reynolds keeps harping about), matching them to the correct note, keeping the right tempo, and later adding the choreography seems like an insurmountable challenge to this amateur. No fudging allowed!

So I've typed out the illusive syllables phonetically and hung them beside my bathroom mirror to work on while I do my hair and makeup each morning. (How very un-nun-like!)

Thus, "Rex admirabilis Et triumphator nobilis" becomes "Rex awed mee rah bee lees, Et tree oom fah tor no bee lees."

If Hubby didn't know what I was up to, he'd haul me off for psychiatric evaluation or exorcism.

Now the last thing I need is to learn I've been unwittingly chanting some voodoo curse, calling down terror on my neighbourhood as I apply my Maybelline. So it became imperative to research the meaning of what I'm singing, and I made an interesting discovery. Did you know the nuns' opening piece of *The Sound of Music* is taken from Psalm 110? When you look at the words and understand the political backdrop of the story's setting, I'm convinced Rodgers and Hammerstein in all their genius had even the nuns making a subtle but strong rebellious statement. As their beloved Austria feels the looming shadow of the Third Reich, their chant proclaims:

"The LORD says to my lord: 'Sit at my right hand until I make your enemies a footstool for your feet.' The LORD will extend your mighty scepter from Zion, saying, 'Rule in the midst of your enemies!' Your troops will be willing on your day of battle. The Lord is at your right hand ..."

So, with the ever-nearing echo of Nazi boots on cobbled streets, the cloistered sisters cling fast to the God who is their solid rock.

A life lesson for us all, in any language and under any threat.

Chess with Keegan
(Appeared February 1, 2018)

"Wanna play chess with me, Grandma?"

"Absolutely!"

Who could resist such an enthusiastic invitation from an adorable 10-year-old? I tried to remember the last time I'd played. Maybe when his dad was his age? I felt sure I remembered the rules, though.

Keegan set up the board and made his first move. A few moves later, he took my bishop with one of his pawns by moving it diagonally.

"You can't do that!" I protested. "Pawns can only move forward."

"Unless they're capturing a piece."

Something about his logic did sound vaguely familiar and I began to doubt my memory. "Who taught you how to play chess?" I asked.

He named one of his friends. Figured. Oh well. I'd humour the kid and play by his rules. Then he tried to tell me if my pawn made it all the way to his end, I could exchange it for a captured piece.

"No, no, no, Keegan. You're confusing it with checkers."

"Well, that's how I play." As if that settled everything.

A few moves later, we began arguing about whether I had his queen in check.

"No Grandma. It's the king you're trying to check."

"No, it's the queen. You need to protect your queen." How on earth could we finish a game when we weren't playing by the same rules? He beat me on the first round, according to his rules. I beat him the second time, but it was a most unsatisfactory win because we were playing two different games.

Finally, in frustration, I grabbed my phone and Googled chess rules. Turns out the kid was right. Don't you just hate when that happens?

Keegan didn't rub it in my face. He beat me fair and square on the next match, and I realized a quick brush-up before we started could have prevented a lot of squabbling.

Does this sound at all like life? You're trying to do your best, maybe in your relationships or at your job — but somebody else isn't playing by the same rules. How can anyone ever win?

Jesus Christ didn't play by the rules, either. He came into a world where the law and all its expanded tenets weighed heavily on people's shoulders. When he went around breaking the rules, the religious rule-makers became so agitated, they plotted to kill him. Religion is crazy, isn't it?

Want to disarm people? Try following Jesus' example. A disgruntled customer comes to the counter, yelling and swearing at the clerk who really has no authority over the situation. But instead of playing by the customer's rules and raising her own voice, the clerk speaks softly.

"I'm so sorry that happened to you. I can understand why you feel angry."

Often, it's enough for the person to start calming down. Playing by their rules only escalates the drama.

A neighbour wrongs you. Instead of retaliating or shaming them on social media, you break their rule and seek peace — even in the middle of your pain and loss. You gain a friend, a loyal neighbour. You teach your children the power of forgiveness. You sleep better at night.

Is that possible? Maybe we should ask some 10-year-olds.

Changing the Atmosphere
(Appeared March 1, 2018)

Portage la Prairie is a happenin' place, isn't it? The announcement of the world's largest pea protein processing facility opening here, followed by the announcement of Simplot's plan to double its production, is breathing optimism into the atmosphere. I'm no economic development expert, but it doesn't take a genius to know the ripple effect means all this good news is only the beginning.

As it should, much praise has been poured out on our municipal councils, city and RM staff, provincial officials, and all involved in making these industrial dreams come true. It takes the efforts of many people working together and putting in long hours to make massive projects reality. We applaud you all!

Today, though, I'd like to suggest there just might be an element to this success that is being overlooked in our media, board rooms and coffee shops. A catalyst that no one can see. A force at work behind the scenes. Dare I speak of it? Consider the evidence and judge for yourself.

In 2014, my church (Prairie Alliance) embarked on a prayer journey where we discerned what God is calling us to be in our community. This led to the start of 24/7 prayer weeks, where ordinary people sign up to pray in one-hour slots, so that prayers go up around the clock for that week. I'm not suggesting for a minute that ours is the only church praying. A movement is definitely afoot across Portage's community of faith. Ours is simply the one with which I'm familiar.

During these prayer times, folks are given a list of specific things to ask God for. This list would fill three of my columns by itself, so I'll point out a few items as they relate to recent news headlines. You can decide whether a connection exists.

The list includes a section where we pray for our front-runners. It names our city and RM council members by name, as well as other community leaders. We ask God to deliver our citizens from pessimism to optimism, from a victim mentality to an empowered one; from a scarcity mindset to an abundance mindset; from fear to joy; from caution to vision. Are you seeing a link?

We've been praying for creative partnerships in Portage – for organizations committed to similar goals, that they can leverage resources for greater effectiveness. Have you seen this happening anywhere?

Here's a sentence lifted right out of the prayer guide:

"Pray for the success of industry and business in Portage; that the resources generated by this success would be poured back into Portage for the good of the city."

You can call it a coincidence. Or you can call it psychological, that what we pray for we somehow, subconsciously, cause to happen. Or you can consider the lyrics to the Chris Tomlin song we've been singing for years, *God of this City*; or Rend Collective's song, *Build Your Kingdom Here*; or the promise of the Bible where it says, "If my people, who are called by my name, will humble themselves and pray and seek my face and turn from their wicked ways, then I will hear from heaven, and I will forgive their sin and will heal their land." (II Chronicles 7:14)

However you see it, doesn't it make you curious to know what else is on that prayer list? It's not top secret; anyone is welcome to jump on board. Trust me, if you live here, you're "on the list." You are being prayed for. Momentum is building.

Everybody's Doing It
(Appeared March 8, 2018)

Right around the time Mayor Ferris challenged me to write a column on mortality, a couple of other related things happened. A Facebook friend accused me of wishing my life away because I wanted January to end. And my mother lamented, "What is it with all the deaths lately?"

I was beginning to get the message.

To the mayor, I said, "Well, we're all dying. I suppose mortality is a relative topic for a column."

To the Facebook friend, I admitted that in many ways I do wish my life away. That's because I believe something C.S. Lewis said: "There are far, far better things ahead than anything we leave behind." Anything! I wouldn't mind one bit if God chose to call me home today, but I'll trust his timing.

With my mother, I held my tongue. But last time I checked, the odds of you and I dying are 100 per cent. I may be lousy at math, but I do understand the concept of 100 per cent.

Everybody's doing it, but hardly anyone's talking about it —even when it's imminent. Why is that?

With Easter approaching, I think it's a great time for us to consider this matter of death and the hereafter. In fact, I think we can talk about this for at least four weeks. You can tune out or tune in, it's your call. Either way, your turn to die is coming. The only piece we don't know is when or how.

I know some people believe that once we die, that's it. We cease to exist. They could be right, but if so, there's nothing more to say.

So I'm going to plunge forward with this series on the premise of my own belief, based on the Christian Bible. It's summed up fairly economically for us in Hebrews 9:27-28: "Everyone has to die once, then face the consequences. Christ's death was also a one-time event, but it was a sacrifice that took care of sins forever. And so, when he next appears, the outcome for those eager to greet him is, precisely, salvation."

So, with that out of the way, I hope you'll keep reading.

"Every man dies, not every man really lives."
If you've seen the movie *Braveheart* about William Wallace, Scotland's martyr to freedom, you are familiar with the quote above. If you knew you were going to die tonight, could you honestly say you have really lived? I hope so. It's not a matter of longevity. I've known people who have packed far more life into 30 years than some do into 90 — and I don't mean bungee jumping or travelling the world or sampling every food known to man. I'm talking about making an impact, leaving a legacy. Using whatever time you have to invest in the purposeful work God placed you on this planet to do. Bringing his kingdom to the people around you, using whatever talents and passions he's given.

If you can't say you've really lived, what would need to happen for you to be able to say you have? I sure hope it's not some superficial bucket list, some tourist trap you've always wanted to visit, a golf course you've hoped to play, or a mindless feat of daring you haven't quite worked up the courage for. I hope it would require a bit of self-sacrifice. That's where life is found. (Check out Matthew 16:25).

Something to think about until we continue next week. See you then!

Why the Cross Does Not Have the Final Word
(Appeared March 15, 2018)

At my desk at City Hall one day, I scanned Portage la Prairie's Fees & Charges Schedule for 2018. It's posted on the City website, should you ever need to know how much it'll cost you to buy a pet licence, photocopy a tax bill, rent a mosquito fogger, have your water turned on, or buy a grave — among many other things.

I perused the cemetery fees with great interest. Adult burial plots range from $870 to $970, not counting opening and closing. No matter how hard I studied the schedule, I could not find a fee for a grave that you want to rent temporarily.

One of the popular songs on Christian radio for the past year has been, *The Cross Has the Final Word*, written by Cody Carnes and recorded by The Newsboys. Although I understand what the song is trying to say, I think it misses the mark. The intent of the key phrase is that the power of Jesus Christ and what he accomplished by dying on the cross trumps everything — sin, disease, war, religion and death.

But it wasn't his cross that achieved all that. If the cross really had the final word, then Jesus Christ would be just another crucified Jew. We may never have heard of him. If an instrument of death has the final word, then death wins. If the cross has the final word, there is no hope for me.

As a kid, I learned how Jesus's followers buried his body in a rich man's tomb, fulfilling a prophecy made centuries earlier. I always assumed this spoke to Jesus's poverty, that he lived without enough means to buy a burial plot of his own. While that's probably true, a more profound thought occurred to me a couple of years ago.

It wasn't until our church started singing a song called *Resurrecting* (by Elevation Worship) that it finally dawned on me. It says, "The tomb where soldiers watched in vain was borrowed for three days." The body of Jesus wasn't placed in a borrowed tomb because he was poor, but because he would only need it for a little while! I wonder what our local funeral directors would say if I walked in and said I'd like to take care of some pre-arrangements, but I only needed my grave for three days.

The final word is not the cross of Good Friday. It is the resurrection of Sunday. It is Christ's empty tomb that really has the final word. Which means it isn't truly empty at all, because it's filled with hope. A song written by two of the worship leaders at my church says, "The empty grave holds my hope each day." I love that, because it speaks not only of life after death, but life right now, filled with hope and purpose every day. Who here doesn't want that?

Titus 3:8 says, "God's gift has restored our relationship with him and given us back our lives. And there's more life to come — an eternity of life! You can count on this."

No matter how far from God you think you are, the truth is that you're never more than one step from him. Easter is the perfect time to take that one step. The late Reverend Billy Graham said, "I've never met a man who accepted Jesus Christ and regretted it."

Next week, I'll share my thoughts on funerals.

Will You Come to My Funeral If I Go to Yours?
(Appeared March 22, 2018)

Do you read obituaries? Have you observed that more people opt for no funeral these days? Ever wonder why? I have my theories, and they could all be wrong. One is that fewer people include a traditional faith experience into their lives, so it might seem incongruent to end such a life in a church with prayers and hymns.

Another theory is that people hate attending funerals and don't want to inflict the same discomfort on their friends.

Or they view their own funeral as being "on stage," one of the top fears for many, topping the fear of death itself. Although it's not likely they'll be asked to speak.

Or maybe deep down, people fear no one will show up. The ultimate rejection.

I've heard people say, "Don't cry when I'm gone." That's not healthy, folks! I don't want my loved ones paralyzed by grief when I die, but tears are a necessary and healing part of the journey. So is laughter. I hope there is plenty of both at my funeral.

"Don't make a big fuss when I pass; just stick me in the ground and be done with it," is another line I've heard. A statement like that is usually made out of genuine humbleness, but what these folks may be forgetting is that their funeral isn't for them. It's for those they leave behind. I found it wonderfully comforting as a grieving daughter to receive the embraces of friends and relatives, to hear my cousins share their memories of my dad, and to hear how much he meant to his friends. I would have felt the loss far more keenly if Dad had declared he didn't want a funeral.

I think pre-arranging your funeral is similar. Some say, "I won't care at that point, so do whatever you want." Again, it's not for you. Pre-planning spares others from a hundred decisions, some of them costly, at a time when emotions run high and energy and focus are at an all-time low. How much better to not have to purchase a burial plot, choose a casket, name a charity, and all those details because they're already decided?

I'm beginning to sound like an ad for a funeral home. I promise, no kickbacks were solicited or received in the writing of this column.

I used to think it would be better to return to the pioneer days where the men of the community gathered to build a box and dig a hole. The women brought food and the pastor said a few words. Death wasn't a billion-dollar business then, and folks didn't go into debt to give their loved ones a "decent" burial. But I came to appreciate funeral home directors when my father died. I understood better the service they provided and the professionalism with which they delivered it.

Maybe I'm a control freak, but I've been planning my own funeral songs since my 30s. As different songs become more meaningful in any given year, I change my playlist accordingly. You might think that's morbid, but these songs burst with such victory I don't see how anyone will return home afterward feeling anything other than hope. You see, I firmly believe it's not so much that life continues after death, but that it finally, truly begins.

I'll share more next week, when we celebrate the reason for this glorious hope.

I Can Only Imagine
(Appeared April 5, 2018)

Easter's over, but no series on mortality would be complete without a few words about Heaven.

Our planet recently lost two prominent citizens. Reverend Billy Graham died on February 21, and renowned physicist Stephen Hawking on March 14. How could two such brilliant minds have held such opposing views on the afterlife? Compare these statements:

Hawking: "We are each free to believe what we want, and it's my view that the simplest explanation is: there is no God. No one created our universe, and no one directs our fate. This leads me to a profound realization that there probably is no heaven and no afterlife either. We have this one life to appreciate the grand design of the universe and for that, I am extremely grateful."

Graham: "Someday you will read or hear that Billy Graham is dead. Don't you believe a word of it. I shall be more alive than I am now. I will just have changed my address. I will have gone into the presence of God."

Is one of these men completely wrong, or is the truth somewhere in the middle? How can we know? It's been one of the top questions of humankind since our beginning. It's the reason people are drawn to mediums who claim they communicate with the spirits of the departed. It's what makes songs like *I Can Only Imagine*, and the recently released movie behind the song so popular. It's why we're so fascinated by those who've had near-death experiences (NDEs). We want to know. We want assurance that something better awaits us, or at least nothing far worse.

Books about people who've had NDEs abound, and their stories share too much in common for us to dismiss. You might be familiar with Howard Storm's book, *My Descent into Death*, an autobiographical journey that changed the author's life from an atheist to a Christian minister. One of the most powerful I've read is by Dr. Eben Alexander, a highly-trained neurosurgeon who firmly believed NDEs are fantasies produced by brains under extreme stress — until he experienced one himself. For seven days, Alexander lay in a coma with the part of his brain that controls all thought and emotion shut down completely. His recovery is a medical miracle, but the real miracle lies in the journey he took during that time, through a sphere where neither time nor place mean anything.

Before he underwent his journey, Dr. Alexander could not reconcile his knowledge of neuroscience with any belief in heaven, God or the soul. Today, he is a doctor who believes true health can be achieved only when we realize that God and the soul are real, and death is not the end of personal existence but only a transition. In his book, *Proof of Heaven*, he tells the story of meeting and speaking with the Divine source of the universe itself. He says it is the hardest story to tell, because our limited language has no words for what he experienced.

This falls in line with the words of Jesus' disciple, John, who received a glimpse into Heaven and recorded everything in the book of Revelation. It's difficult to understand because it was difficult to write. We have no words.

My favourite promise of John's, though, is from Revelation 21:4-8: "He will wipe every tear from their eyes. There will be no more death or mourning or crying or pain, for the old order of things has passed away ..." There's more, and I hope you'll look it up for yourself.

We can only imagine.

The Fine Art of Name-Calling
(Appeared November 29, 2018)

For the first 18 years of my life, I believed my real name was Theresa, after my great-grandmother. Mom explained that "Terrie" was a nickname and registered me as Theresa at school. The other kids would snicker whenever an unsuspecting substitute teacher called out "Theresa" in roll call.

At 13, I decided it might be cool to spell my name Teri. It caught on, and I remained Teri all through high school. That's what you'll see on my high school diploma and our wedding invitation.

Then, because I was moving out of the country, I applied for my birth certificate. Lo and behold, I discovered I'd been legally registered at birth as Terrie. I had never actually been Theresa at all. We teased Mom that she must have been looped on painkillers when she filled out the form.

So I became Terrie once again, and I've stuck with that for 40 years, although others have spelled it Teri, Terie, Terry and Terri. One becomes used to all the variations when one has a name like mine. I try not to let it cause an identity crisis.

Recently, though, I created a Service Canada account online. If you've done that, you know you must first request a special unique code. When my code arrived in the mail, my name was spelled Teri. Even my middle name, Janette, was misspelled. Would this discrepancy cause problems down the road? I didn't want to risk it.

So, down to the Service Canada office I went. I took along my passport showing the correct spelling of my name. I should have realized they'd want my birth certificate and marriage certificate. So, back home I drove for the key to our security box. When I arrived at the Credit Union, friendly Holly led me into the room with all the lock boxes and pulled ours out. I went through everything. No birth or marriage certificates materialized, except for Hubby's. I returned home, where I found mine in a filing cabinet, and circled back to Service Canada.

They entered everything correctly and assured me it was all good.

Several days later when I again logged into my account, my name still came up wrong. Back to Service Canada I went, torn between annoyance at the inconvenience and gratitude for a local office. The lady who helped me before couldn't solve the issue and sent me back to the waiting room. When my name was called again, the second lady went into her computer and assured me my name had been entered correctly and advised me to move forward with my business regardless of how the login name showed up.

Last week, I received the letter I'd been awaiting — still with the wrong spelling of my name. I returned to our Service Canada office. The lady seemed puzzled, but assured me it must be just a glitch and suggested I call the toll-free number and keep toggling between "Press One" and "Press Two" until I reach a human.

All of which left me wondering who named Service Canada.

Worship leader Tommy Walker wrote a song called *He Knows My Name* and it's based on the truth of scripture. King David said of God, "You know me inside and out, you know every bone in my body; You know exactly how I was made, bit by bit, how I was sculpted from nothing into something. Like an open book, you watched me grow from conception to birth; all the stages of my life were spread out before you; The days of my life all prepared before I'd even lived one day." (Psalm 139)

I don't need to worry about what I was or wasn't named, or how it is or isn't spelled. I'm a child of God and he knows my name. He knows yours, too. He is *for* you. You are who he says you are, and ultimately, that is more than enough.

The Racist in Us All
(Appeared January 17, 2019)

Martin Luther King Jr. would be 90 years old this month, which means he was only 39 when he was assassinated in 1963. That's not a lot of time to accomplish all he did, not only for African Americans, but for Native Americans as well.

The United States will commemorate Martin Luther King Day on January 21.

I had never read the full text of King's famous speech, made just before the civil rights march he led on Washington in 1963. I decided to look it up and do more than merely skim it. I expected to find most moving the lines we've all heard, the oft-repeated ones like "I have a dream" or "let freedom ring." Instead, what struck me most was this bit from somewhere near the middle of the speech:

"... many of our white brothers, as evidenced by their presence here today, have come to realize that their destiny is tied up with our destiny. They have come to realize that their freedom is inextricably bound to our freedom. We cannot walk alone."

Nearly 60 years have passed since King delivered those powerful words. But, while many things have improved, racism still runs rampant — on our streets and in our hearts. It's easy for us here in Portage la Prairie to shake our heads at our neighbours to the south and wonder how they could be so blind. So misguided. So ignorant. Meanwhile, Indigenous Canadians continue to experience prejudice every day in subtle and not-so-subtle ways. New Canadians understand what it's like to be viewed as less-than. To take jobs for which they are overqualified because it's all they can get.

Racism hurts a country. It maims a town. It destroys communities. And it resides in every one of our hearts on some level, if we're honest. Whatever colour your skin.

Our community, I'm told, is approximately one-third First Nations people. So wouldn't it seem logical that when I attend a fundraiser, when I observe a Council meeting, when I go to church, when I hear a youth choir, when I show up at my community theatre group's regular meetings, when I watch a sporting event — wouldn't it seem logical that one-third of the people participating in that community event would be First Nations?

Logical, but far from true.

I'm grateful our City hired an Indigenous Community Coordinator whose role is to help give the First Nations citizens of Portage la Prairie a voice. I'm thankful my country opens its doors to immigrants. I'm pleased our government decided to honour Viola Desmond by making her the first Canadian woman to appear on a bank note ... and sad that she's not around to see it. I'm glad my church made one of its key goals and prayers to become one-third First Nations.

Why has PAC made this so specific? Because not only do we desire to accurately reflect our larger community, we want to help bring God's Kingdom to earth, like Jesus taught us to pray. The book of Revelation gives us some pretty colourful images of what God's Kingdom looks like:

"I looked again. I saw a huge crowd, too huge to count. Everyone was there — all nations and tribes, all races and languages. And they were standing, dressed in white robes and waving palm branches, standing before the Throne and the Lamb and heartily singing: 'Salvation to our God on his Throne!'"

The bottom line is: I know my heart needs to soften and grow. And that can't happen when I close myself off from people of different backgrounds. My destiny is tied up with their destiny. My freedom is inextricably bound to their freedom.

And so is yours.

Stewing to Beat Sixty
(Appeared February 21, 2019)

My pale and pasty Canadian self is flying to Florida this week. When I return, tanned or not, I'll have entered a new decade of my life.

Each year, an event called the Deep Thinkers Retreat takes place in Destin, Florida. The organizers accept the first 20 writers who register to come learn from authors Susan May Warren and Rachel Hauck. Between them, these two have written nearly 100 novels, won awards, and made the New York Times Best Sellers list. I've frequently thought about how inspiring it might be to attend one of their workshop/ retreats. (Besides, it's Florida in February!)

But I tend to hum and haw, especially when something proves financially challenging. So every year while I hummed, 20 other writers would sign up before I even started hawing and I'd miss out.

Last July when I received the email about the 2019 retreat, I thought, "Maybe this is the year I should go. I'll be turning 60. It could be my birthday present." Without overthinking it, I registered. Within days, I had both my flights and time off work booked.

Now it's here and I'm not deep-thinking. I'm stewing. *What have I done? How can I possibly function after arriving at the airport by 4:30 a.m. and travelling all day? What was I thinking, choosing the cheapest lodging which means sharing a dorm room with five strangers? What if I cough? What if I snore? What if they cough or snore? What if I can't stay awake for the sessions? What if I get sick? What if the novel I'm working on sucks? What if I don't grasp what they're teaching? What if it rains the whole time? What if it's all a waste of money?*

Why do I second-guess myself, and is asking that question third-guessing? And am I now fourth-guessing?

Unless you're one of those super self-certain people, you probably relate to what I'm saying. Too much second-guessing (also known as fear) sucks the joy out of positive experiences and turns into self-fulfilling prophecy.

Pat Pierson, author of *Stop Self-Sabotage*, says, "The first step is to notice your negative thoughts and intentionally intervene with a better thought. When you tell yourself, 'I will be fine,' your mind doesn't believe it, so instead, start a sentence with 'I choose' and say something you can believe. For example, 'I choose to do everything in my power to create a positive outcome.'"

Psychology expert and author of *Authentic Grit*, Caroline Miller, offers these words to stewers like me. "When we seek out the uncertain and unknown, we push into territory that could lead to our biggest wins. Playing it safe leads to mediocrity."

Reminds me of a story Jesus told in Matthew 25 about the man who entrusted his servants with varying amounts of money. The servant who played it safe by burying his portion was severely chastised, while those who took a risk and doubled their money were entrusted with more. I often wish Jesus had included a fourth servant — one who invested but lost the money. Would he have been punished for losing, or rewarded for risking?

Do you think it's possible Jesus deliberately left out that fourth character because we really can't lose when God is with us?

Now *that* sounds like something worth deep-thinking about on one's 60th birthday. With one's toes in the Florida sand. In February.

Florida in February
(Appeared February 28, 2019)

If all goes as planned, by the time you read this, I will have returned to the frozen tundra known as Manitoba. But as I write these words, I'm sitting on the third-floor balcony of a multi-million-dollar vacation house in the warmth of a radiant sun. I see palm trees and blooming roses, pansies and camellias. I hear the coo of a mourning dove and the gentle bubbling of a hot tub overflowing into a swimming pool. Earlier, I felt the white sand between my toes and watched the sun sparkle so brightly on the rolling waves of the Gulf of Mexico that my eyes could barely take it. It is my 60th birthday and I am torn between feeling blessed beyond belief and horrified beyond measure.

Blessed because I don't deserve to be here — it's only by God's grace that I could make such a trip. That I could spend five straight days learning from seasoned professional writers how to plot a novel, how to create fully developed characters, how to help those characters heal their deepest wounds and face their biggest fears. That I should enjoy the privilege of rubbing shoulders with others who can spend an entire day working on these projects without tiring of it. That together we can help one another plan and plot and, more importantly, learn how to do it on our own when we return to our various homes. That our shared faith could provide a bond of trust and understanding not experienced in our regular workaday worlds.

The horror? It's in the fact that this blessing is delivered on a silver platter called opulence. This grand house stands among hundreds — maybe thousands — of others that go on and on, lot after lot, each one pristine and fitted with every modern convenience. Pools, hot tubs, outdoor kitchens, perfectly groomed gardens. Every sidewalk clean. Every vehicle looking like it just drove off the lot. No trash on the beach. Happy music coming from backyards. Delicious aromas of meat on the grill. More food than anyone could or should ever eat.

The atmosphere of entitlement sickens my stomach and yet I know it resides in my own heart as much as in anyone else's. Many of the stories we write are based on hardship, because without hardship, we have no story. The irony is not lost on me.

How can there be so much wealth in the whole world, let alone in these few square miles that surround me right now? How is all this possible as long as hunger and homelessness still exist, not just on the other side of the planet, but in this country and my own? What would the Compassion children whose photos appear on my fridge think if they could see me now?

When a rich young man asked Jesus what he needed to do to inherit eternal life, Jesus offered an intriguing answer. "Sell all you own and give it to the poor and come, follow me." The young man walked away sad, for he had great wealth.

I'll return home feeling extremely blessed, hopefully a little wiser, but also a little sad. It's my 60th birthday and I still have so very much to learn.

No Such Thing as Unplanned
(Appeared July 18, 2019)

If ever a pregnancy were inconvenient, surely this would have been it. At 26, the woman already had four children — two girls, two boys — ranging from age three through eight. She thought she'd hung her last diaper on the clothesline. Their little three-bedroom home had been fashioned from two former granaries, with no running water and no basement. Her husband had recently incurred a life-altering physical disability. His reduced earning capacity had prompted her to launch a long-dreamed-of career of her own in order to help provide for their growing family. This meant first finishing three years of high school via correspondence, followed by a year of university to gain a teaching certificate. It would require great courage and determination, but they would make it work.

Not a great time to discover you're pregnant.

One could certainly understand and empathize if this surprise interruption brought with it something less than instantaneous joy.

By the time that child arrived, however, these parents had come to terms with the idea. They'd involved the other children in preparing for the new baby. The mother had charged ahead with her education, taking her textbooks with her to the hospital when it came time to deliver so she could study for exams between feedings while she recovered. Two years later, she found herself the only student living in the dorm during the week and returning to her family of five children on weekends.

That fifth baby, that unforeseen little interruption, was me.

I tease my mother that all her studying while she carried me made me smart. But for all my so-called smarts, it took me over 50 years to piece together the notion that my parents may not have had every reason to feel completely delighted when they learned I was on the way. It wasn't until an older relative shared with me a story that started me thinking. Maybe I was not exactly "planned."

This speaks volumes about my parents. That I never felt unwanted or unloved tells me I am one of the truly blessed. One of the "lucky ones," if you believe in luck.

Now, I can look back over 60 years of life and name eight other people who would not exist today if I had never been born — my children and theirs. On my shelf I see three books that never would have been written, not including those still waiting to be published. More stories, articles, plays and columns than I can count. No one else would have put those exact words together in that exact way.

I am left with the conviction that I was, indeed, planned. Perhaps not by my parents, but by someone. Someone who knew more than they did.

Do you ever feel unplanned, unwanted? I'm willing to go out on a limb and say it's safe to assume that a great many of us were not necessarily "planned." Maybe you were not as blessed as I. Maybe your parents made it painfully evident by calling you "the accident" or the "oopsie baby." I don't know who needs to read these words today, but if this describes you, can I make one thing perfectly clear? You are not here by accident. You may be unsure, unworthy, unfaithful, unwise, uneasy, unqualified, unemotional, unavailable or unfit. But you can never be unloved, unwanted, or unplanned by the God who made you.

It Tolls for Thee
(Appeared August 22, 2019)

My third novel, *Bleak Landing*, released two years ago this month. Its first page contains an unusually lengthy dedication. I chose to dedicate that book to the pastors and pastors' wives who have influenced me in a positive way throughout my life. There are 10 couples on the list. I suppose it's an unusual thing to do, but I knew I'd never write enough books for each to have their own and I wanted to honor them all.

In recent weeks, two of the people on that list of 20 have died. In May, my friend and mentor Linda Letellier left this world for the next. I'm thankful to have seen her last fall and for modern technology which allowed me to view her funeral service online from Mountain Lake, Minnesota. The cover of the program showed a beautiful picture of her pulling biscuits from the oven, holding them toward the camera with her huge, hospitable smile. It said, "I'm home. I'm safe. I like it here."

More recently, we said good-bye to Donna Lee, who was my pastor's wife when I was growing up in Amaranth. In a packed-out little country church, we felt inspired by stories of the impact made through her humble, obedient life. She touched many hearts. We walked away encouraged to never let go of God, no matter what life throws at us.

I sometimes wish I lived in a place and time of tolling bells. In our world of rapid communication, we see no need for happy church bells to ring out on wedding days, or for somber funeral bells to let us know someone in the community has passed away. I think the clanging of those bells would serve as helpful and regular reminders that we are here for only a short time, that our turn is coming. The bells remind us we are all part of one another.

Often, people don't want those reminders. I happen to believe they are healthy. If we live each day remembering that the next funeral could be our own, wouldn't we live differently? I don't mean in the "life is short, grab all the gusto you can get" kind of way. I mean it in the "what will really matter after I'm gone?" kind of way.

On the day you die, will the things you're worried about today matter? Your fears and cares? The grudges you're hanging on to? What do you hope people remember about you? When stories are told, will they be of love, generosity, and grace from your hand? Or will you be remembered for lesser things ... your hobbies, your possessions, your obsessions? Will the funny stories about you be tainted with a hint of bitterness or will they be shared with pure and honest admiration? Will others aspire to be more like you? Will those who know you best have sweet memories to inspire and encourage them on their journeys? Will they know how much you loved them?

Each day brings you one step closer to that day. What's one thing you can do this day to make that day everything you hope it will be? Name it, then do it. What's stopping you?

No one has said it more poetically than John Donne: "... any man's death diminishes me, because I am involved in mankind, and therefore never send to know for whom the bells tolls; it tolls for thee."

How About Those *Thoughs?*
(Appeared January 16, 2020)

I am learning to love the word "though."
Last month, I enjoyed the privilege of being guest speaker at a Christmas banquet in MacGregor. The women of the Sommerfeld Mennonite Church were warm, welcoming, and responsive. They laughed in all the right places and grew quiet right on cue. And if you ever doubted the adage that Mennonite girls can cook, doubt no longer. I stuffed myself with delicious food even though I could only sample a fraction of their potluck offerings.

That night I shared with the group some of my funniest stories, but also some serious ones. We looked at a short passage from Habakkuk chapter three, clearly written to an agricultural community during a bleak time.

"Though the fig tree does not bud
and there are no grapes on the vines,
though the olive crop fails
and the fields produce no food,
though there are no sheep in the pen
and no cattle in the stalls,
yet I will rejoice in the Lord,
I will be joyful in God my Savior.
The Sovereign Lord is my strength."

Do you see all the "thoughs" in that passage? The writer is telling us we can rejoice even in the middle of hardship and pain. I encouraged the women to fill in those "thoughs" with their own "thoughs." We all have them. Make a list, whatever yours might be. *Though my marriage is broken, though I am not receiving healing from this illness, though I am still unemployed, though my loved one has an addiction* …you know what yours are, and maybe the list seems extra-long. Once your list is done, add the YET part, like Habakkuk did. *Yet* I will rejoice in the Lord.

Why? Because your story isn't over. God is in the business of great reversals. We see it all through the Bible. Think of Esther. Job. Gideon. Lazarus. But nowhere more powerfully than at the cross of Christ. What our enemy thought was his greatest victory — the Son of God, dead — turned out to be his greatest defeat. Not only did Jesus return to life, but his resurrection made a way for us all to live forever. The greatest reversal ever.

And God can do the same with your pain. Your "though." You may not see it today or tomorrow, but one day you will tell the complete story. The ending will be so triumphant, greater than you could have ever imagined (see Ephesians 3:20).

I've never jumped on the bandwagon of choosing a theme word for a year, but I'm beginning to think "though" might be a great word for 2020. One day, we will have perfect 20/20 vision. We'll see our lives — past, present, and future — the same way God sees them. We'll view with clarity the great reversals he performed in our lives when we continued to worship him no matter what.

And we'll realize the precious value of a little word like "though."

Rickety Bridges
(Appeared March 26, 2020)

I'm one of the fortunate ones. My life has changed little since we began practising "social distancing," as I already worked from home and no children or students live in my house. Everything's cancelled except dirty laundry. I haven't missed my few regularly scheduled activities because staying home is my favourite thing in the world anyway. I had nothing on my calendar which, when cancelled, would have left me disappointed. I've been writing more, reading more, praying more, and working on my quilt project more. If all that's not enough, there's always my neglected piano. Or my neglected hubby. If he has his way, I'll also be baking more. I'm not that desperate yet.

It's surreal, isn't it? Even though little has changed for me so far, the drop in traffic on my usually busy street, the nightly news, the online reports all seem hard to believe. No one knows what will happen, but everyone wonders. We're all afraid. That's normal and understandable.

In my church's online service, one of our pastors shared his favourite C.S. Lewis story and it couldn't be more appropriate for this time in which we find ourselves. Lewis painted such brilliant word pictures, didn't he? (This one is called "Faith in the Face of Peril" and comes from the Collected Letters of CS Lewis, Vol 3, 448.)

Two travelers came to a rickety bridge over a deep, rocky ravine. The first man thought about the goodness of God and convinced himself the bridge would hold till they had crossed over safely. He called this assurance Faith.

The second man looked at the bridge and thought to himself, It might hold and it might not. But whether my life ends today or at some other time, whether here or somewhere else, I am always in God's hands.

The two men started across. The bridge gave way and neither man survived. The first man's faith was unfulfilled; the second man's faith held firm.

I love this story because it forces me to ask, Where am I placing my faith? In our health care system? Science? Government? All of those are doing everything in their power to bring a swift end to this pandemic, to minimize loss, and to ensure we will be able to continue keeping ourselves fed and sheltered. They need and deserve our prayers. Indeed, all of us want to do our part. Will it be enough? Will the bridge hold?

Placing your faith in those things may or may not find fulfillment. But nothing can shake a faith in a good God who holds you in his hands, no matter what. I love the old hymn that says, "On Christ, the solid rock, I stand; all other ground is sinking sand."

Covid-19 has resurrected the original meaning of the phrase "going viral." Let's make faith as contagious as the corona virus. In a time when you're inundated with mixed messages, with words from people who have no clue what our future holds, focus on what will never change. Instead of amplifying your fears, speak what you know to be true. "God is our refuge and strength, an ever-present help in trouble. Therefore we will not fear, though the earth give way and the mountains fall into the heart of the sea." (Psalm 46:1 & 2)

There's that word "though" again. When I picked it for my 2020 word, I had no idea what lay ahead for our planet. Then again, we never do. But we know who is ultimately in charge. We know he can be trusted. And we know he hasn't cancelled a thing.

What If?
(Appeared April 2, 2020

Remember when life was "normal?" Remember how much complaining and criticizing went on when life was "normal?" Yet have you noticed that everywhere we turn people are saying they can't wait for life to get back to normal?

What if it never does?

Listening to the nightly news can certainly feed into our "what ifs," can't it? Maybe we could envision a whole new, better normal by considering different "what ifs." Such as:

What if, years from now, when you ask your grown kids to share their favourite memory from their childhood, they say it was during the pandemic of 2020 because they got to stay home from school and spend quality time with you?

What if crime goes down because the troublemakers are staying home?

What if travel loses its appeal, keeping your vacation dollars here in our local economy?

What if the environment improves because of fewer carbon dioxide emissions?

What if, after this is over, we all scrimp and save until we've socked away enough money to cover six months of living expenses, like financial advisors have been telling us to do all along?

What if you discover a whole new career that you love because you were forced to homeschool your children or take a temporary job or cross-train for different duties at work?

What if, in the race to discover a cure for the corona virus, scientists stumble upon a cure for cancer?

What if traffic accidents decrease because so few are on the highways?

What if sports injuries decline because games are cancelled?

What if, during this pandemic, our medical experts realize they can bring huge relief to our system by paying doctors for phone consults when appropriate? (I received a call from my lung specialist, for the first time ever, with results of a scan done in February. For me, it meant five minutes out of my day as opposed to hours in a waiting room, a round trip to Winnipeg plus parking costs, for the same outcome!)

What if the incidents of ordinary colds and flu diminish because we've made a habit of better hand hygiene?

What if the death toll rises to a million when the enemy of our souls intended it to wipe out all 7.8 billion of us? (As of this writing, 35,000 have died of Covid-19 worldwide. Yes, it's terrible. For perspective, 50 million died in the Spanish flu epidemic of 1918-19.)

What if, after restrictions are lifted, every church in town is bursting at the seams because people are spiritually hungry for the first time?

What if relationships are restored because the harsh reminder of your own mortality caused you to forgive or ask forgiveness or initiate that important conversation?

What if you look back on this and see a hundred ways that God has carried you through?

What if you come out kinder, calmer, more compassionate and patient?

What if God keeps his promise in II Chronicles 7:14 to forgive our sin and heal our land because we, his people, have humbled ourselves and prayed and sought his face?

Many of these outcomes are out of our sanitized little hands. But several of them are up to us. Whether or not they come to fruition will be determined largely by what you choose to do today. Right now. In the middle of it.

I bet you can think of more "what-ifs." God bless you!

Section 2: Marriage & Family

There is no such thing as 'fun for the whole family.'

Jerry Seinfeld

TERRIE TODD

A Rat Tale
(Appeared November 26, 2011)

Some things are only funny 25 years later.
It's been at least that long since we lived in a trailer court that included a concrete garbage corral. We could toss our trash in there and the landlord would come along and burn it when it got full. Really full.

One day, unannounced to the tenants, it all got bulldozed and replaced with a dumpster. Which would have been great, except for the rats who now sought a new home.

They picked our place.

I was washing dishes when through the window I saw the first of the little darlings on our doorstep. He helped himself to some dog food and zipped back below. Evidently our puppy was big enough to keep the neighbourhood cats away while not actually intimidating the rodents. It was rat heaven!

We moved the dog food inside.

We set out traps.

We set out poison.

We tried not to think about it.

That night we were just about to fall asleep when we heard what sounded like small children in steel-toed boots galloping through our duct work. Seriously. Not a lot of sleep that night. I lay there thinking of our dating days and how I'd dreamed of the idyllic life we would have together. Oddly, rats had not entered the picture even once.

The next day we attended the wedding of some friends. It was lovely to get away from our rodentia problems awhile and concentrate on flowers, candlelight and romance. Alas, too soon the festivities were over and it was time to return to our infestation. On the drive home, the bride and groom passed us, smiling and waving as they headed down the highway toward their happily ever after.

I cried.

That night, my redneck hubby determined to get himself a rat. We closed all the heat registers tight except for one, which we carefully removed. Hubby braced a piece of plywood over the opening to create an inviting tunnel and placed some bait there. He announced that dinner was now being served on the upper deck, and set up camp under the kitchen table with his .22, waiting for Mr. Rat to come up for vittles. I went to bed.

I'll spare you the details. Suffice it to say we learned bird shot will create little dents in your wall without actually making holes. But Hubby got his rat that night and by the fragrance emerging from behind a wall a few days later, we knew we got at least one more with the poison. Gave a whole new meaning to "I smell a rat." The odour eventually dissipated and we risked having company again.

What's the point of my tale? Only this. While there are many things in life that will never be funny no matter what, there are a great deal of things that will. Sure, they might make your skin crawl. It might take years. But you'll chuckle, one day.

What's happening in your life right now that someday you'll be able to look back at and laugh? And if that's truly the case ... why not today?

Hats Off to Romance
(Appeared February 18, 2012)
This story also appears in
Chicken Soup for the Soul: Married Life

The smooching in the sketch demanded I find a married couple to act in the drama that Sunday morning. Not having any married couples on our church drama team, I recruited my somewhat reluctant but good-natured hubby to join me on stage.

The theme of the day was the "Roles of Women," and we picked up on Amy Grant's song *Hats* to write a hilarious sketch based on some what-ifs. What if a woman literally needed to change her hat every time she "changed hats?" Within the span of a fast paced, five-minute sketch, "Millie" gets up in the morning, meets briefly with God, provides breakfast for her family, packs their lunches, sees them out the door, goes to work, and meets a friend for lunch. She returns home to children with homework, one with the flu, supper to make, church choir practice to lead, and so on. Throughout the day, she keeps returning to a large hat box placed centre stage, where she finds the appropriate hat for the task at hand — sometimes wearing two or three at once, but never doing any one job well.

By the end of the day, things have careened out of control. As an exhausted Millie frantically sifts through the box searching for her "nurse" hat (did she leave it in Medicine Hat?), her husband walks in wearing a grin.

"Look what I found hidden away in the back of the closet," he announces, blowing dust off a hard hat. "Your LOVER hat!"

Millie replies with an exasperated "Lover hat?!?" and faints into his arms as the lights fade. We knew it would prove a hit with an audience who could readily identify.

My husband agreed to dust off his business suit for the role, but didn't bother to try it on until Sunday morning. Uh oh ... apparently the pants shrunk a little, hanging there in the closet.

Oh well, no time to do anything about it now. Suck it up, darlin', the show must go on.

And it did. I played Millie with enthusiasm, allowing her to get more frantic as the story unfolded and built to the big finish when my knight in binding armor would sweep me into his arms right there in front of the entire congregation!

And he did ... just as his pants split right up the back, revealing to the crowd his white under shorts as the lights faded and our audience burst into gales of laughter and applause.

I went home and put on my mending hat.

On Becoming a Grandmother
(Appeared September 6, 2012)
Also appears in *Chicken Soup for the Soul: Grandmothers*

I thought I was prepared.

I was a mother, after all. I already knew what it meant to love someone so much it hurt. I understood the old adage that to be a parent is to walk around forever with your heart outside your body. I had written in my journal, revealing all the emotions I'd discovered tag-teaming in my heart: happiness, melancholy, anxiety, joy, anticipation, worry. I had seen the ultrasound pictures. I'd crocheted a soft, fuzzy blue blanket, patiently undoing all my bungled stitches and doing them over so it would be a perfect square. I had memorized the verses in Psalm 139 that tell how God wonderfully forms us in our mother's womb. I had prayed for this child and for his parents daily since I learned of his existence. I had written letters to his mom and dad, assuring them how proud I was of them both, how they would be excellent parents.

I'd prayed for myself, too. I'd wrestled with the idea that I was going to be a grandmother. Shouldn't I be wiser first? Or sweeter? Or at the very least, a better cook? How exactly did one cram for this event? I had even admitted to myself that I would soon be sleeping with someone's grandfather. That idea took a little getting used to, let me tell you!

I had bragged to my friends. I had celebrated with my mother. I had gifted my daughter-in-law with maternity clothes and bought the most irresistible little stuffed puppy for the baby.

I had done all of that. I thought I was prepared.

The day he was born, I rode along with his other grandparents to the hospital to meet our mutual little descendent for the first time. We were told to wait in the hallway while the nurses finished up whatever they were doing with him and his mother in the room. Given the hospital rules,

I fully expected my first sight of my little grandson would be in his plastic baby bed and I was prepared.

But when I turned around, I instantly knew that no amount of groundwork could have prepared me for that moment. Instead of the expected baby bed, I was beholding my own firstborn carrying his firstborn in his arms.

I came unglued. Part of me was carried back 26 years to the day I first laid eyes on my son. But those 26 years had passed in an instant, and here I was looking at the next generation, with the same dark skin and the same head full of thick, dark hair. He was beautiful and I was smitten. I didn't even try to check the tears running down my cheeks as I held him in my arms and hugged his dad as tight as I could with the baby between us. What a cherished moment!

This little boy is now in kindergarten and has two little brothers. Every day brings new adventures, new things to learn, new memories to make, and new opportunities to wonder at the marvelous work of our Creator. These little guys have taught me that sometimes stopping to watch ducks is more important than getting in out of the rain. They've uncovered my own impatient ways, the ones I thought I had overcome but now realize the opportunities to demonstrate patience have only become less frequent. They've reminded me that time spent cuddling a sleeping baby in a rocking chair trumps pretty much anything.

Most of all, I've come to realize that no matter how hard I tried, I could not have prepared to love someone so profusely, or to learn so much from someone so small.

How to Live with Me for 35 Years (and counting)
(Appeared September 27, 2012)

First of all, yes. I was a child bride. Now that we've cleared that up, I can tell you October 1, 2012 will mark our 35th wedding anniversary.
    Like most people, I'm super easy to live with — when I'm alone. If I could travel back to 1977 and present my groom with a manual called *How to Live with Terrie*, below are just three of the things it might contain. Too bad I didn't know any of them then.

#1. She'll expect constant praise.
    The first few months we were married, I was crushed when nary a word was forthcoming about the meals I placed on the table. I grew up in a home where expressions of appreciation for food were a natural part of the meal. At the very least, "mmmmm" was heard as we enjoyed whatever was placed before us. If nothing was said, that could mean only one thing: nobody liked it.
    Somehow, I'd failed to notice Hubby's family didn't necessarily share this custom. You came to the table, you ate what was offered, you left. Conversation flowed freely, but rarely about the food.
    Gradually, I got used to this and stopped expecting applause for my efforts. And Hubby has learned to say "thanks for lunch" before he leaves the table.

#2. She'll try to run your life.
    We were about eight years and two children in when Hubby gave me the loveliest surprise for Christmas: a coupon for a weekend away, just the two of us, to do whatever I wanted. Being the planner I am, I prearranged every half-hour slot of our weekend. My schedule included times for rest and recreation, but also long chunks devoted to evaluating our financial, housing, parenting, and every other goal I could

imagine. I created charts and graphs to keep us on track. I was in my glories, knowing we would return home with all our problems solved. I just knew that once Hubby saw how great this was, he'd agree it should be an annual event.

At last, the big weekend arrived. I couldn't understand why Hubby wasn't thrilled with my plan. My schedule lasted about 30 minutes before he had enough. One small goal would have been sufficient to tackle in a weekend.

#3. She'll become a writer and blab your life to the world.

I promised my family I'd provide the opportunity to veto anything pertaining to them before hitting the send button. Hubby's a good sport. Last Valentine's Day, he agreed to let me tell column readers the story of his on-stage pants-splitting adventure. That story later landed in one of the Chicken Soup for the Soul books, many of which are translated into foreign languages and sold all over the world.

One day, we'll find ourselves on a tour bus in Jerusalem and a little old lady will read our nametags and say, "Hey, you're that guy who split his pants on stage after his wife dragged him into a church drama."

But she'll say it in Hebrew and we won't have a clue what she's saying. I'll assume she wants my autograph. Hubby will assume she's saying, "God bless you, you poor man."

It's just as well such detailed manuals don't exist, or most of us wouldn't have the courage to commit in the first place. But had I stayed single all these years, I would still think I was practically perfect. We'd both have missed out on countless rough edges rubbed smoother, and on the multitude of private jokes that accumulate during three and a half decades together.

Life's storms have made us lean hard on God, family, friends, and yes, counsellors to help us hold on. A song sung at our wedding said, "We don't know what tomorrow holds, but we know who holds tomorrow."

True then. Better understood now.

Pennies (stolen) from Heaven
(Appeared February 21, 2013)

Canada's decision to do away with the penny reminds me of some pennies I once purloined. From God.

I was still a preschooler when, each Sunday morning, my dad would give me two pennies to drop in the offering plate. It made me feel like part of the church family to make my own contribution, even though I'd done nothing to earn the money.

One Sunday I watched as the plate passed down the rows of adults. I noticed the occasional person simply passing the plate without contributing, or gently shaking their head at the usher to indicate empty hands. It occurred to me the offering was optional.

It also occurred to me that if I were to hold back my pennies and save them, I could buy myself a treat. Five cents was enough to buy a chocolate bar; ten cents would procure a bag of chips. Yes, I'm that old.

As much as I would love to blame one of my big brothers for planting this sinister idea in my impressionable little mind, I suspect it got there all by itself. I began to implement my plan. When the usher came by, I shook my head "no" like I'd seen the grown-ups do and kept the pennies in my little red purse. Each week, I stacked them higher on a shelf in my bedroom, no doubt rubbing my greedy little hands together like Dr. Evil and congratulating myself on my cleverness.

One night when Dad came to tuck me in, he noticed the growing stack of pennies, now up to six or eight. I must have been holding out for the bigger prize of chips. Delayed gratification began early in my family.

"Where did you get the pennies?" Dad asked.

"Um. I don't remember."

"Sounds like you're having a little memory trouble. Did you forget to put them in the offering?" Like he didn't already know.

I might not have slept much that night had I known the story from the New Testament about the married couple who sold some property, gave a portion to the church, and agreed to tell others they'd donated the entire amount. Their story does not end well. (You can read it in Acts chapter 5.) Though they had every right to keep some of the money, their lying and conspiracy got them in deep enough trouble to be made a disturbing example of.

Dad was far gentler. Eventually, I fessed up. We talked about the plans I'd made for the money and Dad explained how it belonged to God and had come my way only by grace in the first place. I'm certain Dad didn't realize he was giving me an accurate picture of my heavenly Father. Like Jesus did with the woman caught in adultery, Dad did not punish or condemn. His "go and sin no more" message got through, and I knew I was loved.

I wish I could say I never dreamed up another naughty scheme in my life. My schemes only grew more sophisticated with age. But each time I fail, I know where to turn for forgiveness.

Just think. If I'd kept up my deceptive hoarding, I'd have over 50 bucks stashed by now. That's a lot of pennies! Before they're gone for good, I think I'll stack a few pennies on a shelf as a gentle reminder. For even if it were a million dollars, it could never begin to replace the lesson Dad taught me that day: genuine treasure comes in the form of mercy, love and grace.

Braver Than We Knew
(Appeared March 7, 2013)

March 7 is International Women's Day and I want to tell you about one of the women I admire most in all the world, who also happens to turn 30 years old this week. She spent the first 18 of those years in our home.

Mindy entered kindergarten with the same enthusiasm she held for all of life's adventures. She was eager to learn, make friends, and enjoy each day. We could not have predicted what her first few days held in store.

After only two days of school, Mindy's right eye began to water, turn purple, and swell, until it had swollen completely shut. When we arrived at the hospital, medical staff recognized a severe infection and were concerned for her vision. What caused it remains a mystery, but they immediately hooked Mindy up to intravenous antibiotics. That meant staying in the hospital, a first for our girl.

My own tears refused to stay put as her one good eye pled with me to stop the invasion. She could not comprehend the connection between the pain in her eye and the needle going into her arm, nor why I allowed the nurse to hurt her like this.

With the I.V. finally in place, however, Mindy began to settle down and see the hospital stay as simply another adventure. She gladly put on the blue and white striped flannel pajamas supplied and enjoyed the toys and books in the playroom. By the end of the day, she was getting into trouble for scooting too fast down the hallway on her I.V. pole.

That night as I tucked her into her hospital bed and said prayers, I asked if she wanted me to stay with her overnight.

"I think you should go home and help Daddy take care of the boys," she said. "I'll be okay."

I thought she was a terribly brave little girl, but I didn't realize just how brave until I returned the following morning. I found Mindy in her room, having breakfast.

"Mommy," she said, incredulous. "I think the nurses stayed here all night!"

She had thought the staff would all go home to their own beds, leaving her all alone. And that, in Mindy's mind, was quite acceptable.

I should have realized then what a courageous daughter God had given us. In the years to come, she proved it many times. This young lady went on to spend a summer of high school in Army Boot Camp, thriving while some male colleagues quit. After high school graduation she went off to Switzerland to begin work there as a nanny, though she knew no one, did not speak the language, and had little experience caring for young children. She made out just fine, and subsequently travelled to more countries than I can hope to visit.

Today, Mindy is a bright and beautiful married woman (with healthy eyesight) who brings joy and energy to everything she tackles. Between studying for her Master's degree in Counselling, she spends her free time volunteering for a crisis prevention center and a home for pregnant, homeless women. She is passionate about the fight to end human trafficking and works tirelessly to defend the dignity of all women, offering hope and healing to the brokenhearted and abused. Mindy learned early that life can throw harsh and unexpected things at you, but a positive attitude, a determined spirit, and solid faith will take you far.

I really hope I am more like her when I grow up.

One Rascally Long Day …
(Appeared July 18, 2013)

Don't spread this around. Last month I accepted an invitation to spend an entire day, from rising until bedtime, alone with three unbelievably handsome gentlemen. To keep things anonymous, we'll call them Alfalfa, Buckwheat and Spanky.

Alfalfa is six; Buckwheat is three and a half; Spanky is one and a half.

As the appointed day approached, the arguments between Cynical Me and Optimistic Me went something like this:

CM: You're never going to have the energy to keep up with those rascals all day.

OM: Hey, I already know how to do this. I once had three preschoolers of my own.

CM: Yeah, but you were in your twenties then.

OM: So, I'll just let them tear around while I sit and watch.

CM: You'll become exhausted and irritable and then you'll get mean.

OM: No I won't. All I need to do is keep them alive for one day until their parents return. How hard could it be?

By the time breakfast was over, I had prayed for help three times, but I felt pretty proud of myself. Everyone was fed, Spanky had a clean diaper, and the kitchen was sort of clean. So what if Alfalfa decided to stay in his pajamas all day? The cold wind prevented us from playing outside, so we spent the morning reading books. Actually, Spanky and I read books while Alfalfa and Buckwheat jumped from bed to dresser to floor until I made them stop lest someone or something get hurt. So they jumped from crib to floor until something did get hurt: an overhead shelf came crashing down. But hey, everybody was still alive.

After lunch, I put Spanky down for a nap and sent Alfalfa and Buckwheat to their rooms for quiet time.

"But I don't need a quiet time anymore, Grandma," Alfalfa said.

"I know," I said. "But Grandma does."

We survived the afternoon and after supper the weather improved enough to go out. With a big farmyard to play in, I turned Alfalfa and Buckwheat loose and focused my energy on watching Spanky toddle about. Until I heard heart-wrenching screams coming from the other side of the barn. Buckwheat had managed to collapse the rotting top fence rail. His belly still straddled the second rail, his head and hands lost deep in the long, tick-infested grass on the other side. Alfalfa looked on with an amused expression.

From the safety of the mown side, I managed to pull Buckwheat off the fence and checked him over for broken bones, cuts, bruises and ticks. A hug and a kiss and he was good to go. But now where was Spanky? How did that little hooligan disappear so fast? I started calling.

Thankfully, he had only ventured inside the barn. That's when I spotted the big red wagon. Hey, what a great way to contain all three boys — I'd give them a ride! They happily piled in and I began to pull. But half-way down their long driveway, I gave out.

"Say, Alfalfa," I said. "Wouldn't you like to pull your little brothers in the wagon?"

"No."

"Well, you're going to. Hop out."

So Alfalfa pulled Buckwheat and Spanky to the end of the driveway. On the way back, Buckwheat pulled Spanky until, with one heroic last effort, I pulled all three of them again for the last half. I then left the two older characters outside while I wrangled Spanky into the bathtub.

When I called Alfalfa and Buckwheat inside for their baths, Buckwheat had soaked his shoes and socks in a deep, cold puddle and was howling again. But hey, everybody was still alive and Spanky wore a clean diaper and pajamas.

I got Buckwheat into the tub and went to hunt down Alfalfa. Meanwhile, Spanky wandered into the bathroom where his brother splashed around, soaking the entire room. I had to start all over, wrestling Spanky into a dry diaper and pajamas.

Eventually, everybody was tucked into bed, still alive, and their parents returned home. I drove home to a cup of tea and my own bed, thinking about how dearly I love these three little rascals and how thankful I am that God gives children to the young.

My Big Hairy First World Problem
(Appeared August 8, 2013)

The vanity top in our new bathroom has a marble design in black, brown and beige. When I gave my sister the tour, I mentioned that I thought black towels and shower curtain might look sharp, but I wouldn't be buying them any time soon. All the hidden costs of moving will nickel and dime you to death. Nowadays, I suppose it's more accurate to say "loonie and toonie" you to death.

One afternoon a few days later, Sis and Mom showed up with a housewarming gift — black towels and shower curtain! I was delighted.

Naturally, I hung them immediately and they did indeed look chic. We would have the trendiest bathroom on the block, not that I've seen any of the other bathrooms on the block. Hubby was the first to use the new towels the next morning. By the time I saw him, I hardly recognized him.

"What's with the gorilla suit?" I asked.

"It's those new towels," he said. "They're leaving black fluff everywhere."

Shoot, I thought. I should have washed them first. After running them through the laundry, I filled the back of our half-ton with black lint from the dryer, hauled it to the landfill site, and hung the towels back up.

This time, the entire bathroom wore a layer of black fluff. When I swept it up, it barked at me and ran out the front door and down the street where I think I saw it lift a leg on a fire hydrant, although I may have made that part up.

"I want my old towels back," Hubby said. "I don't care what colour they are."

Some people have no appreciation for décor.

I ran them through the wash again.

"You can use 'em, but I ain't usin' 'em," he said.

"Fine," I said. "I ain't scared."

So I did. Black fluff everywhere. I went to work naked that day and no one noticed.

I went online and discovered black towel fluff is a common dilemma. Entire websites devote themselves to black towel fluff. You can even join a black towel fluff support group, although I didn't think I was ready for that.

One person suggested embracing the fluff and listed a host of crafts one could create. Another suggested line-drying followed by a good shake outdoors. I repeated this process four times and the towels still gave off lint. I began to experience nightmares about hideous black-fluff monsters coming to life in the sewers of Portage la Prairie, holding black-fluff monster weddings and producing enough black-fluff baby monsters to take over the entire city.

The loss of sleep started clouding my judgement, as became evident the next day when a woman with fluffy black hair visited City Hall. I lunged across the counter to choke her and co-workers had to pull me off until I simmered down.

My mom and sister encouraged me to take the towels back to the store, along with the shower curtain that worked fine but no longer matched. "What have you got to lose?" they said. "Maybe they'll give you store credit."

So I did. And the store did. I picked out some green towels, washed and hung them. Much better. Hubby says they also give off too much lint, but he is wrong. Black fluff still blurs his vision. He thinks I'm in denial. With martyr-like resignation, he uses the green towels anyway. The man is a saint.

I've since concluded it's not so much the colour as the type of towel. Others told me their horror stories of red fluff, navy fluff, orange fluff, yellow fluff — and the carnage that occurs when they are laundered together. It's bedlam, I tell you.

Why, oh why must life be so darn hard?

Parents, You Really Do Have a Clue
(Appeared April 9, 2015)

Flip through our family photo albums and you'll come across a picture of our older son at age seven, lying on his back, holding a slide rule about 10 inches above his face and studying it so intensely he doesn't notice the camera. Science books at our house actually got read. On Saturday afternoons without fail, our TV blasted *Popular Mechanics for Kids* (it probably didn't hurt that a cute, 15-year-old Elisha Cuthbert co-hosted the show). Today, this young man supports himself and his family as a competent engineer.

On another page, you'll see our younger son at age two with the beloved toy guitar his grandmother gave him for Christmas. In a birthday photo, he gleefully holds a kit of art supplies. His former classmates and teachers remember him as the one forever doodling in class. At the age of nine or 10, he created a pencil portrait of Vladimir Lenin convincing enough to hang on the set for the senior high play. Now, he makes his living as a talented tattoo artist and plays guitar in a band for fun.

In the majority of pictures of our daughter, she is surrounded by people. From the earliest age, her life revolved around others and her generosity with her possessions put me to shame. She became the one other girls, and even boys, came to for advice or just a listening ear. She was the one I'd find crying in her room, not over some personal calamity but over heartbreak a friend was facing. Next weekend, we'll watch our lovely daughter receive her master's degree in Counselling. (I must remember not to wear something with buttons down the front, lest they burst.) Soon she will begin her job at Sonshine Centre in Calgary, specializing in helping women and children live free from domestic violence and abuse.

The point of this is not simply to brag about my kids, though we are certainly proud of them. Here's the thing. Back in the day when their dad and I took those photos, we gave little thought to what our children would do with their adult lives.

We were so busy pushing them to finish their homework, take baths, eat right, be polite, do their chores and not kill each other to think about much else. Yet the clues were all there, though we see them only now, in hindsight. Had we been more intuitive, I'm sure we could have done more to encourage, support and equip them for the roles they were created to play.

Young parents, I want to challenge you in this. In the insaneness of your busy lives, take note of what your children gravitate toward. With some kids, it will appear obvious early on. Others may need to try many different things before discovering their niche. Do what you can to foster their talent, and remember — your child doesn't need to play for the NHL to be a hero. Watch not only for your child's ability, but for his heart. What moves him or her to compassion? To anger? To action? What sorts of events will get him out of bed in the morning? And if you pray, ask God for wisdom. He knows your kid better than you do.

I love Frederick Buechner's words, "The place God calls you to is the place where your deep gladness and the world's deep hunger meet." It takes too many of us 50 years or more to find that place, if we find it at all. Let's do all we can to help our kids discover their place, their calling and their passion. The clues are there.

Confessions of a Party Pooper
(Appeared March 3, 2016)

For four days each year, Hubby and I are the same age. In between these two birthdays last week, our perpetually cheerful eldest called to suggest he bring the family for lunch at our house, followed by an afternoon of sledding if weather permitted. A sort of combined birthday celebration and a great way to wear out three rambunctious boys on a winter Saturday.

Oh. Um. Well. Gee.

I had planned to get some writing done, maybe a little housework. But I knew the correct answer. How long will it be before the boys would rather stick pins in their eyes than go sledding — or do anything, really — with Grandma and Grandpa?

"OK. Sounds good."

I bought frozen lasagna, a bagged salad, pop-in-the-oven garlic bread and a bakery cake. They might be descending on my house and pre-empting my naptime, but I saw no need to be a martyr about it with a home-cooked meal.

I saved my martyrdom for the sledding hill. Though the temperature was a balmy minus seven, the brutal wind threatened to suck my face off and hurl it down the hill without me. I snapped a few pictures of the others and climbed back in the truck where I belonged.

"This is dumb," I thought after a while. "If Grandpa can slide down the hill and live to do it a second and third time, surely I can go down at least once. It's probably more fun than it looks."

It wasn't.

Why anyone would willingly bump down a frozen hill, walloping their tailbone while icy shards stab their eyeballs when they could be curled up by a cozy fake fireplace with a cup of tea and a good book is beyond me. I think I saw my dentures pass me on the way down and I don't even wear dentures.

I survived my one run and quit while ahead.

From there, we packed everyone off to the river for a wiener roast. This required a 15-minute tramp through knee-deep snow pulling sleds laden with lawn chairs and food. Staggering in fruitless attempts to stay upright, I asked the littlest if we were having fun yet.

"I am," he said.

I plowed on, knowing it was the only way for this adventure to be over.

The fire took a while to begin blazing and I fantasized about the hot bath I'd take when we got home. I knew I should be taking a cue from the boys, running around like they were. Instead, I huddled close to the fire, coughing in the smoke and mentally writing the epitaph for my gravestone: "Worst. Grandmother. Ever."

The hot dogs were tasty. Which reminds me, how do you get mustard and ketchup out of mittens?

We packed up and began the long trek back, the boys impressing me with their stamina and good spirits in spite of the cold wind, the snotty noses and the lack of bathroom facilities. Like an old mare returning to her warm stall, I moved much faster on the return trip.

The boys and their parents piled into their vehicle and waved good-bye. Did they see me as nothing but a big spoil sport? Had I crushed their little hearts by revealing the spineless wimp that I am?

It was on my own ride home that it occurred to me. Though I have many clear and fond memories of my grandmother, I cannot say I ever saw her slide down a toboggan hill. Or tramp through deep snow just for the sake of spending time with me. Or eat a hot dog outdoors in February.

Maybe this day wasn't about whether or not I had a delightful experience. Maybe it wasn't about what I would remember, but about what they would. Maybe it was simply about showing up.

I enjoyed that hot bath as if the water came straight from heaven.

TERRIE TODD

Why I'll Never Win Mother of the Year
(Appeared May 3, 2016)

I'll never forget one frigid January evening in 1987. Our third child was all of two weeks old and I was venturing off for my first outing away from him. It was only a grocery shopping expedition, but when you are home with preschoolers 24/7, even food shopping in the dead of winter can seem exotic if you get to do it alone. The plan was to drop all three kids at my mother's house so I could shop in peace.

I carried the baby's car seat out and set it on the hood while I opened the car doors for the other children. I heard it before I saw it. In one horrifying split second, the car seat slid across the hood's icy surface and landed with a sickening crunch, face down on the frozen crushed rock below — with my newborn baby in it.

Few words can describe what a parent feels in that moment, and "competent" is definitely not one of them. I upturned the car seat and examined my son. Snuggled in his snowsuit, he still slept peacefully. It seemed the straps had held him to the seat and only the seat's edges actually touched the ground. Shaking, I loaded him into the back seat facing backwards, with a sibling on either side facing forward. Then I climbed behind the steering wheel, not knowing whether I'd be driving to the hospital or carrying on with my original plan.

All the way to town, I kept asking my older son, "What's the baby doing?" "Is the baby okay?" "Is he breathing?"

I held myself together until we reached Mom's house, but when she came to the door, I became a hormonal puddle. "Mom," I blubbered. "You won't believe what I've done." She let me cry it out of my system, assured me the baby would be fine, and sent me on my way.

I don't know if there's a parent anywhere without a similar story. No mother or father can be on constant alert every second of a child's life (and if you could, I'm not sure you'd end up with adequately independent offspring.) Most of the time, our momentarily lapses in judgement don't carry heavy consequences. But sometimes they do. And when they do, it's imperative for us to remember they happen to all of us. The passing of judgement on one parent by another at these times is unacceptable. If you have managed to keep your child alive to adulthood, it is a far greater testimony to the grace of God than to your excellent parenting skills.

So where is God's grace when a child does not survive?

I believe it's still present. It just looks a whole lot different. It looks like the compassionate support of a caring community of friends and family who know, deep down, that it could just as easily have been their own child. Why wouldn't we extend the same compassion following an accidental death or injury as we do when a child succumbs to cancer? If possible, the parents' pain would feel even heavier as they wrestle self-condemnation. They do not need ours, too.

This Mother's Day, let's remember those who are hurting due to the loss of a child from any cause, at any age. Though I have been spared this grief so far, I watched my sister and brother-in-law bury their only son last year, at age 46. It never gets any easier, and there is no deeper loss. There just isn't.

Of Love and Undershorts
(Appeared February 8, 2018)
This column won a 2019 Word Guild Award

Having married at the ripe ages of 18 and 19, Hubby and I never lived on our own. When we took up housekeeping and life together, we each automatically assumed the role our same gender parent had played and depended on the other to do the same. I guess Mom must have bought Dad's underwear for him, because it took me only 30 years to start questioning why I was doing this as well.

One day when Hubby announced his underwear was full of holes and needed replacing, I declared my freedom.

"You're a big boy. You can buy your own underwear from now on," I said. Or something to that effect. I may have included a rant about how I worked full time like he did and wasn't it enough that I washed, dried, folded and put his underwear away?

Well, technically, we own machines to wash and dry them. But still.

He didn't argue.

But as the weeks went by, I kept noticing the same old ratty underwear showing up in the wash and no new ones making their appearance. I didn't mention it, but I refused to give in. I don't know how many weeks went by. Maybe it was months. Neither of us mentioned the underwear situation.

Then one day I visited Walmart for some other things. I must have been in a particularly benevolent mood that day, because as I passed the men's section, it occurred to me that it would take 10 seconds to grab a package of the underwear Hubby liked and toss it into my cart. Was this really a hill worth dying on? Surely I could be the bigger man and swallow my pride this once.

I did it, proud of myself for conquering my own stubborn spirit. Clearly, I was the more mature one.

When I arrived home later and walked into our bedroom, Walmart bag in hand, a surprise greeted me. On top of Hubby's dresser sat a brand-new package of underwear—the exact duplicate of the package I'd bought.

Without a word, we had both surrendered on the same day.

Hubby was good for underwear for a long time after that. And I can't help thinking God enjoyed a good chuckle.

Author Richelle E. Goodrich said, "If you think the most courageous and difficult thing you can do is stubbornly stand your ground, try graciously giving in."

OUT OF MY MIND

A Lesson from Winter on Love, Sex and Marriage
(Appeared February 14, 2019)

One benefit of these frigid Manitoba mornings is, you don't waste time staring into your closet deciding what to wear. You simply wear it all.

As I bundle up for my morning walks to work, I've been contemplating the importance of doing things in the proper sequence. Long johns before pants, pants before ski pants. Then boots, parka, hood, scarf. Backpack. Gloves. Big leather mittens over the gloves. It all works together quite nicely to help me survive the brutality known as our weather.

But what if I decided to mix it up one morning because I'm bored with the routine or feeling a bit rebellious? Maybe I want to put my long johns on last, or my boots first. What if I put on my backpack and then tried putting my parka on over that? Or maybe I could put on my big leather mitts first. It could be done — maybe. But by the time I managed to zip my coat and tie my scarf while wearing those bulky mitts, I'd be frustrated to tears. I'd be sweating like a boxer. And my workday would be almost over.

Doing things in the right order applies to so much of life, doesn't it? No matter how much we might like to skip some steps, especially if they're hard, life works better in a certain order. We need the education before the good job, and the experience before the better job. We must practise before proficiency comes. We're required to raise children before we can spoil grandchildren. Buckle up before driving off.

Oh sure, we can try doing things cart-before-the-horse. It might even work, with effort. Instead of washing dishes right after we've eaten off them, we could wash them just before we eat. Either way, we're eating off a clean dish, so what's the big deal? But seriously, who wants to be scraping off yesterday's stuck-on spaghetti before you can enjoy tonight's chicken?

You might succeed at driving to the gas station on a flat tire and then putting air in it. You could try washing a dirty floor before you sweep up the loose dirt. It's possible to dress first and then take a shower. It's also really, really dumb.

How about marriage, sex and having babies? These days, people laugh at the idea of saving sex for marriage. Like it's downright dumb.

But is it? Have you ever met anyone who waited and regretted it? I haven't. Present company included. Most things work a whole lot better when done in the right order. Your Creator knows you and put some rules in place that He knows will, if followed, work best for you and the order of your life. Sure, you can change the order and "get along fine." Lots of people appear to do exactly that.

And lots of people don't. They carry around emotional scars from past relationships which deeply and negatively affect their present one — wounds they could have avoided by doing things in the order intended by the One who knows them best, loves them most, and understands their heart.

Valentine's Day is a time to celebrate love and romance and sex.

It's a cold world, friend. Why make your life harder than necessary? Bundle up in the right order.

Filling My Shoes
(Appeared March 21, 2019)

I'm training my replacement at city hall in preparation for my retirement at the end of March. A couple of people have kindly suggested I am leaving big shoes to fill. While the comments are flattering, they're also funny because they bring to mind a whole other story about my shoes.

If you work in an office, you're probably familiar with the way women's shoes accumulate. We arrive at work in our snow boots or walking shoes and change into something dressier for the day. The dressy shoes get left at the office because there's no point hauling them home every night. At city hall, the shoes and boots collect on the floor where we hang our coats. Sometimes they sit there for months.

My first couple of years on staff, I could not bring myself to place my shoes next to the others. I would leave them under my desk instead.

No, it wasn't a germ phobia. Nor was I afraid they'd walk away on someone else's feet.

It was because my shoes were the biggest. I mean, unambiguously, undoubtedly, unmistakably the biggest. My petite co-workers wore the shoe size you'd expect of someone their height. I'm five foot seven and wear size nine. Nothing unusual about that. But when you put a size nine shoe beside a size five shoe, it looks like something you could paddle across Crescent Lake in.

And I have a history concerning my feet.

You see, at the awkward age of 11 or so, I began getting teased about my big feet by an adult who was close to the family and by a big brother who was happy to join the game. I wish I'd been secure enough to laugh along, but I hated it. They said I could be seen coming around the corner because my feet arrived before the rest of me. I grew up convinced I was galumphing around like Bigfoot himself, and no matter how often others said my feet were the right size for my body, it was a hard image to shake.

Eventually, I got over it. I thought. Until I went to work at city hall and saw those dainty shoes beside mine. I couldn't handle it. And I suddenly realized I hadn't "gotten over it" at all.

At some point, I recognized my behaviour was ridiculous and have been placing my shoes beside the others for some time now. It no longer bothers me. Or it might simply be that the people with the Cinderella-size feet have all retired.

The moral in all this? The taunting should not have been allowed. Although it was "all in good fun," and although far worse things happen to kids, I needed someone in authority to nip it in the bud.

Can I encourage all of us to play a role here? Body issues already run rampant. Under no circumstances should you tease children or allow them to mock each other about their bodies, or about anything out of their control. Be their protector. The words of adults, especially family members, carry incredible weight — both negative and positive. So use that power to instill in your kids and grandkids a healthy appreciation for their amazing bodies. Teach them to grant others the same respect. Help them memorize Psalm 139:14, "Thank you for making me so wonderfully complex! It is amazing to think about. Your workmanship is marvelous — and how well I know it." (The Living Bible).

My replacement at city hall is also one of those dainty-feet ladies. But guess what? She's going to fill my shoes just fine.

Section 3: The Writing Life

*My heart overflows with a good theme;
I address my verses to the King;
My tongue is the pen of a ready writer.*

Psalm 45:1

TERRIE TODD

Hey, Haven't I Seen You Somewhere?
(My first column appeared September 25, 2010)

If you're going to write a regular column for the *Central Plains Herald Leader*, you must first introduce yourself to its readers. I used to think I had one of those generic faces every tenth person has, or else a name with a real ring to it. Everywhere I go, somebody says, "Why do I feel I should know you?" or, "Why does your name sound familiar?"

I usually provide one or more of the following possible explanations.

Maybe you saw my face on the front of the *Herald Leader* last Easter, holding a copy of my recently published play. One of my finer moments.

Maybe you saw my hubby, Jon, and me in the *Daily Graphic* 15 years ago after he lost his right arm in a farming accident. NOT one of my finer moments.

Maybe you frequent City Hall. I work there as an Administrative Assistant. Although I seldom emerge from the back offices unless one of our front clerks has candy on her desk.

Maybe you went to see *The Dixie Swim Club* when the Prairie Players brought it to the Glesby Centre last year. I played "Sheree," the athletic, bossy one. One was a stretch, the other ... not so much.

Maybe you saw my byline when I used to write for the Faith page in the *Herald Leader*. Haven't written that column in a few years. My faith, I'm glad to say, remains intact.

Maybe you were a student of my mom, Norma, who taught for years at Portage Christian Academy. I see her looking at me from my mirror a little more each day.

Maybe you're confusing me with my sister, Shanon. She worked for 20 years at Westpark School, starting out as kindergarten teacher and ending as principal.

Maybe you remember me from Red River College when its Portage Regional Centre was across the street from Subway. I worked in their office in the late nineties.

Maybe I cleaned your house. I had my own cleaning service for about 10 years. Can't say I miss it.

Maybe you've been to Portage Alliance Church. I was on staff for 14 years and still attend on Sundays.

Maybe you've seen me dancing with the Prairie Cloggers. I'm the one with the clumsy footwork and the lunatic grin that won't wipe off.

Maybe you work at the Co-op. I've been shopping there faithfully since we moved to Portage in 1983.

And then I realize it's not so much my common face or catchy name. It's the fact Portage la Prairie is small enough to *see* everyone, but a little too big to *know* everyone. The perfect sized town, if you ask me. In the future, if you think you know me from somewhere, I really hope it'll be from this, my column in the *Central Plains Herald Leader*. I'm calling it "Out of My Mind."

I hope you'll go there with me.

Columnist Bids a Fond Farewell

(This column appeared August 16, 2016, after I received abrupt notice that the previous week's column would be my last. I begged and was granted the opportunity to write a farewell column.)

You have to appreciate the irony. I had planned to wrap up my "Jobs that Teach" series with a Labour Day column about how all these jobs led to my becoming a writer. I even planned to include a fitting quote from my favourite old hymn. I had no idea I'd be ending the series a few weeks early or that today's column would be my last. I'm told my style does not meet the editorial vision for The Daily Graphic's future, and I can respect that. If I've learned anything about the publishing industry, it's that it is constantly changing and I consider myself truly privileged to have enjoyed six years of sharing life and words with you. I'm grateful for this opportunity to say good-bye.

The old hymn, however, is more applicable than ever. But we'll get to that later.

Thank you, readers, from the depths of my heart, for your faithful reading and frequent encouragement. Thank you for your graciousness on those weeks when my "Faith and Humour" column was neither faith-filled nor humorous. Thank you for enriching my life by challenging me when I got it wrong. I hope I've been able to inspire you with an occasional laugh, a tear or a new thought. I've written about everything from packing school lunches to lung disease to lavatories. But through it all, I hope I've also served to remind you about the things that last forever: faith, love, hope, family, gratitude and forgiveness.

More than anything, I hope that I have helped you take just one baby step closer to your Creator.

Soren Kierkegaard said, "Life can only be understood backwards; but it must be lived forwards." I'm sad to leave these pages, but I've learned that God generally has something better around the bend and I don't want to miss it because I failed to turn the corner! I can't see what waits around it yet, but I know that Jesus is already there. And that's what walking by faith is all about.

As for the words of that old hymn, I can think of none more comforting or inspiring than these from the heart of Fanny Crosby:

> *All the way my Saviour leads me,*
> *what have I to ask beside?*
> *Can I doubt his tender mercy,*
> *who through life has been my guide?*
> *Heavenly peace, divinest comfort,*
> *here by faith in him to dwell.*
> *For I know whatever befall me,*
> *Jesus doeth all things well.*

Did I mention that Fanny Crosby was blind?

May you be led by the one who does all things well. May you trust him for what's around the next corner. And may you experience the richness of his outrageous love for you. God bless you. Thanks for reading.

She's Baa-aack!
*(Appeared October 12, 2017
after being invited back by the new editor.)*

Well don't I feel silly. After composing a mushy-gushy farewell column for *The Daily Graphic* only 14 months ago, I've been invited back to the pages of the *Herald Leader*. Had I known I'd return so soon, I may have gone a little lighter on the waterworks and the sentimental foofaraw.

But seriously. I'm glad to be back. Nothing's sweeter than knowing your face will end up in the bottom of your neighbour's bird cage or cat litter box.

What have you been up to in the last year? Bought a cottage? Changed jobs? Got married? Had a baby? Had a birthday? Remembered to put out your recycling?

As for me, I've heard rumours. Some are even true.

Book Number Two released in January, and Number Three in August? Both true.

Grandson Number Five arrived in September? Also true. (No girls yet.)

Wedding Anniversary Number 40 on October 1? I know you think that can't possibly be true, but it is. Forty! I remember when only old people celebrated 40th anniversaries, but now kids like us are doing it too.

Quit my job at City Hall? Nope, not true! Although we have seen a record-breaking turnover in personnel, I am not one of the turnovers. I see myself as more of a freezer-burnt pop tart, one of the old-timers after only eight years. I wish that weren't the case. I don't do well with change and too often find myself pining for what used to be. Which, of course, is non-productive and ever so senior citizen of me. After all, everybody knows you can't go back.

Except this column proves that every once in a great while, maybe you can.

As I said in my farewell, "I've learned that God generally has something better around the bend and I don't want to miss it because I failed to turn the corner!" What I didn't know then was that just a few weeks later, I would sign a contract for my third novel — which at that point had yet to be written. Had my column not been cancelled, I'd have stubbornly kept plugging away at it, trying to meet way too many deadlines. You and I would have both suffered — me from overload and you from reading even more mundane drivel than my usual offerings. Lesson learned: when something is taken from you, it might be for everyone's benefit.

And it's not entirely impossible for it to be given back.

Three Facts I Didn't Know I Didn't Know
(Appeared February 25, 2016)

Just for kicks, I decided to turn 57 years old this week. As a teenager, I figured anybody who had passed the big Five-Oh should be darn grateful for any breath of life left in them and view it as a bonus. If I made it to 57, I'd know everything I'd ever be required to know.

However, with information advancing like a cheetah across the Serengeti, I'm the orangutan who's already so far behind I may as well give up. But giving up is not really an option — especially if I want to keep earning a living. Or communicating with family members. Or eating.

So in honour of another year, I thought I'd share three things I've learned since my last birthday. If I can remember what they are.

Number One. It's never too late for dreams to come true.

On this day last year, I had pretty much given up on ever seeing the publication of my novel, *The Silver Suitcase*. In God's humorous sense of timing, it was the day *after* my birthday when the call came. Now the book has taken wing and I've moved on to another. Recently, I cried when I came across a column that ran in this very paper on my birthday in 2012. I'd written it in my disappointment after watching *The Silver Suitcase* do well in an important publishing contest — but not well enough to win, and no second prize was offered. In light of all that has transpired since composing that column, you can see why my own words affected me:

God loves me too much to let me receive things for which I'm not ready. Too much to allow my book to see publication before it's the best it can be. Too much to make it easy for me. Too much to not teach me patience and persistence. Too much to strike me dead for questioning his strange timing. Too much to let my influence outgrow my character. Been disappointed

lately? Maybe God loves you too much, too. Promise me you won't quit. I sure don't intend to.
  Wow. Am I ever glad I didn't!

Number Two. It's always too soon to sit back on your laurels.
  I thought I'd lay the writing aside and focus on my family while I prepared for the visit of my daughter and baby grandson from Calgary. My plan was to spend the long weekend cooking up a freezer full of food and cleaning house.
  Surprise! An email from my agent informed me I needed to put together something called a two-page "Treatment" of my novel in order for her to pitch it to filmmakers at an upcoming conference. Oh, and by the way, she needed it in four days.
  I didn't even know what a "Treatment" was. But after some mild panic, prayer, internet research and Hubby's agreement to vacuum the house, I figured it out and got the task done and delivered. So now I know something I didn't know I didn't know — that a Treatment is a short piece of prose, typically the step between scene cards and the first draft of a screenplay for a motion picture.
  The odds of my efforts amounting to a film are remote, but you have to try, right?

Number Three. The trash will still be there.
  You can publish a book, take home the big award, win the election or the game or the amazing race. You can receive enough handshakes and smiles and congratulatory hugs to last a lifetime. But when you return home, the trash will still need to be carried out. The laundry will still need to be done, the toilets still scrubbed. More importantly, your loved ones will still need to know they count more than any achievement, and what they will remember about you after you're gone is not how much you accomplished but how much you cared.
  And if I don't learn *that* lesson well, nothing else will matter.

Great Minds ...
(Appeared January 11, 2018)

My kids may want to shoot me for yet again turning every insignificant incident into a column, but here I go anyway.

For Christmas, I made a not-very-subtle wish for candles. Specifically, three-wick candles from Bath and Body Works. Burning them in my home office while I write in the pre-sunrise hours before it's time to go to my regular job is often the best part of my day. Nothing like a cup of steaming coffee with my favourite hazelnut creamer, the quiet of early morning, and the warm glow of a scented candle to remind me of something important. You see, for me, the candle represents a spiritual truth: God's triune presence with me, helping me as we work together. As I light the three wicks, I ask him to fill the room with his Spirit, to infuse my writing with his light and fragrance and warmth. To somehow ignite a spark in a reader's heart through the words I type.

Well, maybe that's a tad lofty. But I pray for it anyway. And so, I asked my family for more candles for Christmas. "The kind that smell like something yummy is baking," I said, since I rarely bake any more. Writing is more lucrative and less fattening.

Hubby toed the line by giving me three candles in three different scents from the specified store. Not exactly cookie dough or banana bread scents, but very pleasant fragrances nonetheless: Midnight Blue Citrus, Winter and Goal Digger. These will keep me typing for months, leaving no excuse for not writing.

Then we drove all the way to our daughter's house in Calgary to spend Christmas with her family. By December 29, the remainder of the family had arrived from Manitoba, some by plane and some on wheels. It was our first time all together in ages, and the first time ever for our newest member. Thirteen of us under one roof created delightful chaos, especially when it came time to open gifts.

When dear old mom's turn came, we enjoyed a good laugh. Two of our three offspring had been thinking similar thoughts. While desiring to honour my request for candles, neither of them wanted to risk buying the same scented candle as anyone else. So they didn't shop at Bath and Body Works. To ensure their gift would be unique, they each picked a different store, one in Calgary and one in Winnipeg.

The result? Two identical three-wick Mercury candles in the same Mulled Cider and Cinnamon scent from Indigo. From two different people who, it turns out, might think more alike than they want to admit.

For the record, "Great minds think alike" is not from the Bible. But I'm glad God gave my kids great minds. And the matching candles look (and smell) terrific side by side on our dining table … at least until it's time for each of them to take their turn at my writing desk.

Yes or No, the Struggle is Real
(Appeared May 3, 2018)

I almost said no.
I've become good at saying no. *No, I'm sorry. I can't come to your classroom and talk to the kids about being a writer. I can't speak at your women's group. I'd love to talk to your book club, but I can't.*

It's not a fear of public speaking. That fear flew out the window with my first taste of high school theatre.

It's the fear of exhaustion. Living with a chronic lung disease will do that to a person. You learn to guard and schedule your days like you would for a toddler. *Sorry, that's my nap time. I won't make it through the day otherwise.* Or *No, I'll be up too late. I'll be ill the next day. Not worth it. Besides, I'm subject to coughing fits if I talk a lot.*

I don't say all this, of course. It sounds too pathetic. I just say no. Or I might drop a hint about physical limitation that sounds lame even to myself. After all, I walk a half-hour every day. I hold down a job. I look fine. What's the deal?

I'm filled with angst if I say yes and riddled with guilt if I say no. Guilt, because I've been given so much, and we're supposed to take what we're given and pass it on to others.

So when I'm invited to lead a writing workshop with the Country Quills group which meets in the Tiger Hills Art Gallery in Holland, I almost say no. But guilt wins out for a change, and I agree to come. And immediately ask myself what on earth I've done. Spend several hours prepping for it, still grappling. Then the event is postponed due to a storm, and I spend another month anxious about how I will manage to be "on" for the duration of a four-hour workshop, plus drive an hour each way. Spend another Saturday reviewing my preps from a month earlier because my old brain hasn't retained it.

And somewhere in the middle of that Saturday, I finally begin to realize I feel far more concern for myself than for the people I am going to serve. Had I bothered to ask God what they might need from me? How I could best encourage them? I hadn't.

I ask his forgiveness and try to shift my focus. Before I hunker down for my nap, I read a portion of Ann Voskamp's book, *The Broken Way*. She quotes Auschwitz survivor Viktor Frankl, who said meaning comes when one does something that "points, and is directed to, something, or someone, other than oneself ... by giving himself to a cause to serve, or another person to love." She says, "maybe that's how you peel back everything that distracts and cheapens and derails a life — transcend this life by giving yourself for someone else."

Sunday morning, I drive to Holland with an adjusted attitude, trusting God to increase my stamina and decrease my cough.

And I meet some wonderful writers. I share with them my journey and hear a bit of theirs. Pass on some of what I'm learning. Listen to them read their brilliant words. And begin to hear things like, "This has been so helpful! Thank you for coming!"

Yes, I arrive home exhausted. But the good kind of exhausted, the kind that comes when you've spent yourself with passion and seen others gain from it. Voskamp says, "The abundant life doesn't have a bucket list so much as it has an empty bucket —the givenness of pouring out."

And I find myself hoping for another opportunity to say yes.

The Good, Good Father
(Appeared June 14, 2018)

Father's Day can be a reminder that we're all just a bunch of wounded little kids, can't it?

One of the pitfalls of being a published writer is exposing your work — and yourself — to criticism and rejection. I know authors who don't read reviews of their books because it can be too painful, especially when a negative one comes on an already difficult day.

This happened to me recently. I've always read all my online reviews. Though most are positive, some real stinkers show up as well. It proves you can't please everyone, that readers' tastes vary. The positive reviews keep you writing, the negative reviews keep you humble — at least in theory. I have even taught other artists tricks for handling both praise and rejection.

But for good reason, this review felt like a personal attack. And when the words come from an anonymous stranger, there's little you can do. You can cry. I did not, although that's often my go-to reaction. You can hit something. I didn't do that, either. You can toss back a handful of chocolate chips. I resisted, this time. You can brush it off and tell yourself it doesn't sting. I knew full well it did. You can go on social media, rant about how stupid the reader must be to not "get" what you were trying to say. I've seen authors do this. They are looking for someone to defend them, and it works. Until it doesn't. Either way, it appears unprofessional, immature, and frankly, kind of pathetic.

I distracted myself for an hour with a TV show, and when the show ended, the hurtful words surfaced again. Thankfully, it was bedtime. And thankfully, I have this little routine when I crawl into bed. I recap the events that seem significant from my day — good, bad or ugly — whatever comes to mind. I thank God for each one, then lay it at his feet. He alone deserves the praise for the good stuff, and He alone can handle the difficult stuff. This is also a good time to confess the wrongs I'm guilty of from that day, as they come to mind, and ask His forgiveness.

Then, as I snuggle down into the sheets, I let my bed and blankets represent God's warm loving arms around me. I become an infant, cradled in the embrace of a devoted parent — safe, secure, precious. Loved beyond measure by the one who made me. It's a wonderful way to fall asleep. And it came in handy that night.

The next morning, I looked at the painful book review with fresh eyes. This time, I saw the words of a hurting person wounded by religion. Someone who doesn't know she can go straight to her Creator who loves her like his little child. This time, I was able to pray for her. And yes, even to shed some tears. For her.

None of this would happen on my own. It does not come from years of church attendance or self-discipline or religious rule-following. It's a direct result of embracing the truth of God's commitment to his children. And it's yours for the asking. You have a good, good Father. It's who he is. And you are loved by him. In fact, it's who you are. Loved. By. Him.

"I've been carrying you from the day you were born, And I'll keep on carrying you when you're old." (from Isaiah 46)

To Plant an Oke
(Appeared December 27, 2018)

As a 20-year-old newlywed transplanted from the Canadian prairies to a small Texas city where my new husband would pursue his degree at a Christian college, I took refuge in the school's library. Its books would become a source of companionship, inspiration and emotional health. There, I discovered the earliest novels of Janette Oke and devoured them with passion. I could not have dreamed that, nearly 40 years later, I'd find myself seated in an elegant Nashville banquet room filled with authors, editors and agents from the Christian publishing world while they announced the recipient of the 2016 American Christian Fiction Writers Lifetime Achievement Award: Janette Oke.

Mrs. Oke was not present to receive that award, but it didn't stop my tears from forming as I saw her photo on the screen and heard the wonderful tribute to her and her work. I've never felt prouder to be a Canadian Christian writer!

I thought back to those lonely days of feeling swept away by Mrs. Oke's *Love Comes Softly* stories. The way Clark and Marty came together through difficult circumstances built my faith and my commitment to marriage and family. Not only did those books inspire me to be a better wife and more devoted disciple, but I believe a tiny seed was planted. *Could I be a writer, too?*

As the years passed and children joined our family, my writing opportunities were limited to Christmas family newsletters. Later, when I took the lead of my church's puppet team and then a drama ministry, I began to learn the art of script-writing. This was followed by a column in the church newspaper, which I also edited. Little by little, the seed — perhaps an acorn — received enough water to sprout.

When I had the privilege of hearing Mrs. Oke speak at an Inscribe conference, I felt stirred by her ability to remain so humble and encouraging. Once again, she inspired me. My little seedling grew stronger. I returned home and continued to pursue writing through articles, short scripts and *Chicken Soup for the Soul* contributions. The idea of tackling a novel seemed far too lofty.

Then, while praying for me one evening, a dear friend received a spiritual image. She saw me, sitting on top of an old-fashioned silver suitcase. The case was filled with papers, trying to escape. From that picture — at age 50 — I began writing what would eventually be my first novel, *The Silver Suitcase*. I chose historical fiction largely due to the influence of Janette Oke. (It didn't hurt that my middle name is Janette.) I felt elated when a beta reader of that first rough draft said, "I felt like I was reading a Janette Oke book!"

Although seven years would pass before *The Silver Suitcase* was published, it would go on to win awards, accumulate over 700 reviews on Amazon, and be quickly followed by two other inspirational, historical novels. Next year, it will be translated into Macedonian!

I started a little late in life and will never be as prolific an author as Janette Oke. But I'm confident I would never have started at all had it not been for the seed her books planted in my heart. I believe that little acorn has grown into a sturdy enough oak to become a source of shade, comfort, and inspiration to my readers. Nothing would thrill me more than to one day learn I played a role in planting a similar seed in a young writer's heart.

***

One question I've heard repeatedly throughout 2018 is, "When is your next book coming out?" I wish I knew the answer. I've finished two more books since the last released, but my publisher discontinued its fiction line and my agent is seeking a new publisher. It's a long process when you're committed to the traditional publishing method. Although I've not released a book in 2018, it has been the greatest privilege to receive a couple of writing awards. One of those was the Janette Oke Award given out every other year by Inscribe Christian Writers Fellowship. The essay I've shared on the previous pages helped bring this award home to Portage la Prairie.

TERRIE TODD

A Letter from the Palace
(Appeared May 30, 2019)

Last week, I received a letter from Buckingham Palace. In January, my friend Lucy suggested I send Her Majesty a copy of my third novel, *Bleak Landing*. The book includes a scene from 1939 when King George VI and Queen Elizabeth (our current queen's parents) visited Winnipeg. As I researched and wrote about that event, what intrigued me most was how Prime Minister Mackenzie King and Winnipeg's Mayor John Queen accompanied their Majesties on their various tours. The poor radio announcer, describing for his listeners the actions of the King and the Queen and Mayor Queen and Prime Minister King, got tongue-tied. Rumour has it he grew frustrated enough to swear on air, although that cannot be substantiated.

One hard-cover, large-print edition of *Bleak Landing* remained on my shelf waiting for the right recipient. I took Lucy's suggestion and mailed it to the Queen, along with a nice letter. What did I have to lose but a few bucks in postage?

In the process, I learned about royal gift protocol and what types of gifts royal family members can accept. They may, for example, eat any food they receive. Perishable gifts with a value of less than £150 can also be given to charity or staff. Gifts cannot be sold or exchanged and eventually become part of the Royal Collection, held in trust by the Queen for her successors and the nation.

A list of the Queen's official gifts from 2018 includes over 70 items, ranging from Lego to framed charters to photographs to statues to jewelry to salt.

I imagined my book becoming one of a gazillion items collecting dust in a gigantic warehouse where some poor scribe must document each one in a dusty, ancient record book with a quill pen. (I also imagined Her Majesty riveted to my book late into the night, while sitting in her royal bed sipping Earl Grey from her royal teacup.)

I would wait and see.

Four months later came the frame-worthy reply, written by Her Majesty's lady-in-waiting, Lady Susan Hussey. While the letter makes no promise of the Queen or anyone else actually reading my book, it is filled with the gracious thanks one expects from royalty. When I did a bit of digging on Lady Hussey, I discovered she recently turned 80 years old. A baroness herself, she is godmother to Prince William, and has served the Queen basically her entire adult life. One can only imagine how many of these thank-you letters she has written.

As lovely as it feels to receive a letter from the palace, the royal stationary will never match the value of a much finer letter from a far more powerful source. It's a love letter from the King of kings, and you and I have access to it every day. According to Hebrews 4, the Word of God is alive — meaning it has power to change you, not just once, but over and over. Nothing and no one is impervious to a Bible. Test it out for yourself and see. If Shakespearean English isn't your first language, find a modern translation like the New International Version or even a paraphrase like The Message. If you're not sure where to start, begin with the life of Jesus as recorded by Matthew, Mark, Luke or John. Digest a few verses or a chapter per day.

Then wait and see.

From "As If" to "What If ..."
(Appeared August 15, 2019)

For years, I tried to let the idea go. A story about a Japanese Canadian girl relocated from Vancouver to a Manitoba sugar beet farm during World War II was obviously not my story to write. As if. I'm not Japanese. I'm not a history major. I don't have the experience required to do the copious research. When I realized this fictional girl would start writing letters to the farmer's son, imprisoned in a Japanese POW camp — I knew for sure the story was not mine to tell. Good fiction must be historically accurate and believable. I'd be in so far over my head, I wouldn't be able to see the sun.

Plus, I am lazy.

So I fought it. Great idea for someone else. Not me. While I resisted, I wrote two other books. I think they're good books, but based on publishers' rejections so far, I must be mistaken.

Meanwhile, the "big" story would not let me go.

Then, in June of 2018, I learned about a documentary called *Facing Injustice* in which my friend Terry Tully and his mom, Osono, appear. (I wrote about that last summer when CBC aired it.) One man featured predominantly in the film is Art Miki. Only five years old when relocated with his family, he grew up to play a key role in lobbying government toward redress for the interned Japanese Canadians. He and Prime Minister Mulroney sat side by side to sign the official agreement in 1988.

I watched the film three times. I spent that summer reading books, some about the Japanese internment, some about prisoners of war in Japan, some about sugar beet farming. The more I read, the more I argued with God. The story remained far too big for me.

With an August ninth medical appointment in Winnipeg, I decided maybe I could gain a little inspiration at Folklorama's Japanese pavilion. When I booked my ticket online, I felt intrigued to discover that Art Miki was one of the pavilion's directors. Because I felt utterly unqualified to author this book, I told God if he really wanted me to tackle it, I needed confirmation. I don't often ask God for signs. It seems demanding and faithless and frankly, a little childish. But on my drive to Winnipeg, I told God that perhaps if I could actually meet Art Miki and speak with him, I'd gain some clarity. I knew the odds were slim. Even if he were at the pavilion, he'd be busy. It would be crowded. Would I even recognize him? Would I possess the courage to approach him?

The crowd was so big, organizers were turning people away from the ticket line. I got inside and started looking around. In a row of chairs against the wall about five feet from me, sat Art Miki. I recognized him immediately. I left the food line and introduced myself. Thanked him for all his work on behalf of Japanese Canadians. Told him I was a novelist and a bit of what I was thinking. He told me about Mark Sakamoto's book, *Forgiven*, which they had for sale downstairs. After the show, I bought one of only two copies they had. Turns out the book is a true story that mirrors the more complicated one percolating in my heart. Maybe the concept wasn't so far-fetched after all.

I kept reading. I kept procrastinating. Finally, last November, I plunged in. Three chapters into the girl's story, it was time to start writing the soldier's. I felt stuck. I knew I needed to get this guy from Winnipeg to Japan somehow, but I couldn't just randomly make stuff up. I prayed for guidance. I'd promised myself I'd stay off Facebook all weekend and just write. But Hubby asked me to log in and check whether his co-worker's grandbaby had arrived. When I logged in, the first thing I saw was my friend Anita's Remembrance Day post. She'd left a tribute to her great-uncle, Isaac Friesen, who served with the First Battalion, Winnipeg Grenadiers and ended up in a Japanese POW camp. Five minutes after asking God to show me how to get this kid to Japan, I'm reading about Isaac's battalion. I found everything I needed to get my fictional soldier where I needed him, including routes taken, dates and other priceless details.

My "as if" began to feel more like "what if."

In February, I attended a writers' retreat where bestselling author Rachel Hauck worked with me. "If you don't write this story, I will," she said. She meant it as encouragement.

I replied, "Yes, please do. I really wish you would."

When she saw my tears, she asked why I felt such a powerful connection to this story. I could only shrug and cry harder.

"I think it's yours to tell," she said. It was my 60th birthday. I kept at it.

Last Friday, August 9, 2019 — one year to the day since I met Art Miki at Folklorama — I finished the first draft of *Rose Among Thornes*. All 100,000 words of it. It will take a miracle for anyone to publish a book that long by a relatively unknown author. But what if …?

Will this book ever be published or is it meant only as a personal exercise in depending on God's leading? Time will tell. While I wait to find out, I will repeatedly rewrite and revise the story, because that's what good writing is all about.

In his book *The Artisan Soul: Crafting Your Life into a Work of Art*, Erwin McManus said, "… if God refuses to mass-produce but insists on an intimate process that in the end forms each of us into the image of Christ, why would we choose a lesser path for our own lives?"

Is there an idea that won't let you go? Are you resisting out of fear or self-doubt? Ask God for guidance. No, he won't always grant "signs" when you ask. But occasionally, he does. He loves your honesty. He honours your persistence. He strengthens your faith. And he loves more than anything to walk alongside you on your journey.

ACROSTIC STORIES

Each year, I enter the Brucedale Press Acrostic Story contest. Sometimes, I even win! An Acrostic is a story that is 26 sentences long. Each sentence begins with the next letter of the alphabet, in order. For this contest, every contestant must begin with the same three words as provided by the organizers. Each year after the winners are announced, I use my story for one of my columns. The next five columns are acrostic stories; the first earned first place.

TERRIE TODD

Ziggy 'Fesses Up
(First appeared October 23, 2010)

Adored by many, His Worship Mayor Zigfried Johnson stepped to the podium to address the citizens of Quincy one final time.

"Before my 25-year career as your mayor draws to a close," he said, "I have something I must tell you. Confession is never easy, but it is good for the soul. Disclosures of this nature are uncommon from a man in my position, and I sincerely hope this will not result in your becoming cynical toward my successor. Even I voted for him, and I am confident he would never stoop to the type of behaviour which I am about to divulge."

Five hundred voters held their breath, awaiting the mayor's next words. George Xander, although voted in by an overwhelming majority this time, would never be as loved or trusted as Mayor Johnson had been. He had, after all, run against Johnson in every election held since they were college boys together and had lost every one. If not for Zigfried's voluntary retirement, a new mayor would not even have been considered by the good people of Quincy. Just what was their beloved leader about to share? Kay Johnson, his wife of 49 years, stood by his side looking adoringly up at her Ziggy, assuring her fellow citizens that his revelation would not be of a licentious nature.

"Let me begin by taking you back to that Election Day 25 years ago," the mayor continued. "Maybe you remember that I won by only one vote that first time. Never one to settle for such a close count, my worthy opponent here, Mr. Xander, demanded a recount. Of course, the election officials complied."

"Perhaps it was fate, perhaps it was something else," the Mayor continued. "Quincy residents may remember the near tornado conditions that prevailed that day, but what you probably don't know is that as the votes were being recounted, an assistant opened a window, causing ballots to go flying around the Council Chambers. Results were delayed, but after all the ballots were gathered up and counted yet again, it was confirmed that I had indeed won by one vote."

"Six months later, while moving the heavy oak table in the Council Chambers, what did I discover but four uncounted ballots wedged inside a drawer in the table. Three of them were votes for my opponent, George Xander. Unless there were still more uncounted ballots hidden somewhere, George, not I, had actually won the election by one vote. Vigilantly, I searched the room for more lost ballots to no avail, then discreetly shredded the four I'd found and remained your mayor for the next 25 years."

With tears in his eyes, the Mayor removed the chain of office from around his own neck and placed it around his successor's. Xander humbly received the adornment and stepped up to the microphone.

"You are forgiven, my friend," His Worship Mayor George Xander said, silently recalling the windy day he'd stood outside that Council Chamber window enjoying a cigarette, when two ballots had come floating his way — both votes for Johnson, and both quickly stuffed deeply into his own pocket.

Ziggy Johnson smiled and sighed, a 25-year weight off his weary shoulders at last.

Save the Last Dance ...
(Appeared July 23, 2011)

Applying Grandma's advice, I resolved to find myself a man who didn't dance. Because she herself had married a guy who could really cut a rug, my grandmother spent much of her 85 years waiting while other ladies cut in, one after another, for their chance to promenade with the only male on the dance floor. Charlie Hooper was a regular Fred Astaire and it was this trait that had made my grandmother, and so many other girls, fall in love with him. Dashing and debonair, he made Grandma the envy of Xenia County when he proposed to her that hot August night. Even at their wedding, the lovely bride danced only once with her graceful groom.

For me, though, things were going to be different. Goodness knows I loved to dance, but I would not be taken in by fancy footwork and smart stepping. However lonely I might be, I would not be swayed by such shallow and superficial shenanigans. It mattered not that I went alone, danced alone, and returned home alone afterward.

Just as I was finally beginning to believe that my partner-free dancing was more fun anyway, I met Kelvin. Kelvin Kellogg was the best dancer I had ever seen. Light on his feet and always in step, he moved as smoothly as a cat. My heart skipped a beat when I first laid eyes on him, tripping the light fantastic on the dance floor of the Xenia Community Hall. Not wanting to weaken my resolve, however, I did not join the lineup of young ladies waiting their turn to dance with this young Patrick Swayze. Older women even swallowed their pride and practically begged Kelvin to twirl them around the floor just one time.

Perhaps it was this reluctance on my part that caught Kelvin's eye. Quietly, I made my way to the cloak room after the last dance was over and as I turned around to go, who was standing right in my path but Kelvin Kellogg.

"Ready to leave?"

"Silly question," I muttered, not looking him in the eye.

"The band will play one more if the prettiest lady in the room will dance with me," Kelvin coaxed, holding out his hand.

Under any other circumstances I'd have zipped right past him and gone on home, but such a charming invitation was more than I could resist. Visions of red roses and a long white gown were already dancing in my head as Kelvin took me in his arms and waltzed me around the room to Elvis Presley's *I Can't Help Falling in Love with You*. With our eyes locked tightly on each other, it seems we did fall in love that night and the rest is, as they say, history. Xenia residents came out in droves to celebrate with us and to dance with the groom at our wedding reception.

You'd think I would regret repeating my grandmother's mistake, but I've learned two things Grandma never did. Zeal for dance is much too precious to keep to oneself; and after the band plays its final song, I will always be the one who gets to take my dancing man home.

Quintessa Takes Flight
(Appeared July 10, 2014)

Airborne at last, Quintessa stretched her neck to view the panorama below.
"Bloody business, this," she mumbled. "Can't say I'm particularly enchanted to be a mosquito, but it sure beats the larval stage."
Dare she admit how much she loathed the idea of seeing, let alone sucking blood? Eventually, she knew she would probably have to concede to nature, but for now she would play the role of the royal aviator and set her inner monarch free. Focusing on her flying after all those long days wriggling in a scummy birdbath felt like heaven, even though her peers already seemed to be zeroing in on warm-blooded targets. Gluttony and greed might be appropriate for the lower classes, but not for this little princess. Her goals were loftier and far more glamorous than those of the riffraff surrounding her.
"I'd much rather become a flight expert than merely go on a feeding frenzy," she told herself. Just because she was a Culex didn't mean she must settle for the life of a savage.
"Keep your blood, you ugly vertebrates! Let me fly!"
Mosquitoes around her swarmed toward what appeared to be a farm, where horses, cattle and pigs created an all-you-can-eat buffet, but Quintessa buzzed past the uncivilized offering, her proboscis high in the air. Not for her, these barbarian habits, these boorish customs, these beastly obsessions and brutish dependencies. Only the crème de la crème was good enough for Quintessa.
Pressing past the horde, she felt chagrined to find herself inexplicably drawn to the heat and smells emanating from the farm. Quintessa, however, remained as strong as her wilting wings allowed, convinced only the weakest of her species would dive for the nearest available food without first enjoying the freedom of flight and fancy.

Resting for a moment on a low tree branch, the little mosquito panted and tried to calculate how much longer she could fly without ingesting blood. She knew she could live on nectar and plant juices like her male counterparts, but if she were ever to reproduce, imbibing remained her only alternative.

"Tasteless, absolutely degrading," she muttered. Unless she chose to abandon the ultimate goal for which she was hatched — to lay eggs — she knew she must submit to protocol. Vampirism seemed the only means to succession of her self-appointed crown.

Weakening rapidly now, Quintessa's attention was drawn to the raucous cawing of a crow above and she immediately sensed a possible solution to her predicament. X-ray vision might have come in handy to help her home in on the bird's body, but she relied on her heat sensors until she found a tender spot to latch onto, beneath a wing. Yellow feet suddenly dangled in mid-air as the crow took off, and Quintessa felt electrified to find herself once again airborne, without draining an ounce of her own energy.

Zoonotic arboviruses such as West Nile lay dormant while the Princess Quintessa reigned supreme on her private aircraft, feeding and flying and fulfilling her life's destiny all in one glorious jaunt from the loftiest of heights — at least for now.

Payday for Stacey
(Appeared July 2, 2015)

Appreciating the finest of Billy Bob's culinary art, Stacey Quentin wolfed down the slightly burnt beans and chased them mercilessly with strong coffee. Billy Bob might not be the greatest cook on the prairie, but he was the best Virgil McCoy's Cattle Company offered; besides, Stacey knew the tastiest sauce was hunger. Cooking was something she had never aspired to, no matter how much the cowboys — especially Grady Drummins — taunted her about it.

Driving cattle and studying the teachings of Socrates, an unusual combination to be sure, were the two things Stacey loved more than anything. Even though she was a girl, she pulled her weight on horseback while holding her own in discussions around the campfire about the classical Greek philosopher — a subject for which Grady Drummins showed a surprising affinity. For eight weeks, she'd kept up with the men on the long drive from Texas to Kansas and only once had she required assistance from one of the cowboys. Grady hardly thought of her as a girl anyway. He had roped the calf Stacey's lasso missed and carried it in his arms, laughing as though it was light as a feather.

"I think you need a little more practice, Plato," he said as he deposited the calf at Stacey's feet and walked away with a grin.

Just you wait, she thought. Kansas City would be upon them soon and with it, payday. *Laugh if you like, Grady Drummins, but I earn a man's wage and deserve every penny of it.*

"Marry me, Plato," Grady called out in jest every time Stacey got within earshot. "No man needs a womanly woman when he can have one who knows how to wrangle cattle *and* quote Socrates."

"Once made equal to man, woman becomes his superior," Stacey quoted through clenched teeth, determined to show Grady Drummins his place one day soon.

Payday arrived at last, and Stacey was able to bathe and slip into a pretty frock before lining up with the other drivers to collect her earnings in Kansas City.

"Quentin, Stacey," called out the payroll master with a bored drawl. Roy Fisher thought he'd seen everything, but when a young lady stepped forward to collect a driver's wages, he laughed in her face. "Stacey Quentin," he called again, looking around the room to see which of the cowboys might have been gifted with such an unfortunate name.

"That's me," Stacey insisted as she reached for the roll of cash.

"Unless one of these fellas is willin' to sign for it, I can't let you have this here money, Miss," the payroll master said, holding the roll high above Stacey's head. "Virgil McCoy has his rules and they don't include payin' cowboy's wages to a mere cook."

"Wait just a doggone minute," a deep voice boomed from the back of the line. "Xanthippe herself couldn't have proven more worthy than Miss Quentin here, one of the finest cattle drivers I've ever had the privilege of working with. You can hand over what she's got coming to her right now or I'll hand over what *you've* got coming."

Zany as it seemed, Grady Drummins had stood up for Stacey and referenced Socrates' wife in one fell swoop, convincing her she'd be a fool to not welcome his next proposal of marriage, whenever it might come.

A Kitty's Tale
(Appeared June 6, 2019)

Always curious, Xerox stuck her nose into the empty cereal box I'd placed on the kitchen floor for her. Before I could count to three, her entire body had disappeared inside, and as I rushed around with my morning coffee, the cereal box eventually stopped moving and began emitting a soft purring sound. Cats are hilarious, and Xerox — so named because she was an exact duplicate of her mother — had me smitten from the moment my friend Kathy introduced her to me three months ago.

Distracted by my assignment to write a good-news story about a local business, I grabbed my bag and headed off to work, hollering, "Goodbye Hon, have a good day" over my shoulder to my husband Quinn.

Evening had arrived by the time I returned, exhausted and still with no story to write. For once, couldn't one of our local businesses impress me with a little "above and beyond" service?

"Great meal, Hon," I said absent-mindedly as I finished stacking dishes in the dishwasher. "Hey, where's Xerox? I haven't seen her since I got home."

Jingling her favourite mouse toy with the little bell around its neck, I turned toward the spot where I'd left the cereal box that morning.

"Kitty, kitty, kitty! Last time I saw her, she was sleeping in that —"

My cereal box was gone, and my husband's face was suddenly the colour of the concrete sidewalk.

"No. Oh no. Please don't say it." Quinn added two words that confirmed my worst fear. "RECYCLING DAY!"

Shouting for me to follow, Quinn ran through the back door and around to the curb where he'd wheeled out our recycling bin — complete with the cereal box — several hours earlier.

The very idea that he could possibly have tossed our darling Xerox inside was too horrible for words!

"Unusual that you didn't find the empty cereal box a tad on the heavy side, don't you think?" Vindication was already forming in my heart as sarcasm dripped from my lips. "What on earth were you thinking? Xerox will be long gone by now!"

"You would think so, but look at this," Quinn chuckled as he reached into the deep bin and pulled out the meowing kitten.

Zeus's Zero-waste Recycling Company had provided my good-news story by taking everything else and leaving in the bottom of the bin a small bowl of water, a scrap of fabric, and an unruffled kitten who looked up at me like she'd planned the whole event solely for my benefit.

Section 4: Health, Fitness and Life in General

My son, pay attention to what I say; turn your ear to my words. Do not let them out of your sight, keep them within your heart; for they are life to those who find them and health to one's whole body.

Proverbs 4:20-22

Diary of a Mad Yogi
(Appeared January 22, 2011)

Day 1. Shopping for Jillian Michael's popular *30 Day Shred* video, instead I find her *Yoga Meltdown*. The back of the DVD promises fast results, so I take it home. The premise of this workout is to take traditional yoga poses and put repetitious movement to them for cardio work, followed by holding each pose for 15 seconds for strength-building and balance. I watch carefully and try to replicate the moves Jillian and her two minions demonstrate. I'm doing swimmingly until about 30 seconds in.

Can anyone besides these three freaks of nature actually *do* a chaturanga push-up? This is like a normal push-up, except your hands are under your chest, elbows tucked in tight to your body, and you move s-l-o-w-l-y. You stop with your nose inches above the floor and hold there for 15 seconds. Impossible. I skip this and keep going.

I discover I can do the Warrior Three pose by keeping one hand on the coffee table.

While attempting the Camel pose, I get stuck. This is *not* how I pictured my own demise. My poor hubby will come home to discover my stiffened corpse, requiring a custom-made, camel-shaped casket.

Lastly, we learn the Dolphin pose. I always wondered why dolphins are always smiling. Now I *really* wonder. These moves are not humanly possible (hence, all the animal names). Clearly, the video is a fake. It's amazing what they can do with computer animation these days. I will be so sore tomorrow!

Day 2. I am too much of a cheapskate to pay for a DVD and not use it. And am very surprised to find I'm not sore at all! I try again. It seems slightly more possible, but what will my chiropractor say next time I'm in for my regular attitude adjustment and he finds me twisted like a pretzel?

There is a Level 2 workout on this disk, but I don't even watch it. At this rate, I figure I'll be ready to move up to the next level by my 300th birthday.

Day 9. Somebody should tell these work-out video makers to think ahead before they say stupid random things their customers will have to listen to over and over again. Next time I hear "who's your daddy?" I'm going to slap somebody.

Day 19. I've got rug burns on my elbows and knees from the Berber carpet. I find an alternate outfit.

Day 31. The push-ups are not getting better, but I can do the Warrior Three pose without hanging onto anything. I am very proud of myself!

Day 45. I dare to watch the Level 2 workout. At this rate, I will be ready to move on by my 100th birthday.

Day 51. I can do all the poses except the stupid chaturanga push-ups. I modify and keep going. Is it my imagination or is it easier to get up again after getting an apple from the bottom of the fridge?

Day 66. Is it my imagination, or are my jeans looser?

Day 80. Is it my imagination, or am I having fewer aches and pains?

Day 89. Is it my imagination, or was that a proper chaturanga push-up I just did? At this rate, I will be ready to move on to Level 2 by my 52nd birthday next month.

Out of My Guardian Angel's Mind
(Appeared February 26, 2011)

*N*ote: *This week's column features a long-winded guest columnist.*

I was having a pretty easy day 'til she decided to put the car in the ditch.

Hi, I'm Tenshi the Guardian Angel and I'm here to tell you Terrie's story. I think she's too embarrassed to tell it herself.

We'd just had an unusually mild weekend. You know what happens when winter hits again after a few days like that. Ice. Everywhere. People falling down on it, breaking ankles and limbs. Angels and tow trucks racking up overtime. It was one of those bitterly cold, windy days that makes me wonder why anyone lives here and makes me thankful my charge has an attached garage on her house, a reliable car and indoor employment. Pretty cushy job for me!

Terrie had an appointment with her hairdresser after work, out in the boonies north of Bagot. She's been navigating that road over a decade and, although it makes her nervous, I've managed to keep her out of trouble. This particular day she drove preoccupied with her trip to Denver just two days away. She was heading down that gravel road a little on the fast side. I don't recommend this. I stayed on the alert.

When she hit an icy patch, I could tell she was finally in the moment when she started saying, "Oh ... oh ...."

I managed to keep her ol' Caddy from spinning around or flipping, but when it stopped it was up to its windows in snow.

I saw a bad word forming at the back of Terrie's head and before I could cover my ears, it shot out her mouth.

"Now what?" she said next. This chick has no cell phone. I don't recommend this. "May as well start shoveling." She popped the trunk open. There was no getting out the driver's side, so she climbed uphill to the passenger side and pushed hard on the door. She thought she was heaving on it with all her strength, but I heaved my share, too. I slipped out and helped pull her out of the car, where one look told her she could shovel all day and all night and still not get that car out.

I figured she'd have enough sense to wait in the car and put on the ski pants and leather mittens from the back seat. Instead, she closed the trunk and marched down the country road in the biting prairie wind, leaving the warm clothes behind! I don't recommend this. Brings to mind the ol' cliché about fools rushing in.

This is not the woman you want in charge at your next disaster, folks. In her befuddlement, she thought the nearest yard site was her destination. By the time she reached it and realized it was abandoned, it was too late to turn back. Nothing to do but keep walking.

All the way, she kept saying, "Lord, please send help, please send help."

What was I? Chopped liver? I thought. I took stock of her outfit. A hood and scarf, good. Mittens were nothing to write home about. Still wearing those 10-year-old boots from Payless. Well, they'd keep her vertical on the ice, anyway. While she envisioned her fingers frostbitten and falling off, her writing and secretarial careers both grinding to a freezing halt, I focused my attention on blowing warm air on her fingers, toes and nose.

A half hour and two miles later, she arrived at the Hell or High Water Salon, looking like a Popsicle. The white kind. What flavour are those, anyway? Doesn't matter.

Hot tea, extra sweaters, and sitting under an old-fashioned hair dryer were just the cure.

The car got rescued the next day, none the worse for wear. Terrie was okay, too, once she quit shivering. Except for her ego. And once her hair was done, that was pretty much taken care of, too.

Impressive thing: of all the humans who ministered to her that night (thanks Doreen, Brian, Dan and Jon), not one pointed out how foolish she had been. I definitely recommend this.

Living with Chronic Nocturnal Positional Paroxysmal Bechesthesis

(Appeared June 22, 2011)
A revised version of this story also appears in *Chicken Soup for the Soul: Inspiration for Nurses*

It started some 15 years ago. I would start coughing as soon as I lay down. Inconvenient and annoying, but not a huge deal. The professionals suggested it might be some mild type of asthma I'd just have to learn to live with. I did.

Then one fall I went on a weekend retreat with several girlfriends at a cozy family cabin at Clear Lake. Since three of us were sharing a room, I crawled into my sleeping bag and warned the other two about my coughing habit.

One of them, a nurse I'll call Marci, took on a most somber tone. "Oh," she said. "You have Chronic Nocturnal Positional Paroxysmal Bechesthesis."

My inner drama queen immediately took the spotlight. This sounded serious. How much time did I have left? Months? Days? Should I be quitting my job, putting my affairs in order? No matter what, I would be brave.

"Really?" I said. "What's that?"

"It means you cough when you lie down," Marci said.

The other friend, whom I'll call Lisa, let out a snort heard in Toronto and the two of them started chortling so hard they rolled off their beds, which in turn got me laughing so hard I started a coughing fit that lasted long into the night. Which, in turn, made them howl even harder. You get the picture.

Good times.

I'm not laughing so much now.

Frightening new symptoms had me visiting the doctor, who ordered a chest x-ray. "Something unusual going on in your lungs" led to a CT scan. Of course, each of these steps is separated by weeks, during which one becomes convinced one is dying and every hangnail and eye twitch becomes yet another symptom. The internet is most helpful in self-diagnosis of anything a hypochondriac might fancy.

The scan results were both comforting and confusing. Good news, it doesn't look like cancer. Weird news, we don't know what it is. So next week I see a specialist, who will most likely stick a garden hose down my gullet and I may just come home that day still in the dark.

I share this because anyone who has reached my age has probably already played this waiting game and may be there now. This "how sick am I, anyway?" business is distracting, isn't it? But here's the thing. From the moment we're born, we are all terminal. We don't know when or how, but we will all die. Why we act like this is a big secret puzzles me. Occasionally, contemplating a face-to-face meeting with our Maker is not a bad thing. Learning to wait isn't easy, but it's not a bad thing. Accepting that I don't have to know everything is not a bad thing. Appreciating each breath as a gift from my Creator is not a bad thing. The only "bad" thing is wasting an experience by not growing through it and not sharing it with others.

So, at the risk of losing readers to boredom ... and at the risk of feeling like an idiot should this turn out to be nothing ... I'll share. Maybe we can learn and grow together.

The Theatrical Side of the Lung Saga
(Appeared August 27, 2011)

My friend Nita thought I should combine my ongoing lung ailments with my love for all things theatrical and write a new musical for the stage. I came up with some great (if not precisely original) titles, like *My Fair Lungs, The Lung and I,* and *Oklunghoma!*

The heroine is diagnosed with Bronchiectasis. It means her bronchial tubes, instead of being smooth and cylindrical, are, in medical terms, knobbly and wobbly. Her lungs are scarred. Alas, her long-held dream of modeling for anatomy textbooks is over. How this developed remains a mystery. That week of smoking in Grade 7? (Don't tell her Mom.) Her 12 years of cleaning houses for a living, inhaling Comet and Javex? Possibly. Mold in the walls of her former home? Could be. In any case, it's a done deal now. The audience grows restless. The chorus breaks into a rousing number called *She Might Get Better, She Might Get Worse*. But by this point the plot is so weak, the opening night crowd has left their seats and are demanding a refund.

We've known awhile that I have this condition, but my doc was digging around for something more sinister because Bronchiectasis, while it explains the coughing, is not supposed to hurt. Mine does.

But nothing more dramatic was apparent, so my doctor's latest attempt at earning his keep was a free sample of acid-reflux medicine. Not the problem. So, here I sit with my mystery and a complimentary membership to the "shot-in-the-dark of the month" club.

Cynical as that sounds, I do not resent the medical community. Lord knows, I couldn't do what they do.

On a recent visit to my lung doc, he walked into the examining room to find me wearing a pair of bright yellow glasses with a big red clown nose. "What's up, Doc?" I said.

Poor man probably thought I got off on the wrong floor. I didn't have the heart tell him it was a test to see how long it would take him to notice. Since he passed, I said I just wanted to brighten his day, what with his depressing job and all.

"I don't think it's depressing," he said. I guess that means he's helping at least a few people, even if I have yet to join their ranks. Oops, there I go again. My pastor tells me cynicism is not a spiritual gift.

Darn.

Anyway, I'm living with some new rules which involve more sleeping and less doing. Religiously huffing my way through Jillian's hateful exercise routine. Trying desperately to not become an old crank. (Don't ask my long-suffering spouse how I'm doing on that front.) And stubbornly rehearsing the list of bodily parts that still work right. It's a surprisingly long list. The one who knit it all together knew what he was doing, and I'll trust him to decide when it's time to let it unravel.

When you come right down to it, isn't it mind-boggling that our bodies function at all? And for that, I can only be grateful.

Thanks for asking.

A Souper Dooper Adventure
(Appeared July 19, 2012)

Relearning how to do a task you've been doing mindlessly for 35 years is a challenge, and this was not one I particularly wanted to tackle. Like my mother before me, I have always taken a certain amount of pride in how quickly I can throw a meal together. I thought Kraft Dinner was a food group and frozen pizza made perfectly acceptable Friday night fare. (Just so you understand the learning curve here.)

But, determined to do my part for my wellness journey, I am learning to shop for and prepare food I'd barely heard of before. On Friday evening, I singlehandedly cleaned Sobeys out of kale (which I previously thought God created solely for decorating our salad bars) and leeks (which don't actually leak. Who knew?)

On Saturday, I set out to create something called "Black Forest Cream of Mushroom Soup." I've made plenty of homemade soups before, but not like this.

First of all, you need to know that when it says, "Preparation Time: 40 minutes," it really means three hours. I guess they forgot to include the time it takes to juice five pounds of carrots to form the stock, the hours of chopping vegetables, the necessity of going online to watch a video about how to clean and cut a leek, the need for a clean t-shirt partway through, and the kitchen cleanup afterwards.

Secondly, when it says, "Serves five" it really means "serves five adult elephants." You'll need a big pot.

Have you ever cleaned, sliced and sautéed two pounds of fresh mushrooms at once? This soup also includes bushels of fresh spinach, carrots, onions, corn, celery, leeks, garlic, almond milk, canned beans and assorted fresh herbs. For the next couple of hours, I cranked up the music and juiced, peeled, chopped and blended like a madwoman. I was Iron Chef! Julia Child! That little rat from Ratatouille.

Everything was going swimmingly, too. Until the big, shall we say, eruption.

The instructions said to take raw cashews and puree them with almond milk. Then fill the rest of the blender with some of the hot soup mixture, puree it all together, and add it back into the soup pot. With my left hand on the blender's lid, I hit the button with my right. My right hand, that is, not the right button. The wrong button, actually.

That's right.

The high-powered force pushed the lid off, spewing the mixture onto the counter, the floor, the upholstered dining chair on the other side of the counter, the wall, the microwave and me.

Did I mention it was hot?

It's a good thing the puree smelled yummy, because my kitchen looked like an air sickness bag had exploded while the plane executed a loop-de-loop.

And yes, I said a bad word.

But they tell us nothing bad ever happens to a writer – it's all material. Lucky you.

By this time I had so much invested in that soup, I'd have eaten it even if it tasted like dirt. It didn't. Even my grandsons finished their bowls at supper that night. I froze several future meals and I learned you really can teach an old cook new tricks.

But I think I'll rename the recipe. Volcanic Veggie Vexation has a nice ring to it, don't you think?

Getting Rusty
(Appeared October 3, 2013)

My last saxophone lesson was in mid-May. When it ended, I bid my farmer/teacher a happy summer and the sax stayed in its case until early July when I pulled it out to amaze my visiting mother-in-law.

She was amazed all right.

I couldn't remember a thing! I hastily put the instrument back in its case and there it stayed. I'm to begin lessons again in November. My instructor will take my hard-earned dollars for teaching me the same old things over. My long-suffering husband will have to listen to the same juvenile beginner tunes, with the same excruciating squawks. Apparently, playing a sax is not like riding a bike.

Or could it have something to do with the fact I started learning in my fifties?

***

I did some sewing recently. Hadn't sewn much for years and forgot how much I enjoy it when it's something more dazzling than re-attaching buttons or hemming slacks.

I was dazzled all right.

I couldn't even thread the machine, let alone the needle. Good thing the old woman who sleeps with my husband keeps a pair of magnifying glasses around the house.

***

Last week, I returned to Jillian Michaels' Yoga Meltdown video workout after giving myself a four-month break. It's not that I intended to give myself such a long break. It was supposed to be a week or two, while we moved. Then I gave myself an extension. And another. I'm generous that way. Finally decided to discipline myself and get back into it.

I was disciplined all right.

Strangely enough, it wasn't until two days later I felt the sore muscles — mostly from that despicable Camel pose.

Does it seem to you that the older we are, the less time it takes to get rusty? You can't afford to quit for a minute, or you're right back to square one. This is why we spend the first several years of our life in school. Youth is the time to study new languages, memorize poetry, scripture and multiplication tables, and learn how to ride a bike or play an instrument.

What's the point of learning anything new at this stage if you forget it all at lightning speed? I may as well sit on the couch watching *The Bachelorette* and not bother. This is not encouraging.

Or is it?

When I took another stab at my saxophone playing, I realized I could navigate through my beginner book without help and in a lot less time than it took the first go around. In spite of myself, maybe I wasn't entirely lost after all.

The quality of my finished sewing project is far superior to anything I cranked out when my eyes were only 12 years old, in spite of the ease with which my nimble fingers could thread a needle way back then.

That I found the yoga more difficult after a break tells me it actually was making a difference before the break. It means if we stick with our exercise programs, we really can enjoy some small measure of control over our strength and flexibility as we age — key factors in avoiding falls, broken bones and aching joints.

Guess I don't get to quit yet. Bummer.

All this talk of camels and needles reminds me of a Bible verse I once memorized. "It is easier for a camel to play a saxophone than to pass a rich man through the eye of a needle." Or something like that.

Maybe I learned that one in my forties.

Just Me and My Man-Flu
(Appeared January 9, 2014)

By the time you read this, I hope I am either recovered or dead. As I write, I battle a hostile, hideous bully of a viral bug determined to flatten me with aches, chills, fever, coughing fits and bad hair. Not to mention delirium. Ever since my husband discovered me studying the Kleenex box for directions, I take no responsibility for any delusions or inaccuracies you may uncover in this week's column, nor for any domestic violence that may ensue in your home should you choose to read it aloud.

In 2012, I unwittingly started a dumb tradition of beginning each new year with a virus ... cold, flu, who knows? But since I don't get sick the rest of the year, I really can't complain.

Well, actually, I can. Quite well.

In fact, I've done so much whining and whimpering with this one that I strongly suspect I have, against all odds, come down with none other than the dreaded MAN-flu. I wouldn't be surprised if I could give any man a run for his money in the self-pity department. I looked online to find out whether females can actually catch Man-flu, and it seems I am the first in the history of the universe, which pleases me in some twisted way.

One study found Man-flu may be a legitimate complaint due to the male's higher level of testosterone and therefore lower level of immunity. But I prefer the more imaginative explanation given by Z. Aston Meddows-Taylor: "All flu bugs require their host to survive so they can feed off their host. Big bad flu bugs don't pick on women as they fear they'll kill them, eliminating their food source. They only go after big hairy men who can resist them. The weakling flu bugs only go after women, as men shrug them off at the slightest hint on contact."

Gotta give the guy credit for creativity.

Maybe it's a cold. I Googled the differences, but they're complicated, especially when one's brain is already slowly leaking into one's lungs and getting horked up in quarter-sized gobs with every cough.

The only thing I know for sure is, between my shivering one minute and sweating the next, God will not spit me out of his mouth any time soon. (And if you don't get that joke, look up Revelation 3:16.)

Speaking of God, I decided on Day Five of my flu to try focusing on all the things I could thank him for in the midst of my wretched misery, starting with the fact I wasn't barfing. I felt thankful I no longer had little kids to look after. Then I added our warm house, working furnace, water heater, cozy blankets, hot tea, lemon juice, honey, a job with sick benefits, chocolate and Tylenol. I listed my appliances, sunshine, a hubby to run errands and listen to my grumbling, and the pretty Christmas lights I had no energy to take down. Also flannel jammies, velour housecoat and rabbit-fur slippers made by a First Nations friend. Lo and behold, before I knew it, my thank-you list outnumbered my flu symptoms.

It generally outnumbers most anything, once we take the time to make one. Happy Flu season. Stay well!

How My Daughter-In-Law Drove Me to Drink
(Appeared September 18, 2014)

When our son married the love of his life in 2005, we knew we would love her, too. We just didn't realize how much. As time marches on, we are discovering Dara to be an interesting blend of Annie Oakley, Martha Stewart, Lynn Jennings and Granny Clampett.

I had little respect for her pantry full of weird hippy food the first few times I snooped. "There's nothing to eat in this house," I'd grumble. What were they feeding my grandson? What was with the bags of black beans? What was quinoa and how was it pronounced? What kind of animal did hemp hearts come from? What did one do with couscous?

But that was back when I took my health for granted. Funny how things start to look different when you stop doing that. My newfound interest in nutrition soon had me cooking differently and noticing the benefits, too. I'm thankful Dara feeds my grandkids more nutritiously than I fed her husband.

When she tried to introduce us to her home-brewed kombucha, however, I felt skeptical. I'd never heard of it, for one thing. It smelled suspiciously like wine, for another. And the deal-breaker was the floating blob of slime in every bottle. Seriously? People drink this stuff?

It was apparently loaded with probiotics, which I understood. But knowing it was made from either tea or berries, that it was fermented, and that it contained something called Hyaluronic acid all made it sound like a perfect storm for me and my Interstitial Cystitis.

Then I went on a two-week stint of antibiotics for a lung infection. I hate taking antibiotics, but if I must, I make sure I take probiotics at the same time. Why do so few doctors tell you that antibiotics kill your good bacteria along with the bad? Sure, the pharmacist hands you a list of possible side effects, but provides little if any explanation for why the side effects occur or what you can do to prevent them.

Good probiotics cost a fortune at the health food store, though, so I decided to take advantage of the free, homemade kombucha Dara offered. I drink an ounce with each antibiotic tablet, and it seems to be succeeding at keeping typical antibiotic side effects at bay. And it even tastes good.

Turns out kombucha has been around a little longer than I have, at least 2,000 years. It boasts a rich anecdotal history of health benefits like preventing and fighting cancer, arthritis and other degenerative diseases. Its beneficial claims include detoxification, joint care, digestive health and immunity boosting. It helps provide your body what it needs to heal itself by aiding your liver in removing harmful substances, promoting balance in your digestive system, and being rich in health-promoting vitamins, enzymes and acids.

While Russia and Germany have conducted extensive studies on the benefits of kombucha, no major medical studies are being done in the west. Could the reason be that no one in the drug industry stands to profit from researching a beverage the average consumer can make for as little as 12 cents a litre?

Although there's a lot of information available online, including how to make kombucha, I wanted to share a little about it here for those who, like me, hadn't heard of it. You can do your own research, but the general consensus seems to be that with regular, daily consumption, you can notice improvement in immune system functioning and energy levels within about a week, the healing of more minor ailments within a month, and the healing of more radical illnesses within a year.

So you could say my daughter-in-law made a believer (and a drinker) out of me. But I draw the line at swallowing the slimy floating blob. I don't care how healthy she tells me it is.

I'm Pickin' Up Good Vibrations
(Appeared April 16, 2015)

Apparently, April is Oral Health Month. Have you noticed how in the movies, they always give the villains crooked, discoloured teeth while the good guys display straight, white ones? What makes me laugh are movies where the story takes place in the 1600s, but the heroes still have all their teeth, perfect and gleaming. In reality, life expectancy back then was 35 and the life expectancy of one's teeth even shorter. Someone fortunate enough to reach my age would pretty much be gumming it.

If you promise not to hate me, I'll tell you a secret. I've never had a cavity. Back in the early 1970s, our provincial government funded sessions where dental professionals came into the schools each year with a giant set of teeth and a massive toothbrush to teach kids how to brush properly. I took it to heart.

When my wisdom teeth required extraction in my thirties, my dentist did one side at a time and those wise old choppers were reluctant to divorce themselves from my gums. At one point, I think the man braced one foot on my forehead for leverage. Afterward, I developed the dreaded "dry socket" that leaves nerves exposed and keeps you in pain for weeks. A month later when I went in for the opposite side, I was told I was highly unlikely to experience the same thing. Or maybe I misheard and they actually said, "highly likely." You can guess the rest. What a nightmare.

It was enough to make me deeply thankful for my otherwise good teeth.

Apparently, one of the reasons for my good fortune is a low acid environment in my mouth — which, ironically, has a downside. Tartar buildup becomes more stubborn than normal. Or so they tell me. So every six months I find myself lying prone, my head in my hygienist's lap as she chisels away on my teeth. (Have you noticed dental hygienists tend to be beautiful? I wonder if it's a requirement?) It's a long process and sometimes I need to return for a second session because my hygienist's arms grow tired. Once, I saw her break into a sweat as she worked loose a chunk of plaque the size of a Volkswagen.

She talks me into an electric toothbrush.

Two weeks later, I buy one, take it home, and let it charge overnight. I study the instructions, squeeze out the paste, stick the contraption inside my mouth, and press the button. Immediately, my entire head starts vibrating. Toothpaste splatters the walls and I see about 14 of my own eyeballs arranged in a jagged row three inches in front of my face.

People use these on their kids' teeth? I think. If someone had tried sticking one of these in my mouth when I was a toddler, I'd still be in therapy. With a mouthful of dentures.

But, I'm a grownup. And having shelled out big bucks for this thing, I'm determined to make it work. I shove it around all four quadrants of my mouth, entrusting the sadistic little device to deliver as promised. After two minutes it starts to pulse, telling me I can stop. Thank Heavens.

The room stops spinning. I mop my face, my hair, the mirror and the sink. My teeth do feel cleaner, at least that's what I tell myself. And, like most things, I suspect I'll get used to it. If not, you can be sure you'll be reading about it in the weeks to come.

Take care of those teeth and gums!

In Which I Discover the Fountain of Youth
(Appeared June 11, 2015)

I auditioned for the Prairie Players' fall production of *Arsenic and Old Lace* and was assigned the role of Elaine. Elaine is 20 years my junior. There will be no living with me now.

Our director, Stephanie (bless her heart), seems to think I can pull it off. I knew I liked that girl. If I make a complete fool of myself, at least I won't have as long to live with the humility as I would if I actually were 20 years younger.

Most thespians agree the best part of being involved in a play is the camaraderie with the cast and crew throughout the production. But did you know memorizing all those lines keeps actors young, too? It's true.

The benefits to our brains of memorizing anything are well documented, including the improvement of brain function, neural plasticity, focus and so on. Ever notice how easy it is for a child to learn a second language while adults struggle? It's because the youthful plasticity of their brains makes it easy to chart new neuro pathways. Learning something new forces your brain to chart new paths and can help ward off dementia. The added benefits to your heart and spirit when you memorize scripture or meaningful poetry are greater still.

Regardless what you believe about the power of God's word, memory training of any kind can stave off cognitive decline. According to a blog post on the Best Colleges Online site, "Memory-forming can become a healthy lifelong habit. Researchers from the National Institute on Health and Aging have found that adults who went through short bursts of memory training were better able to maintain higher cognitive functioning and everyday skills, even five years after going through the training. Practicing memorization allowed the elderly adults to delay typical cognitive decline by seven to 14 years. Students who start practicing memory training now can stay sharp in years to come."

Having the ability to memorize a script for a play, yet being too lazy to memorize scripture, frequently leads me to "should" on myself. *Shoulding* on yourself is never a healthy practice. Either do the thing you think you should, or stop *shoulding*, I say.

So a few weeks ago, after our youth pastor invited the congregation to read Psalm 103 aloud together, I decided to try memorizing it verbatim. I printed it out and sticky-tacked it to the wall beside my bathroom mirror where I could work on it while fixing my hair and makeup each morning. Then I review it each night when the makeup comes off. By adding a line or two a day, it came surprisingly easy. And it's a lovely improvement over my usual habit of rehearsing my grievances during this activity. Plus, it took no extra time out of my day!

Two weeks later, I recited the passage to my hubby. It worked so well, I decided to go to the beginning and tacked up Psalm 1 and 2. Two weeks after that, I recited both chapters. I'm now working on 3 and 4. At this rate, I could learn the entire book of Psalms between now and 2018. (I might have to take a break to learn Elaine's lines.)

I'd sure like to make this a lifelong habit. You with me?

If I'm going to portray the youthful Elaine, I'm going to need all the help I can get. Now if I could just recall where I put that script.

Practically a Spa Day
(Appeared November 2, 2017)
This column won a 2018 Word Guild Award

One of the perks of living with a chronic lung disease is that you can occasionally book a day off work while your doctor runs a garden hose down your throat and takes a look around. I try to think of it as a spa day, with my own handsome chauffeur to drive me around.

We rise at stupid o'dark in the morning for the drive to Grace Hospital & Day Spa, and I hope my doc is getting a good sleep. A nice lady who calls me "Hon" checks me in. A fellow appropriately named *Manny* leads me into the prepping area where he gives me one of those fashionable one-colour-suits-all, one-size-fits-none gowns. A nurse tucks a warm blanket around me to lull me into thinking she's on my side. Then she sticks a needle in the back of my hand, a blood pressure cuff on my arm, and a clothes pin on my finger. Another expertly steers me into the treatment room. I assume the rubber chicken stuck to the ceiling is to boost patient confidence in the skill level of medical professionals.

My doc hands me a shot glass full of vile stuff to gargle. This numbs the back of my throat which deactivates my gag reflex ... although yours is probably kicking in about now. After he introduces a drug to my IV, the colourful supply bins on the shelf start dancing a mildly hypnotic jitterbug.

They have me clamp down on a mouth guard, like a football player. Then a teensy-weensy camera goes down my gullet, and I watch on the little monitor in front of me exactly what the doctor sees. Of course, by this time, I am so looped I think I'm watching a documentary on cave exploration. Every time the doc squirts more saline solution, I cough and the TV screen goes all snowy, like our old black and white used to do every time our next-door neighbour, Eddie Haddad, used his electric razor. Frustrated us kids to no end if we were in the middle of Bonanza.

Anyway, the whole deal is done before I have time to enjoy the sauna or mineral pool or a manicure. I'm wheeled to the recovery room which I'll share with seven of my new closest friends who have also been scoped, although it's not polite to ask where. I'm given another warm blanket. This is followed by a pleasant, dozy hour of quietly contemplating the meaning of everything. A cool glass of apple juice confirms that my swallowing mechanism is up and running again.

I'm unhooked from all tubes and set free to dress and leave the spa — with some precautions, like no driving for 24 hours. Why couldn't they say no cooking?

On the ride home, a song comes on our Christian radio station, reminding me that every breath in my lungs come from my Creator, the one who gives me strength and lifts me up.

I thank God for my lungs, my driver, a sunny day, a job with sick benefits, and for my good doctor and nurses. I can feel grateful and laugh at all this because I know that the one who's ultimately in control is the same one who's holding me in his everlasting arms.

Contact me if you're facing your first bronchoscopy. I'm an old pro — and it's practically a day at the spa.

It was a Dark and Spooky Night
(Appeared October 30, 2010)

The spookiest event of my life did not occur at Halloween. Let me take you way back before the turn of the century.

It's Christmas vacation, 1976. I'm a 17-year-old girl driving 500 miles home to Manitoba. I load my Dodge Dart and take off immediately after my last class, planning to drive halfway and spend the night with family friends.

It's dark by the time I start looking for the turnoff that will take me to their farm. I turn left onto a gravel road and soon realize my mistake. This is not a road at all, but a driveway leading to an abandoned looking house. Better get back on the highway. I put the car into reverse and drive straight back, forgetting the driveway had taken a sharp turn. Ka-chunk! My car will go neither forward nor backward. I am hung up on railroad tracks. In the middle of nowhere. With no phone. On a freezing night. I see a headlight coming toward me. A train?

I decide there is no point in doing nothing. I look down that daunting driveway. Is that glimmer of light coming from a window of the shabby old house? I walk toward it, praying with every step. I hear dogs barking. Large dogs. I pray harder. And louder. My heart is thumping faster than my footsteps. The dogs gather round me, barking and growling as I knock on the door.

No answer.

I knock harder. Finally, a young child opens the door and I step inside.

"Is your mommy or daddy home?"

While I wait, I look around. The scene before my eyes is one of the most disturbing I have ever witnessed. Every surface is littered with stuff. I swear I see the grime on the walls and floor moving in the dim light of the bare bulb. Through the living room door, I see children clad in dirty pajamas, watching TV.

An ominous string of coloured lights blinks at me from a skinny Christmas tree.

While one of the kids goes upstairs to rouse an adult, I find a phone between a carton of sour milk and a soiled diaper. I describe my location to my friends so the police will know where to start looking for my body.

A man comes downstairs, tucking in a grungy shirt while he lights a cigarette and yells at the dogs. We head outside together. I understand the foolishness of a young girl getting into a stranger's car, but I have asked for God's help and have no choice but to believe he has provided it.

We drive in the man's car to mine, where he assesses the situation. I don't know how he accomplishes it, but he frees my car from the tracks. He refuses the $20 I offer in gratitude and I'm on my way again, breathing thankful prayers all the way to the right farmhouse.

There, I'm greeted by friendly faces, a hot bath and clean sheets.

I fall asleep pondering how sometimes angels come very cleverly disguised indeed.

Strange Doin's are a-Brewin'
(Appeared October 15, 2011)

Beware the Ides of October. Strange things happen this time of year. At least, to me.

In the Spotlight

We have a motion-sensor light at the back door of our garage. Neither Hubby nor I saw that thing come on once all summer. In fact, if we thought about it all, we assumed it was turned off or burned out.

Until the first night of frost. I had picked our tomatoes and brought them inside earlier in the day. It wasn't until I was ready for bed that it dawned on me: I had forgotten about one plant because it was in its own pot, separate from the garden. I was already in my ratty old bathrobe but determined to save those last two or three tomatoes. You know where this is going.

I grabbed a flashlight, slipped my feet into some flip flops, and headed stealthfully out the patio doors. Wouldn't you know it, the motion-sensor light came on. Hello, neighbours!

Not Exactly Martha Stewart

I almost always keep a frozen pizza on hand for emergencies. I won't bore you with what constitutes an emergency or how often they occur, but here's what happened last time I pulled one out. Now, I don't always buy the same brand but whatever looks like the best deal of the shopping day. Not all brands are packaged alike — some come with a cardboard circle on which the pizza sits until it's time for the oven. Some don't. Recently, I'd been purchasing the sans-cardboard kind, so I popped the pizza into the oven and set the timer. You know where this is going.

When the pizza was ready, I couldn't figure out why it was so difficult to slice. Man, oh man, that thing was tough! Finally picking it up enough to look underneath, I discovered a cardboard circle now fully fused to the pizza crust after having been in the oven for 25 minutes.

Hubby and I scraped it off as best we could and ate it anyway. Not bad, actually.

Powerless

Late one Friday afternoon, the power went out at work. No computers, no fax machines, no lights. Just a bunch of workers with nothing better to do than gawk out the window at the police officer trying to direct traffic at our busy corner. And a boss smart enough and kind enough to tell us to go on home and call it a day.

I pulled into my driveway and pressed the button on my garage door opener. Normally, it works if you barely touch it, so I was surprised when the door stayed down. I pressed the button again. Nothing. Surely if the battery were dying, I could squeeze one last use out of the remote by mashing the button good and hard. This resulted in a broken garage door opener, while the garage door still refused to go up. You know where this is going.

I let myself in another way and soon discovered the power was out at my house as well.

Since none of this could possibly have anything to do with my being scatterbrained, inattentive or just plain deficient, I gotta chalk it up to the freaky time of year. Beware!

When God Surprises You
(Appeared September 6, 2018)

I had been at my housecleaning gig for nine years when my husband suffered an unfortunate accident that resulted in the loss of his right arm. About six weeks later, while we were still reeling from this change, I stopped to pick him up from the Portage campus of Red River (then Community) College where he taught an Accounting course.

While I waited, weary and dirty from a day of cleaning houses, I sat in a chair in the hallway. Suddenly the manager, Irene, breezed by.

"I need to talk to you before you go," she said to me. "About some work."

I watched her disappear into her office. *Forget it*, I thought. *I am not interested in adding one more cleaning job to my list, especially one the size of this.* I felt tempted to sneak out, but she caught me and called me into her office.

To my surprise, it was not a cleaner she was looking for but an evening clerk. Someone to man the office from regular closing time until evening classes began. The work would be cyclical and varied. It paid more than I currently made. And if I wanted, I could take classes free of charge as long as they were relevant to the job.

It might have been a no-brainer, except that it would mean I'd be at work during those critical after-school, homework-coaching, chore-nagging, supper-preparing, kitchen-cleaning, piano-practicing hours. How could I do that to my family, especially during this confusing time when my husband was trying to navigate the chaos of his new life? I prayed and sought advice from my mother and sisters, who encouraged me to go for it.

What I couldn't see then was that God was holding a unique door open and if I didn't step through it now, the next several doors after this one would probably remain closed.

Though the hours did prove challenging, I spent the next four years at that job. The rusty hinges of my office skills were quickly oiled as I got up to speed with computers and took several courses toward the Office Administration certificate — free of charge.

By this time, I'd also been hired one day a week organizing creative arts at my church, and I kept that job (it later grew into full-time, but that's a story for another day). I quit all but two of my cleaning jobs (offices that could be cleaned on the weekend and for which I recruited the help of our teenage daughter).

I look back on that period now as one of the craziest in my life and the life of our family — juggling three part-time jobs while raising three kids — and Hubby and me with only three hands between us. "Help me, Jesus" became my breathing prayer.

It's a good prayer to pray. And a life-giving breath to breathe.

I was still 14 years away from walking into city hall and landing at the administrative assistant's desk where I've worked for nine years now. But in hindsight, I can see how one thing led to another and another. I sometimes wonder how life would have unfolded had I said "no thanks" to Irene's unexpected invitation that day. I'm grateful I didn't. I'm grateful Irene looked past my grubby cleaning lady appearance to see something else and to pull open that door.

Falling Down on Escalators
(Appeared March 14, 2019)

They say nothing bad ever happens to a writer. It's all material.

So when I fell on an escalator at the world's busiest airport last month, it took me only minutes to realize I could glean a column out of the embarrassing experience. But first, the humiliation.

Thankfully, the escalator was going down and I was nearing the bottom. A small rolling bag balanced on the step behind me, its handle in my right hand. My left hand held a half-full water bottle. A light blanket was draped over my left arm. My backpack hung squarely across my shoulders. Somehow, I lost my balance, and when you lose your balance on an escalator there's no retrieving it. Or perhaps there's no retrieving it when you're just days shy of your 60th birthday like I was.

In any case, down I went. In one of those surreal, slow-motion moments, I became aware of several voices all asking the same question: "Are you all right?"

"No," I squeaked. "Can you help me up?"

I put out a hand and a kind man pulled me to my feet, not letting go until I stood on solid ground. Someone else retrieved my bag and blanket. My water bottle had dumped its contents across my hand.

I stood off to the side to assess the damages. One more person asked if I was okay. With a shaky voice, I replied "I will be. Thanks."

I'd landed on one hip. *That's gonna hurt tomorrow*, I thought. My right hand throbbed. No broken bones, just a bruised ego. It's crazy how shaken I felt. I suppose it came from seeing how frighteningly fast something like that can happen and realizing how much worse it could have been. And how far I was from home.

I carried on, thankful I had lots of time to find my gate. Pretty soon the signs pointed up. I needed to take another escalator. My first instinct was to find an elevator or stairs. I walked past.

Then my mind returned to an event at age 17, visiting a ranch belonging to one of my high school teachers, Mr. DeVries. After a pleasant trail ride, the horse I rode (I'll call him "Lucifer" to protect the innocent) took off unexpectedly as soon as he came within sight of home. Apparently, his saddle had not been properly cinched. I found myself hanging off the side of Lucifer for hours, or at least a second. I remember the taste of dirt as I hit the ground. Mr. DeVries saw the whole show. He caught the horse and walked it back to me.

"You need to get back on," he said.

I did, determined to show Lucifer who was boss and Mr. DeVries that I wasn't a sissy — even if I really wanted to cry.

Lucifer took off again. I landed in the dirt again.

This time, Mr. Devries made me climb back on the horse, but walked the animal to his stall. I slunk into the house for a soothing shower and a little cry.

I don't recall being on horseback since. It's never been a priority. But it all floated to the surface that day at the Atlanta airport.

I turned around, walked back to the escalator, and stepped aboard.

Thanks, Mr. DeVries.

Explaining Social Media to My Fifteen-Year-Old Self
(Appeared July 4, 2019)

My one- and three-year-old grandsons in Calgary don't question how their grandmother can appear on their mom's cell phone screen and talk to them from far away. Why would they? As I watch them so naturally engage with technology, I imagine describing it for the kids of the 60s and 70s. The following script springs to mind as I try to explain social media to my 15-year-old self. Since my initials back then were "T.O.", I'll call my young self TO and my current self TT.

TO: So, tell me what the year 2019 is like, when we turn 60. Are we even still alive?

TT: We are!

TO: Is it like the Jetsons? Does our car fly?

TT: No.

TO: It folds into a little suitcase, though, right?

TT: Um, no. Although those little smart cars are getting closer. They're just not that smart yet.

TO: Bummer. Do we go from room to room on people movers?

TT: Not unless we're at the airport.

TO: Do we have a robot maid? Is her name Rosie?

TT: No, we have a human maid. Her name is Terrie.

TO: Do kids watch TV on their wrist watches?

TT: Well ... they can. Hardly anyone wears a watch anymore, though. If they do, it does a lot more than tell time. Most people just use their phones.

TO: What do you mean, their phones?

TT: Our phones have little screens on them, so ...

TO: Oh, the Jetsons have that! Like a TV?

TT: Well, not like any TV you know. More like a computer.

TO: A computer? Computers don't have screens. And they weigh a ton.

TT: Not anymore. You can carry them around in your pocket now, and nearly everyone does.

TO: You must need an awfully long cord!

TT: No. They're wireless.

TO: Wireless? You mean like a transistor radio?

TT: Sort of, yes. And they do it all. Make phone calls, tell the time, the weather, send text, take pictures—

TO: Yeah, right.

TT: No, really. You can look up stuff on the internet—

TO: What's an internet?

TT: Oh, gosh. Let me think. It's like … an encyclopedia … with everything you ever wanted to know and more. Except you can simply say, "Alexa," and ask your question, and it will answer you. Or you can ask Alexa to play a certain song or tell you a joke or give you the square root of 104,691. Or you can simply say "call Carl" and next thing you know, you're talking to Carl.

TO: Far out.

TT: And you can use it to post stuff on social media.

TO: What is social media?

TT: Oh, that's how you connect with people to share stuff about your life … news, photos, recipes, opinions, links to other things on the internet. People get into big arguments on social media. Even with people they've never met.

TO: Sounds like a time waster. I don't understand how the stuff you "post" gets from your computer to someone else's.

TT: It's like email.

TO: What's email?

TT: Oh my goodness. We are a dinosaur, aren't we? It's like regular mail, but instantaneous. And without paper. I type it in, hit "send" and it displays on someone else's screen.

TO: So I guess our typing skills aren't completely useless.

TT: Not at all. I've used them to write books, columns and more. Speaking of books, we can read those on our phones, too.

TO: Get out.

TT: No, really. You can carry hundreds of books around in your pocket.
TO: Even big ones? Like a Bible?
TT: Yes, even Bibles. In several different versions.
TO: No way. So do you use your phone to talk to God, too?
TT: Um ... no. We still talk to God the same old-fashioned way. Directly. Instantaneously. Any time, day or night. No wires needed. Just pray.
TO: But that's how I do it now.
TT: Right. It's still the same.
TO: So I guess God is ahead of his time.
TT: You could say that. He hasn't changed. Though you have changed a thousand times, He has not changed once.
TO: I think I'm a little relieved.
TT: I think I am too. Anything else you want to know?
TO: I imagine you've done away with bad hair days, moodiness, and all-around general selfishness by now, right?
TT: Sigh.

TERRIE TODD

The China Cabinet
(Appeared September 12, 2019)

In 1979, I was living with my husband in Longview, Texas when my parents came to visit. One of the places I wanted to show my mother was a cluttered antique dealership I passed every day on my drive to work. I'd never stopped there myself, but I'd spotted some items I felt sure would capture Mom's fancy.

I wasn't wrong. She loved it! What I didn't expect was that Mom would purchase a china cabinet. She had wanted one like it since she was a little girl. With no space in their motor home, my parents had to leave the china cabinet at our place, and Mom decided right then that it would be mine one day. We got to enjoy it for the next three years.

When we returned to Manitoba in 1982 with all our earthly belongings stuffed into a cargo van, the china cabinet came with us. We had also acquired, for free, a solid oak WWII surplus desk. (Side note: I love that I write novels set during WWII at this desk!) We laid the china cabinet on its back on top of the desk, stuffed with towels and bedding. Along the way, we stopped for a month in South Dakota where Hubby helped relatives with harvest. By this time, I was chasing our toddler around and carrying baby number two. We unloaded only what we needed and left our van packed to the gills. When we headed for Manitoba in November, we reached the Canadian border near closing time. The customs officer took one look at our overfilled van and said, "I ain't goin' through all that stuff. Get outta here."

We arrived a couple of hours later at my parents' house in Portage la Prairie. Mom's china cabinet was finally home.

It moved with her to Winnipeg in the late 90s. When Mom downsized five years ago, the cabinet went to my sister's house back in Portage where it displayed her collection of nativity sets. Now my sister is downsizing, and the china cabinet stands once more in my home. Since our kitchen already has a built-in cabinet for such things, I don't need the old girl for china. Instead, we placed it in my office — an arm's length from the old desk on which it once rode over 2,000 kilometres. It displays the books I have for sale and my writing awards. I think it looks great!

Keats wrote, "A thing of beauty is a joy forever." I don't know about forever, but this china cabinet still has many good years ahead of it. Barring a house fire, I've no doubt it will be here long after I shuffle off this mortal coil. Maybe it will even hold china again someday.

But for all its history, memories, and beauty, the lovely china cabinet is only a *thing*. As much as we value it, Mom, Sis, and I would gladly exchange it if doing so meant we could change things we cannot change for ourselves or our loved ones. If the cabinet could buy perfect health, peace of mind or eternal life, we'd trade it in a heartbeat. If it could mend the wounds that break our hearts or fill the voids left by those we've lost ... well, I guess everyone would want it. Then I'd have a new set of problems, wouldn't I?

I'm grateful to know the true source of all healing, peace and life, and the one who paid the price for them. His name is Jesus. He's pleased when we learn to love people and use things. Getting it the other way around leads only to misery.

Section 5: Special Days & Seasons

Live each season as it passes; breathe the air, drink the drink, taste the fruit, and resign yourself to the influences of each.

Henry David Thoreau

TERRIE TODD

Easter

The angel said to the women, "Do not be afraid, for I know that you are looking for Jesus, who was crucified. He is not here; he has risen, just as he said."

Matthew 28:5-6

TERRIE TODD

Why My Grandsons Won't Be Getting a Clucking Bunny (at least, not from me...)
(Appeared April 16, 2011)

Please don't think of me as the Grinch who stole Easter. I adore chocolate and daffodils and fluffy chicks and bunny rabbits and little girls in frilly frocks.

I just think that if we truly needed a kids' story to replace the real Easter story, we could come up with something more credible than a clucking rabbit who lays chocolate eggs and delivers them to children for no apparent reason. So I decided to come up with one. A Manitoba-friendly, parent-friendly, wallet-friendly one. Here it is.

Once upon a time, a long time ago, before colour was invented, the world was all in black and white and shades of gray. A little girl named Ruby and a little boy named Jim were exploring in the forest near their home.

By and by they came across a little house in the middle of the forest. The house was made of snow.

"I wonder who lives here," Jim said as he approached the door. But before he could raise his hand to knock, the door opened (which was a very good thing because knuckles rapping on snow do not produce much sound). A little skunk stood in the doorway.

Now skunks were the only creatures who had any colour, for they held the colour key. While the rest of the world was black and white and shades of gray, skunks had red heads and orange legs and yellow bodies and blue tails and purple feet and green stripes down their backs. They stood out like the little girl in the red coat in *Schindler's List*.

"Welcome! Come inside," the skunk said.

Since neither of the children had ever seen a skunk before, they went inside. The skunk offered them hot chocolate, which they happily accepted. What they did not know was that the skunk was an evil skunk who had put sleeping powder in their hot chocolate and Jim and Ruby were soon fast asleep. Because the writer of this tale had a word count limit, however, they soon awoke, tied up the evil skunk, grabbed the colour key, and ran home where their parents tucked them into their cozy beds and they slept soundly until 10:37 the following morning. When they awoke, the world was all in colour, for the evil skunk had been defeated at last.

And that is why, to this very day, skunks are black and white and the rest of the world is in colour. Except for Manitoba in early spring, when it is all black and white and shades of gray. This is why children must sleep late on Easter weekend. For if they do not, the world will remain black and white and colour will not come.

There, now isn't that much better? And so believable, too. No need to thank me.

The Real Hero
(Appeared April 23, 2011)

Those who seek and receive professional counsel for their life and relationships are considered heroes at my church. If this includes you, you know the process can be both encouraging and difficult, but worth it. Taking time to root around beneath the surface has an inevitable tendency to expose emotional rubble we don't always want to look at. And we all have our rubble.

One of the most overwhelming and recurring thoughts I've had through my own counseling process has been the staggering size of God's heart. The hurts and disappointments in my own life are miniscule compared to what others have suffered, but when you multiply those hurts by the billions, for every person who ever breathed, all with our pain and scars, one question surfaces. If God truly sees it all, how can he bear it? We hear on TV about abused or malnourished children and we want to change the channel because our hearts cannot handle it. The atrocities of war fill volumes. Hunger and disease run rampant. The age-old question about why God allows all the misery crops up ever so easily, leading many to conclude he may be loving or he may be all-powerful, but he certainly cannot be both.

And then our protest is silenced by the shadow of a cross.

Not only does God see it all, but if the Bible is true, he loves each hurting individual with a love we can only imagine. So how can his heart stand it? His capacity for pain must be at least as great as his capacity for love. God's heart breaks for the abuser as much as the abused, the perpetrator as well as the victim. And on some level, we are all both.

When Jesus died on the cross, it was not only for the sins you've committed, but also for the sins done against you. Not just for forgiveness, but for healing. I don't claim to understand this, but Isaiah 53:5 foretold it: "He was pierced for our transgressions, he was crushed for our iniquities; the punishment that brought us peace was upon him, and *by his wounds we are healed*."

As you celebrate Easter weekend, may God grant you a fresh picture of his great big heart. We simply cannot put him in a box, understand, or explain him with our little human hearts and brains. We cannot fully appreciate the battle at Calvary, when all the forces of darkness rallied everything they had and hurled it all at my hero as he hung there. Every vulgar thought, every loathsome deed, every emotional or physical wound ever inflicted. All of it, flung at him as though he committed it all himself.

The suffering will one day come to an end. We have the ultimate Hero. He took it all. He paid the price. It is finished. We win!

Outrageous Grace
(Appeared April 5, 2012)

I adore cats. I don't currently belong to one, and I suspect I'd get annoyed with the hair in the house if I did. But as a kid, I had several.

My most memorable? Frederica, the calico. Freddy, for short. She was beautiful, a good mouser, and a prolific mother — much to my parents' annoyance. Each batch Frederica delivered would invariably contain the same combination of three kittens: a calico like herself, which we'd name Harriet; an orange and white one we would name Elmer; and a solid orangey/brown one named John. We borrowed the names from the three Wiebe brothers — local single fellows who frequented our home. Since calico cats are always females, Harry got changed to Harriet.

It was a dark day when the elderly Mrs. Dumanski from across the street came to our house asking in her thick German accent whether the dead cat in the middle of the street was ours. I asked her to repeat the question, but by that time my mother had come to my rescue. I waited in my room while Mom hurried out to check.

It was Freddy. A car had hit her while she carried home a mouse for her babies. A family friend took Freddy's body to the beach where he gave her a respectful burial.

I mourned for weeks, fearing that God was punishing me. You see, just days earlier I'd been playing at my cousin's house and our aunt caught us smoking homemade cigarettes on the back steps. I had rolled the "cigarettes" from torn newspaper and stuffed them with recently mowed grass. It's a miracle we didn't set fire to the whole place!

Here's the thing. Why did I assume God was punishing me? Had I been taught this, or did I put it together myself? Had the children's song, "Oh be careful little hands what you do ..." given me a skewed picture of a Father up above, looking down in love, arranging for a car to drive over my beloved cat because I had led my younger cousin astray? The guilt made my sorrow still deeper and I felt miserable.

Years later, I would learn the difference between punishment and discipline.

A wise parent knows the best kind of discipline matches the crime. After repeated warnings about slamming a bedroom door, Dad removes a child's door from its hinges for a week. Dishonouring curfew results in grounding. An abused computer gets taken away. Logical, appropriate consequences bring about the growth and improvement of the one disciplined.

Punishment, on the other hand, simply makes the criminal pay with little concern over whether rehabilitation is even possible.

God disciplines his children in love. But our punishment was paid by someone other than us — also in love.

Now, when I look back at that brokenhearted little girl weeping over her lost pet and taking the blame, I know that what I needed then was the same outrageous grace I would need every day of my life. I can easily picture Jesus pulling her into his lap, holding her tight and comforting her.

"It's okay to be sad," he tells her. "I know you loved Freddy, but you did not do this. This is just life in a broken world. Your sin is covered already. You will never pay for it. You can never pay for it. I already have."

And that is the story of Easter.

The Value of a Good Question
(Appeared April 17, 2014)

What is the most significant question anyone has ever asked you? (Not counting that one.) Think about this now. Probably, you'll quickly eliminate those which you've been asked repeatedly:
- Would you like fries with that?
- Did you remember to put out the garbage?
- Can I interest you in a great offer on long distance services?
- Got milk?

Your mind skips instead to the "biggies" you have been asked only once or still long to hear:
- Do you take this woman to be your lawfully wedded wife?
- Will you accept the position?
- For one million dollars, is that your final answer?

And then there are those questions we all hope we're never asked:
- Sorry to wake you, Ma'am, but is this your son?
- Where were you on the night of ...?
- Have you ever used ... lied about ... been convicted of ... cheated on ...? You can fill in the blank.

Sometimes one seemingly simple question holds enough power to send us into a tailspin. Jesus Christ proved himself a master at asking questions. Often, he answered others' questions with another question — a technique I find irritating when it's used on me because it forces me to think, and I don't always want to think. When the religious leaders of Jesus' day tried to catch him off-guard with tricky questions, he came back with clever questions of his own, beating them at their game and leaving them speechless. (For more on this, check out Matthew 12:9-14 and 22:15-22.)

Whichever question you deem the most significant pales in comparison to the life and death question Jesus asked his disciples in Mark chapter eight. It's the same question he will eventually ask you and me: "Who do you say I am?" Like his disciples, we can easily deliver the things others say about Jesus. A good man. A prophet. A holy man. An example. A legend. A little misguided. A naive idealist. A boat-rocking, rabble-rousing rebel.

But what others say won't matter one whit when the day comes that you find yourself face to face with Jesus and he asks, "Who do YOU say I am?" This Easter season, you owe it to yourself to check out the claims he made about himself and decide what your answer will be.

What was it that riled those leaders so much they wanted him destroyed? Do you really think he'd have been put to a brutal death for being a good teacher, a loving healer or even a little misguided?

It was his claim to be the Son of God, the long-awaited Messiah, the Resurrection and the Life, that got him nailed to a cross. How dare he? If that's who he was, it meant he possessed authority, a closely guarded commodity already diminished by the presence of a foreign government. Any further threats, even from God himself, were unthinkable. No wonder they would do anything to prevent this man from influencing the crowds. Too bad they were so short-sighted they missed the most significant question of all: "Who do YOU say I am?"

Don't let it happen to you.

Hands I've Held Dear
(Appeared April 2, 2015)

Whether or not you're a country music fan, you've probably heard the old song *Daddy's Hands*. Whenever I hear it, a lump forms in my throat. My dad had a rather unique left hand, injured in an accident when he worked in a gypsum mine before I was born. With surgeries and skin grafts, they managed to save it, but Dad's left hand remained at a strange, stiff angle and his use of it was limited. Still, I loved Dad's hands. To me they represented love, care and tenderness because he was a loving, caring, tender dad.

When I met and married my husband, I loved his hands too. One morning in 1995, after he switched from an office job to farm work, I noticed how his hands had taken on that greasy look of mechanics and farmers. Sitting across the breakfast table from him, I said, "You know, I've always loved your hands, but it's going to take a while for me to get used to them looking like this." I couldn't have guessed in a million years that later the same day, Hubby would injure his arm in an accident and we'd be saying goodbye to his right hand.

Following Hubby's amputation, I found myself unable to sleep and would get up to read my Bible. Passages about the hand of God and the arm of God jumped out at me from everywhere. You can imagine how comforted I felt to read the following:

"Do not fear, for I am with you; do not be dismayed, for I am your God. I will strengthen you and help you; I will uphold you with my righteous right hand ..." Isaiah 41:10. God's strong, safe hands endure forever.

My dad lives in Heaven now and I know he has two strong, healthy hands. I look forward to seeing that. I know my husband's arm will be fully restored one day, too, and I really look forward to seeing that.

But the hands I long to see most are the only hands that will bear scars in Heaven. Nail scars. And those scars were no accident. They represent Jesus' own choice to endure pain and death on a cross out of love for me and you. An old hymn says, "I shall know my Redeemer when I reach the other side by the print of the nails in His hands."

This weekend, as we remember Christ's sacrifice and celebrate His resurrection, please take a good look at your own hands and consider the ones that took the nails for you.

What's on Your Key Ring?
(Appeared March 24, 2016)

Next week will mark seven years since I began my job at City Hall. Along with a list of administrative assistant's responsibilities, I was given something I wasn't expecting: a key to the mayor's office. Little did they know what kind of twisted mind they were entrusting with that key.

Having a key to the mayor's office on my key ring could land me in a boatload of trouble. I could do all sorts of things, from leaving a whoopee cushion on his chair to papering his walls with my newspaper column. I could stick a label on his coffee maker saying, "Voice Activated" and then try to suppress my guffaws while he yells at it to start. I might even be able to plant his computer keyboard with damp cotton balls and grass seeds, then position it in the sunlight and watch the response as alfalfa begins sprouting between the keys.

So far, I've refrained. Though I suspect someone will be watching me more closely now.

You're wondering what all of that has to do with Easter.

In the days before Jesus Christ came, access to the Hebrew God was strictly limited. (Okay, so the Mayor is not God and his office is not holy. Work with me.) Only the temple priests could enter the Holy place, and only the *high* priest could enter the *Most* Holy Place, and then only once a year. On the Day of Atonement, the high priest could enter to make atonement for the sins of the people. A heavy veil hung in the opening to this holy of holies. According to one Messianic Jewish Fellowship article, the veil was made using many layers of cloth. The curtains overlapped, creating a three-foot thick maze. So great was the division between God and the people.

Enter Jesus Christ of Nazareth.

At the exact moment that Jesus died on the cross that first Good Friday, the veil to the Most Holy Place split from top to bottom, seemingly of its own accord. Those present must have felt terrified! This split signified that the barrier between man and God was destroyed forever. From that moment on, anyone who places their faith in Jesus can come into God's presence at any time. He held the key and he opened the door. It means we can go directly to him for whatever we need. Forgiveness. Comfort. Strength. Courage. Wisdom. Healing. Eternal Life.

I was entrusted with a key to the mayor's office because of good references and a reliable history of work experience. You could say I earned it, but I could also lose it with one irresponsible decision.

But I did absolutely nothing to earn access to God, nor can it be taken away. It's a gift, and a very expensive one, bought for me by the Son of God himself. Bought for you, too.

And that, friends, is what Easter is all about. Celebrate it with all the gladness and gratitude it deserves!

Waiting for the Reunion
(Appeared April 9, 2020)

If you ask people what they miss most during this time of isolation, you can be reasonably sure it's not their workplace or Rotary meetings or sports practise or shopping or the theatre or restaurants or even church. If you ask what the first thing they want to do when restrictions are lifted, most won't say they're going to run straight to the pub or go work out at the gym or purchase concert tickets.

Oh, they'll do those things eventually. But for most of us, what we're looking forward to the most is a reunion with loved ones. Grandparents ache to hug their grandkids again. Children and teenagers are eager to see their friends. Young couples in love will enjoy that first embrace more than any other. Every "first-time-back" meeting will be a place of joy, smiles, and connection. Church lobbies everywhere will look like mass hug-fests the first Sunday we gather again. The longer we must wait, the more precious that day will be.

It's fun to imagine the rejoicing, the cheers, the smiles, the bursting into song, the bounce in people's steps when that day comes. We're social creatures, made for community. For what some call "fellowship."

And in a way, that's what Easter is all about.

When sin entered our world—and along with it, sickness and death—it doomed us to a future separated from God and eventually from each other. God is perfect and cannot fellowship with sinfulness. Our sinfulness broke his heart, because he *wants* community with us.

So he made a way.

He sent his son, Jesus Christ, to pay the price for our sin. Because Jesus was perfect, when he died on the cross, it took care of the sin part. But only his resurrection could solve the separation part. Three days after his death, he rose from the dead. Because he did, we can too. This is why death holds no power over those who believe in him. It's why Christians can feel deep joy at a funeral, even while we're sad and grieving. We know there's a great reunion coming, and we look forward to that day more than any other.

1 Corinthians 15:55 asks, "Where, O death, is your victory? Where, O death, is your sting?" The writer, Paul, told believers not to grieve "as those who have no hope." He didn't tell us not to grieve. Of course we grieve. But we grieve with the knowledge that our separation is temporary.

The death and resurrection of Jesus Christ changes everything. It teaches us how to grieve. It teaches us how to die. It teaches us how to wait.

Easter 2020 will be one for the history books, won't it? Whether you're stuck at home with kids who can't participate in their usual traditions, or home alone longing for a family gathering, or worried because someone you care about has contracted Covid-19, or grieving the loss of a loved one—may this Easter serve to remind you why it's the most important holiday on the calendar. There's a great reunion coming that Easter made possible.

The longer we must wait, the more precious that day will be.

Mother's Day

*Honour her for all that her hands have done,
and let her works bring her praise at the city gate.*

Proverbs 31:31

TERRIE TODD

Heartstrings
(Appeared May 10, 2012)

It is late May 1981 and I am in the springtime of my life. I'm in the hospital, cuddling my newborn son against my breast, a large pillow between him and the Caesarian incision. I gaze into his beautiful little face and realize a love I had never known. I have heard it said that "to be a mother is to walk around forever with your heart outside your body," and for the first time, I understand. I realize with amazement that I would gladly die for this child.

Fast-forward to early September 1999.

I am standing on the observation deck at Winnipeg International Airport watching a Royal Airlines jet take off for Vancouver. My handsome, six-foot-four son is aboard, excited to be off on his own for the first time.

How did this happen? Had this changing of life's seasons transpired while I had my back turned? I blink back the tears and make some wisecracks to dissolve the lump in my throat. I'll have a good bawl sometime in the next few days when I'm home alone and can do it up right. For now, I am thankful for his two younger siblings who keep me grounded with their chatter, singing and bickering on the ride home.

If the season of raising children is summer and the empty nest fall, then it is the younger siblings who make the turning of the leaves gradual, gentle, tolerable.

When a child arrives, we know the day will come when he or she will leave. We prepare ourselves as best we can, and the thought that was almost unthinkable when they were still in our arms becomes a little more endurable through the high school years. Still, there is that ache, that beating of the heart so many miles away ... though we know this is the natural order of life and wouldn't really want it otherwise.

It's why mothers need each other.

It's also why we need God. For just as we could not bear the changes of our Canadian seasons without shelter, we need His constancy, His faithfulness, His shelter to endure the changing seasons of our lives.

Now enjoying this empty nest season of my life, I'm so thankful for a God who never changes. I know that my children are in His hands ... that they were never truly in mine to begin with. And that there is no better place for any of us to be.

Happy Mother's Day.

Don't Look Now, But Your Mother's Prayers May Be Following You
(Appeared May 9, 2013)

It was Mother's Day, 1981. Technically, I was already a mother since I would give birth to our firstborn a week later. Overdue, I felt as massive as a mammoth, as bulky as a bear, as huge as a hippo. I was retaining so much water, I couldn't wear my own shoes and had to schlep around in my husband's moccasin slippers.

To multiply the merriment, I developed a revolting rash all over my body — for which my doctor could give me nothing, for the baby's sake. So I spent nights tossing and turning (as much as one can "toss" when you're the size of a whale) and trying not to scratch.

Labour finally began late Friday afternoon and on Sunday afternoon, our nine and a half-pound son was born via C-section. It gave a whole new meaning to the words "long weekend."

And I had never been so helplessly in love with another human being in my life.

With practice must come proficiency, because we repeated the performance two more times — without the rash, with much shorter labour times, and without requiring surgical deliveries. But with the same overwhelming rush of love every time.

Funny how that works, isn't it? Methinks the flood of parental love is God's way of ensuring we don't ring their scrawny necks when they keep us up all night because they are teething or throwing up or wetting their beds or staying out past curfew or getting married the next day or birthing babies themselves.

It's also God's way of teaching us a little about himself. Although we could never love our children perfectly the way he loves his, becoming a parent gives us a window into God's compassion. Nothing breaks our hearts like knowing our child is in pain or seeing him or her make bad choices. God's heart breaks for us, too, but he is wise enough to give us freedom of choice and to allow our pain to make us stronger even though he could take it away in an instant. Most parents will tell you that if it came down to it, they would die for their child. In God's case, he did.

My father used to tell the story of how, as a young man drafted into the Canadian Army during World War II, he knew his mother was praying for him. Though well aware of her faith, he possessed little interest in God himself. The day came when Dad received word his mother had died. That night, he dreamed of a light. His mother was following the light and in his dream, he knew he would eventually follow it, too.

At the time, Dad had no idea what the dream meant, but it made an impact on him nonetheless. Years later, he came to faith as well, and realized the fulfillment of his dream. No wonder one of his favourite hymns went like this:

I'm coming home, I'm coming home,
To live my wasted life anew,
For mother's prayers have followed me,
Have followed me the whole world through.

All mothers make sacrifices. Missing a night's sleep is one thing. Giving up things we might like for ourselves in order to buy those skates or music lessons for our offspring is another. But praying for our children is both the greatest privilege and the most powerful sacrifice any parent can make. Don't underestimate it.

Happy Mother's Day!

A Mother's Legacy of Faith and Perseverance
(Appeared May 8, 2014)

Last week, I stood near my mother as the body of her third husband was lowered into the ground.

The first time I witnessed this, in 1986, cancer had claimed the life of my father; the second, in 1991 when my first stepfather succumbed to heart disease after only 20 months of marriage. Mom had been married to John (who affectionately introduced himself as "Mister Norma the Third") for 15 years when a rare disease called Progressive Supernuclear Palsy ended his life here on earth. None of these departures were swift or straightforward, and Mom found herself playing caregiver each time, though her formal education never trained her for the role. I hated seeing her at yet another graveside. At 82, standing between her tall sons, stepsons and grandsons, Mom looked small and frail to me, maybe for the first time.

My mother's strength is becoming legendary. She has outlasted enough of life's hurricanes to rank among the most cherished of retired ships. She deserves to be honoured in a safe and sunny harbour, with no more battles to fight. Instead, she must remain here to keep sailing, whatever storms are yet to come. Knowing Mom, she will do so with grace, wisdom and ridiculous portions of spunk. An old hymn by W. C. Martin says:

... it holds, my anchor holds:
Blow your wildest, then, O gale,
on my bark so small and frail;
By His grace I shall not fail;
For my anchor holds, my anchor holds.

Understanding the temporal nature of these separations is one of the things sustaining Mom while she awaits her turn to join the party. It's inaccurate to say she "lost" three husbands because she knows exactly where they are. Or, more precisely, whom they are with. Nothing can surprise the author and finisher of her faith, and he tells us that to be absent from the body is to be at home with him. He tells us we don't grieve as those who have no hope. He tells us he is the resurrection and the life, and that everyone who believes in him will live, even after dying. And in her favourite Bible verse, he tells Mom to be still and know that he is God.

I recently learned that years ago, when farmers cleared a field of trees for planting, they traditionally left one tree standing. The surviving tree was spared for a purpose — to provide shade for the farmer and his animals on a hot summer day, or shelter from a sudden storm. These days, I imagine my mother must sometimes feel a bit like that last standing tree. I hope she knows how much shade and comfort she continues to provide to those she loves.

Oh, my mother hasn't done everything perfectly and she'd be the first to tell you so. But by her determination to carry on, Mom models for her children how it's done. How you don't abandon the one you promised to love when they become weak and sick. How, although you become angry, frustrated, discouraged and confused, you don't stay stuck there. How you don't allow loss to paralyze you. And how, when calamity falls, you turn to the one who calmed the raging Sea of Galilee with his words.

Mothers, as we celebrate your special day this weekend, I encourage you to reflect on this. What are you modelling for those who come behind you? How will your children do life better because they watched you? Have you shown them where to turn for rescue during the storms of life? And will you continue to offer shade and shelter, even if you one day find yourself the last tree standing?

Never Too Old to Need Mama
(Appeared May 7, 2015)

I should have known things were going too well. The Prairie Players' performance of *Sleeping with a One-Armed Man* at the Glesby Centre went swimmingly last week. We felt overwhelmed when an audience of 265 showed up and collectively donated $1,380 to Manitoba Farmers with Disabilities. Thank you to everyone who came. Your generosity and support are deeply appreciated!

Next, we drove off to the ACT Festival in Dauphin. I hoped the team would do as well as they had at home. I hoped the adjudicators wouldn't criticize us into the ground. I wondered if I'd find my way, especially since I was staying at my niece's home and would need to navigate country roads after dark with my dicey night vision. Would the weather turn horrid? Had I packed the right outfits? Would my old car hang together? Would my sometimes precarious energy levels fizzle before the weekend ended?

Not only did I arrive with no wrong turns, but the adjudicators offered much praise and helpful suggestions for making our play better. I enjoyed extraordinarily restful sleep in my niece's spare room. The weather was perfect. The camaraderie delightful. The food too good to be true. The cherry on top occurred at the Saturday banquet when I won TWO fantastic prizes in the silent auction fundraiser! I rarely win anything, but this time I needed help lugging my loot to my car: a large flowerpot filled with gardening supplies and a beautiful hand-crafted deacon's bench!

I headed for home the following afternoon belting out happy songs, feeling like a competent playwright, a capable adult and a truly fortunate individual. In Neepawa, I stopped and used the free McCafe coupon we'd each found in our goodie bag.

It should have occurred to me that my car might be equally thirsty.

It's not that I didn't look at the fuel gauge. I just didn't look at it soon enough. And when I did, it told me seven litres and a range of 110 kilometres remained. Already past Westbourne, I should reach the filling station at the intersection of Highways 16 and the Trans-Canada, no problem. Right?

Wrong. My singing stopped.

At least I had enough warning to pull onto the shoulder. Now what? It's a busy highway but flagging down strangers when you're alone is not widely recommended. I called home and left a message. Then I tried my sister's house and didn't bother with a message. I debated. I could call CAA and wait a couple of hours or I could try Mom. She's generally looking for something to do on a Sunday afternoon.

But what competent, capable, 56-year-old calls their mother to rescue them from the side of the road?

Then again, what 56-year-old is fortunate enough to have that option?

I dialed Mom's number. She arrived in 20 minutes. I climbed into her car and the first words out of her mouth were not, "what were you thinking?" or "I can't believe you ran out of gas." As we made eye contact, she said, "I smell a column in the works."

Indeed. I had already been scribbling notes while I awaited her rescue. Think she's on to me?

She drove me to the nearest station where I purchased a jerrycan and the two of us figured out how to fill it. Back at my car, we emptied it into my tank and got behind our respective steering wheels, both smelling like gasoline. Mom followed me back to the station, waited while I filled, and continued to trail me into Portage in case I did some other dumb thing.

Thank you, Mom. You are part super-hero, part cheerleader, part guardian angel. And all grace.

Rest assured, mothers. It may not often look this obvious (or this pathetic), but your kids will always need you — no matter how competent, capable or old they grow. Happy Mother's Day!

Father's Day

*The righteous man walks in his integrity;
His children are blessed after him.*

Proverbs 20:7

TERRIE TODD

God's Got a Great Big Fridge
(Appeared June 18, 2011)

It was the first and hopefully last vocal solo of my life. Portage Alliance Church choir, 1985. There was a short alto solo in the Easter cantata and if I concentrated hard and curled my toes just right, I could reach the required D-flat. Man, was I nervous! But the words were priceless and I knew if I could just convey them well, I would surely change the world:

What will you do with Jesus?
Neutral you cannot be.
One day, your heart will be asking
What will he do with me?

I envisioned lost sinners falling to their knees in repentant droves as I sang the closing line and they finally realized they were playing a high stakes game with their eternal souls.

The best part was that my dad was in the audience. He was already ill with the disease that would end his life a year later, and it would be one of his last times in church. I don't know how big a struggle it was for him to get there, but he was there.

The repentant droves did not materialize that day, but after the concert, Dad gave me a big hug and said, "It was beautiful!" Whether or not it was beautiful is beside the point. My dad thought it was, and that's what mattered. I may have been a 26-year old mother, but daddy's approval was still mighty important.

Do we ever outgrow our need for parental approval? Is it healthy? Beats me. I do think it's universal, though. Many years ago, I remember being discouraged about a play I'd written that no one wanted. I felt rejected and untalented. Then a friend pointed to my fridge and the artwork proudly displayed there by my children. She told me that regardless what others thought, God loved my play because I was his child. Even if it was never produced, the script was on God's fridge and when the angels came by, he proudly pointed it out and said, "Look at this! My girl did this!"

I have hung onto that mental image ever since. I've got tons of stuff on God's fridge, and so do you! I guess God has a mighty big fridge.

This weekend is Father's Day. If you're a dad, I encourage you to lavish your children with praise and encouragement. Let them know you're proud of who they are and what they do, whether they're two or 52.

If you still have a dad, don't take him for granted. If your relationship is far from ideal, can you enjoy and celebrate what is good about it anyway? Tell him you love him while you can.

And if you've lost your dad, rest in the knowledge that you have a heavenly Father who sees you all the time, loves you beyond measure, and is thrilled to call you his child. He even displays your best work on his fridge!

(By the way, what do you suppose God keeps inside his fridge? Angel food cake? Divinity Squares? Heavenly Hash ice cream? All fat-free, of course!)

Happy Father's Day!

Remembering Dad
(Appeared June 12, 2014)

Mom tells me I'm like my dad. I figure she says so because she doesn't want to take credit for my slightly warped sense of humour.

Dad was a trickster who loved a good laugh. I don't know if I actually remember this event or if it only seems like I remember it because I heard the story so often. In any event, I couldn't have been more than three. (At least I sure hope I wasn't, because any older and it might indicate I'm not as clever as I fancy myself.)

Like many children, I had a favourite doll. I spent a great deal of time and attention on that little dolly, changing her clothes, feeding her, and lugging her around. One day while my back was turned, Dad decided it would be hilarious to smear a little peanut butter on my dolly's bottom and hang around to watch the reaction.

I didn't disappoint. Whether delighted or disgusted, I can't say. But "astonished" would be an understatement. Dad got his chuckle that day and many times over as he retold the tale through the years. Like a prize fish, my eyeballs probably grew with each telling.

Fast forward.

I was a 25-year old mother with two real babies of my own. (Dad's peanut butter prank must not have traumatized me too severely.) One morning I was busy vacuuming our home when the vacuum suddenly quit. What? Had I blown a breaker? Was my machine kaput? I inspected the switch, then followed the cord around the corner. There, in the middle of my kitchen, stood my father, the end of the cord in his hand and a big goofy grin on his face.

He had stopped in unannounced to see the kids and me, a rare treat. While I made tea, Dad squished into the rocking chair with the children to read a Dr. Seuss book. It's a memory I treasure.

A mere two years later, we laid my father's body in the grave. If there's anything positive to be said for cancer, it usually provides plenty of opportunities to say good-bye and tell people how much they mean to us. I'm thankful for that. Not everyone gets the chance.

Last week, an evil man killed three young RCMP officers in Moncton. Did their families have any opportunity to say what they needed to say? I suppose when your loved one is a cop, there's more daily awareness that every goodbye could be the last. But what's true for police officers and their families holds true for all of us. We never know. It's a lesson I sure don't want to learn the hard way, do you?

So, in honour of Father's Day, I'm sending special affection to two favourite dads I am grateful to still have in my life: the father of my children and the father of my grandchildren. You make me proud, guys, and I love you both to pieces. Thanks for loving me, too — warped sense of humour and all.

A Father's Patience Remembered
(Appeared June 18, 2015)

Call me spoiled, but I owned my own car before I had a driver's licence. And what a sweet ride it was! A 1974 ogre-green Dodge Dart.

I was never one of those teenagers itching to get behind the wheel. My 16th birthday went by without much thought toward my licence. Then my 17th came and went.

I guess Dad decided enough was enough. I attended a Christian boarding school 800 kilometres from home, and each time I had a break from school, Dad would make the round-trip to fetch me home, then a second round-trip to take me back a week later. When presented with a deal on the Dart, my parents saw it as an opportunity to save time and money in the long run. They bought the car.

Now to convince Terrie she needed to learn to drive before it was time to return for Grade 12.

I passed the written test with no problem and received my learner's permit. Mom let me drive the 25 kilometres home, but I think she had only one nerve left when we got there.

Home alone a few days later, I decided to practice parallel parking in our spacious backyard. Dad had some brand-new eavestroughs waiting to be installed and I decided they would work well to represent the cars I needed to park between. How I drew that conclusion when I couldn't even see them from the driver's seat is beyond me. Maybe I figured I'd feel them, like speed bumps. I laid the troughs along the ground and started maneuvering the car into place.

Did you know a 1974 Dodge Dart will flatten a brand-new eavestrough like long johns through the wringer?

At least I learned one thing that day.

Dad calmly hammered his eaves trough back into shape, but it never looked the same.

The next time I climbed behind the Dart's steering wheel, Dad rode shotgun and we were going all the way from

Amaranth to Winnipeg to pick up Mom. I putzed along at about 65 kilometres an hour for the first while, Dad patiently telling me to take all the time I needed and accelerate when I felt comfortable doing so. Eventually, I reached the speed limit and cars stopped whizzing around us.

Naturally, I assumed we'd pull over and switch seats long before we got into city traffic. But to my surprise, Dad navigated me all the way to my aunt's house in Winnipeg where Mom waited, no doubt wondering what was taking us so long. That trip gave me the confidence I needed to take my driving test and pass. I figured I was good to go.

But Dad had one more lesson for me. Before he'd allow me to hit the highway on my own, he needed to know I could change a tire. First, he explained the process. Then he parked himself in his favourite lawn chair to watch the show, a cold drink in one hand and a fly swatter in the other. I had to change the tire from start to finish, all by myself.

I haven't changed a tire since.

Ten years later, my father passed away. Dad's concern for my safety and his patient teaching are memories I cherish. Given the option, I still avoid driving in general and parallel parking in particular. But I've maintained my maximum number of driver's merit points for nearly 40 years, so Dad must have done something right.

I miss that guy.

Happy Father's Day.

Nine Things I'd Do with Dad
(Appeared June 14, 2016)

I'm thankful to have had a father for the first 27 years of my life. But 27 years are not enough to pack in all the things a father and daughter can and should do together. Here are nine things I'd love to do with Dad if I could. Most of them cost little or nothing.

#1. Go for a walk. My dad left us before the beautiful walking path around our Crescent Lake was created. I sure would love to show it to him.

#2. Cook something. Dad had his specialty creations from the kitchen: apple kuchen, potato pancakes made from hand-grated potatoes, and venison roasted with lemon slices. I'd get Dad to teach me his secrets for these delicious dishes.

#3. Go shopping. I don't recall ever shopping with Dad, but I think it would be fun to pick out something for him (probably a tool) and something for me (probably an outfit). This could be followed by …

#4. Go for ice cream. Dad loved soft ice cream, while I prefer hard. We could go somewhere that offers both. He'd chuckle when it melted on my chin and I'd say, "Before you laugh too hard, better check your moustache."

#5. Help with a Do It Yourself project. Dad was a bit of a MacGyver when it came to jerry-rigging solutions. I could have learned a lot if I'd paid closer attention to some of the things Dad fixed or created. I like to think I'd take advantage of the opportunity if I had it now.

#6. Plant a Tree. The baby evergreens Dad planted in his backyard in 1981 now tower above my sister's house. I could have been out there helping him, but I wasn't. How much more precious those trees would be now if I had. If he were here, I'd get him to help me plant a tree in my yard and cherish the memory every time I looked at it.

#7. Interview him about his childhood. It's ironic that the books I'm writing now take place during the Second World

War era, when my dad served in the Canadian army. I could sure use his memory if I had access to it! I'd also love to ask him things like: Is there anything you regret not having asked your parents? What was the happiest moment of your life? What are you most proud of? How did your experience in the military mold you as a person? What is your earliest memory? Who were your friends when you were growing up? What was your favourite thing to do for fun? What was school like for you as a child? What were your best and worst subjects? You get the idea.

#8. Play a Duet. Dad couldn't read a note, but he played the accordion in his early days and the piano when I knew him, all by ear. Decades after taking piano lessons myself, I picked up the E-flat alto saxophone. A piano/saxophone duet only works if you have music written in two different keys ... or if the pianist plays by ear. Dad would have been able to pick up by ear whatever I was playing on my sax and make it work. Or at least, we'd sure have fun trying!

#9 Pray. One thing I seem to have inherited from my father is the inability to rein in the tears while praying. Dad knew something truly powerful occurs when we pray, because we are approaching the throne of our Creator and the King of kings. If I could once again hear my father praying for me, my children and my grandchildren by name, I would be reduced to a puddle on the floor. The best kind.

I hope some of these spark ideas for you. Happy Father's Day!

Ahead by a Century
(Appeared June 13, 2019)

If my father were still here with us, he would have turned 100 years old this year. He's been gone since 1986. Although I'd have loved for him to be around longer, I tend to think he was one of the blessed ones who took only 67 years to complete his assignment on this earth before moving on to a much lovelier life.

When my father was born in 1919, women had been allowed to vote for three years, although they would not be declared "persons" in Canada until Dad was 10.

World War One had ended the previous fall (although it would not be called that until the Second World War), but the subsequent influenza epidemic still raged on. As a result, the 1919 Stanley Cup series was suspended after five games.

From mid-May until late June, the Winnipeg General Strike became the largest strike in Canadian history. More than 30,000 workers left their jobs. Factories, shops, transit and city services shut down. The strike resulted in arrests, injuries and the deaths of two protestors.

In books, ranking near the top were Willa Cather's *My Antonia,* James Joyce's *A Portrait of the Artist as a Young Man,* and *The Good Soldier* by Ford Madox Ford.

Movies hitting the big screen in 1919 included hits called *The Miracle Man, Male and Female,* and *Daddy Longlegs.* The big stars of the day were Charlie Chaplin, Lillian Gish, Mary Pickford, and Gloria Swanson. Of course, the movies were silent — forcing the viewer to read intermittent title cards displayed separately from the moving picture to inform dialogue and key plot points. Theatres provided an organ or piano player who accompanied the on-screen story, enhancing its drama or comedy. Of course, I'm sure that by the time Dad got to see a movie, talkies had been invented since they came out in the late 1920s.

As a Manitoba farm boy through the 20s and 30s, Dad was not acquainted with the luxuries of indoor plumbing and electricity. While Chrysler and Ford were introducing their latest automobiles to the world, Dad's family relied on horses and actual horsepower. It's weird to think he grew up that way, but lived to see television, the moon landing and computers. Dad would be completely blown away if he could see us driving cars that tell us where to go. He'd marvel at how easily we can stay in constant contact with others whether they are across town or on the other side of the world. He wouldn't believe how simple it is to "ask Alexa" to answer a question or play a specific song.

With all these changes, one of the things remaining the same is the value of a good father — or, in the absence of that, a good father figure. No matter how technologically-advanced this world becomes, every one of us needs and craves the security, love and validation that only a good father can provide. I feel blessed to have had one of the good ones. I'm pretty sure Dad never attended a parenting seminar or listened to a podcast in his life. He never heard a TED talk or read *How to Talk so Kids will Listen and Listen so Kids will Talk.*

But I saw my dad embrace my mother. I watched him cry. I tasted his home-cooking. I listened to him sing his made-up songs about me as we drove down the gravel road in his old Fargo pickup. I saw him reading his Bible. Best of all, I heard him pray for me each night when he tucked me into bed.

You could say Dad was ahead of his time. Maybe even ahead by a century. Happy Father's Day!

Thanksgiving

Piglet noticed that even though he had a Very Small Heart, it could hold a rather large amount of Gratitude.

A.A. Milne

TERRIE TODD

A Thanksgiving Lesson from Alfalfa
(Appeared October 9, 2010)

Grandpa and I took our three little rascals to the Assinboine Park Zoo on what may have been the last summery Saturday for this year. The place has sure changed since our kids were little, and even more so from when I was. The cost of admission is higher even though the variety of animals is less, unless my memory fails. I remember black and brown bears, even a grizzly. I recall zebras and giraffes and gibbons. Relatively few primates seem to live there now. I thought the zookeepers might be interested in our three monkeys, but they declined my offer.

The perspective of a child is always fascinating. Four-year-old Buckwheat announced that his favourites were the bats. Which was interesting, because none of the rest of us saw any bats. The highlight for Spanky, not quite three, was catching a ladybug and carrying it in his hand most of the day. Meanwhile, seven-year-old Alfalfa's favourite thing was the Polar playground.

I think my favourite part was the butterfly garden, a chance to sit and relax amidst the sweet fragrance of the flowers (a definite step up from the scents offered by the animals). The butterflies fluttering by made me want to sit much longer than three rambunctious rascals allowed.

When we returned the boys to their parents, we stayed for the evening and I had the privilege of tucking Alfalfa into bed. As he said his prayers, I needed to bite my cheeks to keep from laughing out loud. He was so exhausted, he could barely squeak. But he wanted to thank Jesus for the good day we'd shared and found it necessary to name every animal he could remember seeing. As his voice got smaller, his pauses grew longer. "Thank you that we got to see the polar bears and the lions and tigers and camels and snow leopards and ... kangaroos and monkeys ... and butterflies and buffalo and eagle ... and frogs and ... chipmunks ... and ... a type of bunny..."

We said "amen" and kissed goodnight, but I think he was gone before my "I love you" even hit his ears.

Alfalfa had just demonstrated a wonderful way to fall asleep, thankful for every detail of his day. And I'm pretty sure he's not even familiar with Johnson Oatman Jr.'s old hymn, *Count Your Blessings*.

When I lay me down to sleep, I'd love it if God sometimes chuckles. I want to fall into slumber rehearsing all the blessings of my day and feeling truly grateful for them — even on the ordinary days. My comfortable home, a hot shower, clothes to wear, books to read, food to eat, a job I enjoy, likable co-workers, freedom to live without fear, grandsons to snuggle, columns to write and readers to read them, a body that functions, a car that mostly works, soft mittens and warm slippers, a bottle of my favourite lotion, a cozy bed to lay my tired body in. Our public library and whoever invented such a thing. My church. Sidewalks. Garbage pick-up. Dishwashers. Dahlias. I could go on, but I know you have a list of your own. May it put you to sleep smiling tonight.

When upon life's billows you are tempest-tossed,
When you are discouraged, thinking all is lost,
Count your many blessings, name them one by one,
And it will surprise you what the Lord has done.

Happy Thanksgiving.

Five Ways to Be Grateful, Even When You Don't Feel Like It
(Appeared October 8, 2011)

It sounds cliché, but grateful people are happy people. Yet gratitude requires a daily choice, doesn't it? It's so much easier to see what we don't have than to consider all we have. So today I'm giving five tips to help you win the battle.

#1. Here's a fun exercise you can do online. Log on to www.globalrichlist.com and key in your annual income to see where you fall in the world's richest ranking. I was in the top 12 per cent. Look at the lineup of people to see where you show up on the scale. Sobering, isn't it? And something to be thankful for.

#2. Choose someone who has been a positive influence in your life and tell them so. Not good with words? That's why God invented Hallmark. There's sure to be a card on a store shelf that says it perfectly for you, if you take the time to look. Or take your person to lunch, a game or a movie. Paint them a picture. Use your imagination and find a way to express your gratitude.

#3. Pick the thing that's bugging you most right now. Frustrations at work? With a family member? Your health? Now answer two questions: in what ways could this be much worse? What can I learn from this difficulty? Then be thankful that it is not worse and be grateful for the opportunity to learn something from it.

#4. Ask yourself: who is doing something good for someone I love? A nurse at the manor? Your child's teacher, youth pastor or coach? The neighbour collecting for Heart and Stroke Foundation? Tell that person "thank you" for what they're doing to benefit your loved one. It will mean more than you can imagine.

#5. Write down 99 things you're grateful for today. Think of it as your own little *Book of Awesome*. Here are mine, in no particular order: Coffee with hazelnut creamer. Hot showers.

Coconut-scented bath products. Toothpaste. Floss. My computer. This column. Sunshine. Warm slippers. Toast. Canada. Chocolate. Sight. Literacy. Music. Roast beef. Fresh tomatoes. Prayer. Eyeglasses. Cork boards. Kleenex. A garage. A garage door opener. Furnaces. Washing machines. The Bible. Family. Blue jeans. Curbside garbage and recycling pick-up. Crescent Lake. Candles. Wayne the Squirrel. Pickles. House plants that don't die. Doctors who call me. Cameras. Indoor plumbing. My job. Baby animals. Ball point pens. Friends. My piano. My pillow. The flip side of my pillow. An email from my daughter. Cinnamon-Apple tea. Flannel sheets. Grocery stores. Inter-generational dancing. The word "shenanigan." Tweezers. Duct tape. Balki and Larry's dance of joy. Hair dye. That little kid on the internet who conducts orchestras. Electric blankets. Hugs. Dishwashers. People who snort when they laugh. Skin. Q-tips. Fuzzy socks. The laughter of children. Laminate flooring. Pretty scarves. Good teeth. Daisies. My co-workers. The delete key. Free parking. Gravity. Coupons. Peaches. My church. Birthdays. Thrift shops. Shingles. Live theatre. My car. Rocking chairs. Free draws. Sleep. Police officers. Tylenol. Mountains. Smiles. Tears. My satin blouse. Distance education. Brakes. Breaks. Cookbooks. Storage space. Toilet brushes. Paved streets. Electric lights. Toys. Self-sticking envelopes. God's unstoppable love.

Happy Thanksgiving!

Five Things I Don't Have that I Don't Want
(Appeared October 17, 2013)

For most of the three decades I've been part of Portage Alliance Church, the congregation has celebrated Thanksgiving together a week after the actual holiday with a full-blown turkey dinner. That way, our church shindig doesn't interfere with family events and we can keep the gratitude, festivities and feasting going.

So, in keeping with the extended season, I thought I'd do the same. After all, thankfulness should be a habit all year 'round.

If you're like me, you find it challenging to be grateful all the time. But I love what some smart person once said: "If you don't have all the things you want in life, think of all the things you don't have that you DON'T want."

They are countless, but I'm picking five that come to my attention immediately. I challenge you to make your own list.

#1. Orphanhood. My Compassion child, Tarion, lives in Ecuador. Last year, his mother died of complications with Diabetes. Meanwhile, I've endured 54 years of my mother and she's barely slowing down. (Kidding, Mom.) Seriously, I can't imagine experiencing such a devastating loss as a child and am enormously grateful to still have my mother. I'd keep her for life if it were up to me.

#2. Homelessness. Last week, I listened while CHVN Radio broadcast for three days from Siloam Mission in Winnipeg. I heard stories about life on the streets and how even nights at the shelter, while safer, are so much less inviting than the privacy and comfort I enjoy in my own home. I am truly thankful to have never experienced this misfortune.

#3. Blindness. As I write this, the golden October sunshine streams in through my windows, highlighted by the reds, oranges and yellows of the autumn leaves and accentuating the warmth of the Persian melon walls surrounding me. I use my eyes from the moment I scowl at the beeping alarm clock until I simply cannot hold them open any longer, savouring the last paragraph of that "just one more chapter" before snuggling down for the night. While I complain about needing bifocals and probably even trifocals, I cannot fathom life without eyesight and I deeply appreciate mine.

#4. Paralysis. I've heard of three people who have suffered strokes following surgery in recent months, leaving them in worse condition than before the surgery. As I observe their long struggle to fight their way back, I am overwhelmed with gladness for my mobility. Getting dressed, walking to work, my fingers flying over the keyboard, cleaning our house, preparing a meal; I hope I never take any of it for granted.

#5. A Hellish Destiny. This one trumps all the others combined. Although death is on the list of top human fears, it is not one of mine. Not because I'm a brave or good person, but because I don't have to dread what happens when I die. I may have been pawned off cheap by the enemy of my soul, but Jesus Christ redeemed me with his own life. I John 5:13 tells me, "These things I have written to you who believe in the name of the Son of God, so that you may know that you have eternal life." That's what I call a confidence to be grateful for!

What do you not have that you don't want? Cancer? Unemployment? A prodigal child? Divorce? Disability? I'd love to see your list.

Remembrance Day

This is what the Lord says to you: 'Do not be afraid or discouraged because of this vast army. For the battle is not yours, but God's.'

2 Chronicles 20:15

TERRIE TODD

Why I Wear a Poppy
(Appeared November 6, 2010)
This story also appeared in
Chicken Soup for the Soul: O Canada!

In 1919, the year my father was born, the first Remembrance Day was observed throughout the countries of the British Commonwealth. Originally called Armistice Day, this day commemorated the end of the "war to end all wars" on Monday, November 11, 1918, at 11 a.m — the 11th hour of the 11th day of the 11th month. Remembrance Day is a day that "Canadians pause in a silent moment of remembrance for the men and women who have served and continue to serve our country during times of war, conflict and peace."

Dad was 20 when Canada went to war again. He was drafted into the army, but spent his years of service on Canadian soil, as an officers' chauffeur on the west coast. Although he never saw battle, he hated every minute of his time there. He missed home, he missed his family, he missed his own mother's funeral. When he returned, he married and settled down to raise a family and rarely spoke of his years in the army. My father was not your typical, flag-waving veteran. Dad never joined the Legion, never made a speech about being proud to serve his country, never spoke of how privileged he felt to wear the uniform. I wear a poppy one day a year to honour him, regardless.

Some time ago, I spoke with a fellow Canadian who refuses to wear a poppy on Remembrance Day. "War is against my religion," was the explanation. I said nothing, partly out of cowardice, but mostly out of surprise, knowing this person's ancestors had fled from a land of bitter religious persecution to the relative safety of Canada. I wondered how those same ancestors would feel about this stance? Had no one fought for their freedom, those who fled to Canada would eventually face the same thing all over again — with nowhere left to flee. Is it really too much to wear a poppy one day a year to honour that dedication, regardless of one's point of view?

In 2008, I saw my young friend James go off to Afghanistan. He called me a few times from that desert land, just to unload some of the horrific experiences he was facing. Each Sunday, I'd see his parents and his wife in church and wonder how their hearts could bear it — the worry, the wondering. We all breathed a sigh of relief when he returned safe and sound, knowing others had not and would not. It doesn't seem too much to wear a poppy one day a year to honour James and his comrades, regardless.

Remembrance Day is not about condoning war or glorifying weaponry or celebrating death. It does not make a statement about your politics or your religion or your conscience. More than 1.5 million Canadians have served our country in this way, and more than 100,000 have died. They gave their lives and their futures so that we may live in peace.

That's why I'll be wearing a poppy on November 11.

Glorious and Free
(Appeared November 12, 2011)

Surprisingly, not everyone grants me the attention I so clearly deserve. Last week, I met my third grandson, Rorin Bennett Todd. He was 48 hours old and slept through the entire meeting. I nuzzled him, talked to him, counted his fingers and toes, rubbed his back, kissed his velvety cheeks and stroked his brown hair. He made only tiny puppy squeaks, but I know he was saying "I love you too, Grandma, and when I get big I'm gonna read your column every week."

The blessing of three healthy children and now three healthy grandchildren is one I hope I never, ever take for granted. When I consider the millions of miracles that must go right (and how often they do!) in order for a child to be formed and delivered without complications, it quiets my heart in awe. God has been kind to us.

With all these boys in the family, my perspective on Remembrance Day has changed. As a kid, I recall assembling in the Amaranth Elementary School's hallway. It meant listening to talk of wars fought by old men, wearing a poppy on an annoyingly wayward stick pin, singing *Oh God, Our Help in Ages Past*, reciting John McCrae's *In Flanders Field*, and suffering through that interminable minute of silence. Then we got the rest of the day off, and if we were lucky there was snow to play in.

Not until I was a mother myself did it hit me. It was not old men who went off to war.

One Sunday near November 11, I looked around our church at all the guys in the conscription age range, including my own sons. Why, they were just *kids*! I imagined this was 1942 and these guys were all going off to fight. I tried to wrap my head around what that would mean for our church, for our town, for my family. Tried to fathom the slow or nonexistent methods of communication available once they were gone. And, worst of all, wondering which ones would not make it back.

Then our daughter joined the Canadian Forces for a brief stint in high school, spending a summer in training at Cold Lake, followed by a short time in our Reserve Force. We were proud of her, but no one was more relieved than I when she decided militia life was not for her. While she was there, I simply refused to consider what it would mean if another country declared war on Canada.

And today, while other grandmothers in other parts of the world welcome little ones into war-torn environments, I have lived my entire life so sheltered, so naive. So free. I will not pretend I understand it; I will only be humbly and deeply grateful.

I cannot assume this privileged life will be guaranteed for Rorin and his brothers. But for them, and for each child on our planet, I offer this ancient Hebrew prayer this Remembrance Day:

May God bless you and keep you. May God make His face to shine upon you and be gracious unto you. May God lift up his countenance upon you and give you peace.

A Bone to Pick
(Appeared November 9, 2017)
This column won a 2018 Word Guild Award

Well, my goose is cooked now. Local chiropractor Dr. Bruce Narvey has been giving me regular attitude adjustments since I was pregnant with our youngest son, who turned 30 last January! Dr. Narvey has served our family through thick and thin — even going above and beyond by treating Hubby in a Winnipeg hospital following his 1995 arm amputation. And if all that isn't enough to earn my undying loyalty, the fact that he reads my books ought to be.

Why then, one wonders, would I name a villainous character after him?

On my last visit to his torture chamber — I mean, office — our conversation sounded something like this:

"I have a bone to pick with you. Just one."

When a chiropractor has a bone to pick, it can't be good. Where exactly did he find this bone?

"Oh?"

"Yeah. I finished the book. It's very good. But …"

I always dread the but.

"Did I get something wrong?" My mind skimmed the details of the novel, wondering which historical fact I may have misrepresented.

"Well, I can't help wondering why the one real jerk in the book has the same name as me."

Oh.

Woops.

I laughed. I remembered naming that character. I knew he was going to be a mean one, but *Mr. Grinch* had already been taken. *Ebenezer* seemed too obvious, as did *Adolf*, *Goliath*, and *Lucifer*. Then too, there's the trick of giving your character a name appropriate to the era and ethnicity. I usually look up the most popular names for the year of a character's birth and choose from that list. This time, I thought I'd try to use a little subliminal psychology. I figured if the name sounded like "brute," perhaps readers would be subconsciously predisposed to fear him.

Hence, *Bruce* was born.

And honestly, it never occurred to me. But sitting in his office, the opportunity seemed too good to pass up.

"Well," I said. "You must have a little bit of bully hidden under the surface, or you wouldn't enjoy cracking people's bones."

This is not a wise thing to say to a man who's about to crack your bones.

"I do not have any bully in me whatsoever. And I am most certainly not a Nazi sympathizer."

Oh. I'd forgotten that detail about my fictional Bruce. And about Dr. Narvey's Jewish heritage.

We laughed and teased some more. I got my adjustment and walked out better aligned than when I walked in, and with a column already beginning to write itself.

The Second World War ended more than 70 years ago. One reason I like writing novels about life here in Canada during those years is because of the heroes who fought to end the atrocities overseas. It occurred to me that if no one had prevented Adolf Hitler from completing his mission, Bruce Narvey and I would not be picking bones or laughing together. He would not be my chiropractor or my friend. The Narveys and their people would have been wiped off the planet before Bruce was even born.

And I stopped laughing.

Lest we forget, indeed.

Never Been to War
(Appeared November 8, 2018)

I found a treasure while browsing the bookshelves at our local MCC Thrift store recently. Compiled by Priscilla Galloway and published in 1999, *Too Young to Fight: Memories from our youth during World War II* includes reminiscences of 12 writers who were children or teenagers during the war. Many of their contributions include photos. I saw the book as a tremendous research tool for future novels, even though I assumed it was American. I figured many of the stories would cross over.

To my delight, when I took a closer look at home, I discovered it's a Canadian collection. In fact, one of the contributors, Joy Kogawa, wrote an entire novel based on her experiences as a Japanese Canadian during the war. I recently read that book — *Obasan* — and mentioned it in one of these columns. She refers to war as "state-sanctioned racism," and for good reason.

I'm about halfway through *Too Young to Fight*, and I can easily imagine some of these real-life stories happening to my fictional characters.

One reason I enjoy writing about the lives of ordinary Canadians during the war years is because those stories have, for the most part, been overlooked. Books and movies are made about the battles, the espionage, the truly big adventures in all their drama and horror. But those of us who didn't live through it know little about what life was like here at home.

This collection provides a brilliant glimpse into those lives, often seemingly unaffected by war on the surface. But many recall experiencing deep fear, knowing how children their own age suffered the direct ravages of destruction across the sea. Some became well-acquainted with British children sent to Canada to be kept safe and feared the same could happen to them. Separation from parents and everything familiar. Where would they go when their turn came?

Several wrote of difficult adjustments after the war ended. What had become normal was now topsy-turvy. Some were, for the first time, becoming acquainted with a father they'd never known — in some cases, a father who we'd now say suffered from post-traumatic stress disorder but for whom therapy was unavailable. One English child, sent to Canada at the age of four, returned to England at the age of nine to parents she barely remembered and a baby brother she'd never met.

Some lost their fathers and big brothers entirely.

The quote that summarizes it most powerfully comes from Jean Little's section of the book. She closes her chapter like this:

"Real war wounds maim you for life. Fear haunts the dreams of children caught in war even when they become grandparents. Although I lived through the war years cocooned in my cozy Canadian childhood, the life stories told to me by people who had survived World War II, and a book written by a teenager who had not [Anne Frank], taught me that war has no happy ending. Although I still live in a cocoon called Canada, I try not to forget."

And neither must we.

My singer/songwriter friend Keith Kitchen of Swift Current has recorded a song called *Never Been to War*. The music video (directed by Derek Selinger) recently won the 2018 Best Music Video award at the Edmonton Short Film Festival. It's a song of gratitude and innocence, afforded to us because of the sacrifices of others. The video, made in cooperation with the Royal Canadian Legion, is well worth your time this Remembrance Day. You can easily find it on You Tube by typing "Never Been to War" in the search box.

Christmas

For God so loved the world, that he gave his only begotten Son, that whosoever believeth on him should not perish, but have eternal life.

John 3:16

TERRIE TODD

Heartbreak Hotel
(Appeared December 11, 2010)

The room we were given was small and seemed less than pristine, but we were exhausted and thankful for a place to sleep. We'd just driven all the way from Manitoba to Fort Worth, Texas to witness our son's Aerodesign contest and university graduation, all on the same weekend. We checked into the official hotel of the competition.

Next morning, I found Hubby examining red spots on himself.

"We've got bugs" he announced. On the off chance he was not simply being paranoid, I sprang out of bed like Tigger on steroids. There were definitely some kind of teensy critters moving around on the sheets. Eee-eww. We avoided the bed as we got dressed and packed, then reported it to the front desk. No one else from our group had found their room thus occupied, and we still needed a bed for another night.

"Tell you what," the desk clerk said. "I'll give you the Elvis suite for the same price as a regular room."

We weren't sure what the Elvis suite might comprise, but *Movin' on Up* was playing in my head as we took the elevator to the top floor, wondering what we'd find when we got there. Rhinestone-studded taps? Glowing Viva Las Vegas signs lighting up black velvet paintings on the walls? A bed shaped like a giant sideburn?

For starters, there was a star on the door.

"Finally," I thought. "Somebody recognizes my true status."

The door opened to a classy three-room suite with a beautiful mantel over a bricked-in fireplace. No hunka-hunka burnin' anything in there! A plaque on the wall informed us Elvis Presley had been a guest in the room in 1974. (A quick calculation assured me it was not the room in which he died.) Other famous guests were listed below ... Bob Hope, Jimmy Durante and others. (They have no doubt added my name to the plaque by now.) It was a lovely room with lots of amenities, plenty of space, and best of all, it was free of creepy-crawlies! We had a good rest.

I couldn't help but wonder how an establishment which can keep up other rooms, lobbies and grounds so beautifully could be so lax with others. Was this some sort of "two-tiered" system where cleanliness can be afforded only by the rich and famous? Imagine the indignation of one of the privileged ones had he been assigned the run-down room with the bugs.

The experience got me thinking of a certain inn in Bethlehem and a guest who turned out rather famous but did not turn up his nose at the humblest of accommodations. Can you imagine him saying "Excu-use Me! I don't DO straw. Now where's the Baby Dior blanket I ordered?"

"Think of yourselves the way Christ Jesus thought of himself. He had equal status with God, but didn't think so much of himself that he had to cling to the advantages of that status no matter what ... He didn't claim special privileges. Instead, he lived a selfless, obedient life ..." Philippians 2:5-8

Over My Dead Body
(Appeared December 6, 2012)

Have you thought much about what might happen to your life's work after you're gone? You might after you read this story.

As my Christmas gift to readers this year, I've decided to do something different. Rather than a continuing fictional tale, each week will bring you a stand-alone true story about the history behind some of our favourite Christmas carols.

Hark, the Herald Angels Sing has become one of my favourites. Maybe it's because of the wonderful way the Peanuts gang sing it at the end of *A Charlie Brown Christmas*. Maybe it's because the song contains the entire gospel of Christ within its verses (basically, God and sinners reconciled).

In any case, until I did a little research, I had no idea that neither the writer of the words nor the writer of the music would have wanted the two joined. Did you?

In 1739, Charles Wesley penned the lyrics with the request that only slow, solemn religious music be coupled with his words. It was sung to a different, probably depressing, melody that is no doubt long forgotten.

A hundred years later, Felix Mendelssohn, a Jew, wrote the joyful melody now so familiar to us, to commemorate the 400th anniversary of the Gutenberg printing press. It was called *Festgesang an die Künstler* and he made it clear he wanted his music used only for secular purposes.

Long after both Mendelssohn and Wesley were dead, an English organist named Dr. William Cummings joined the joyous music to the profound words. Almost 200 years later, you and I still sing along to this beloved carol. We would remain unfamiliar with both music and lyrics if someone had not come along and joined the two.

Do the original writers roll over in their proverbial graves every time this carol is sung? I sure hope not. I hope they look on from above with glad hearts, both now understanding the depth and beauty of their contribution to the world.

And I hope the rest of us can learn to hold loosely to those things we "create." Firstly, because most things improve with a little collaboration. Secondly, because after we're gone we have little say about the things we leave behind. And thirdly, every shred of creativity we possess is only a gift from the One who first created us.

I hope you enjoy the carol more now that you know the story. For fun, try reading it through as simple prose, without the tune ringing in your head if you can:

Hark, the herald angels sing, "Glory to the newborn king! Peace on earth and mercy mild, God and sinners reconciled." Joyful, all ye nations rise. Join the triumph of the skies! With the angelic host proclaim, "Christ is born in Bethlehem!"

Christ, by highest heaven adored, Christ the everlasting Lord! Late in time, behold him come. Offspring of a virgin's womb! Veiled in flesh, the Godhead see. Hail the incarnate Deity! Pleased as man with men to dwell, Jesus, our Emmanuel.

Hail the heaven-born Prince of Peace! Hail the Son of Righteousness! Light and life to all he brings, risen with healing in his wings. Mild he lays his glory by, born that man no more may die. Born to raise the sons of earth, born to give them second birth! Hark! The herald angels sing,

"Glory to the newborn King!"

Our Finest Gifts We Bring
(Appeared December 13, 2012)

You may not have heard of Katherine Kennicott Davies, but she wrote what I used to consider the dumbest Christmas carol of all time. *The Little Drummer Boy* (originally titled *The Carol of the Drum*), which the American woman wrote in 1941, became famous when recorded by the Trapp Family Singers of *Sound of Music* fame.

My opinion of this song was formed between the ages of 13 and 18, when I still knew everything. I knew the Bible records no drummer boy at the Bethlehem stable, not in any of the four gospels. That whole "ox and lamb kept time" thing? Please. And a newborn baby smiling at him? Probably just gas. Never mind that a newborn can't focus his eyes that well. And whoever heard of lulling a baby to sleep by beating on a drum anyway? As a young mother, I'd have appreciated the gift about as much as I'd appreciate bedbugs. Furthermore, I always thought the song annoying to sing, what with the obnoxious rumpa pum pums interrupting its storyline.

That is what I used to think.

I finally got it one Christmas in my late thirties when, as usual, I was involved with the annual Christmas banquet at Portage Alliance Church. The drama team was staging a short play I had written and the music team would perform several songs, including *The Little Drummer Boy*.

Our drummer that year, who was no longer a boy, would play a solo part. As I watched him beating his heart into the piece, I finally clued in to what the song was all about. The drummer boy had nothing else to give.

Neither did I. No gold. Certainly no frankincense or myrrh, even if I knew what those were. I couldn't play a drum, either.

But I could write a play.

All of a sudden, the lyrics changed a bit for me. "I write my plays for him, pa rum pum pum pum. I write my best for him, pa rum pum pum pum…"

And finally, the clincher: "Then he smiled at me." Not as an infant from a manger bed, but as my risen Lord. Smiling. At me and my little play.

The song has been one of my favourites ever since.

Last year, Winnipeg musician Sean Quigley won praise for his video, posted to YouTube, featuring a fantastic rendition of *The Little Drummer Boy*. Quigley's video, shot at familiar Winnipeg locations, took full advantage of heavy snow. I find it mind-boggling that Quigley played all the instruments, sang the vocals, recorded everything and shot, directed and edited the video himself.

At only 16, Sean Quigley grasped what I had missed.

"Drummer Boy speaks to me so much," he told media. "The whole song is a story. It's about this boy who gets word of Jesus being born and he goes to see him and he doesn't have anything to give him; he's like 'I don't have money, I don't have gifts to give you. But I can play my drum and that's more than enough'."

If you haven't seen Quigley's video, I encourage you to watch it soon. Go to YouTube and search "Drummer Boy Sean Quigley." Watch the joy on his face.

What is your drum? How will you make a gift of it this Christmas?

OUT OF MY MIND

And Heaven and Nature Sing
(Appeared December 5, 2013)

Through the month of December last year, I began a tradition of researching and writing about the stories behind our most loved Christmas carols. For Part One of this year's series, I've picked *Joy to the World*.

What would you do with your child if you noticed, between the ages of five and 13, he'd picked up Latin, Greek, French and Hebrew in addition to his mother-tongue? Would you suspect you had produced a linguistic genius? What might you expect from him? What would you do when you grew tired of him criticizing the music at church every Sunday? Would you dare him to come up with something better, since he thought he was so smart?

That's what Isaac Watts' father did when Isaac was 18 years old, and the boy responded to the challenge. The next Sunday, Isaac produced his first hymn, with enthusiastic response from the congregation. For the next two years, he wrote new hymn texts every Sunday and more than 600 hymns in his lifetime. It's no wonder he became known as "The Father of Hymns," even though the religious establishment considered him an outcast. A nonconformist, Watts was banned from both Oxford and Cambridge, and received his education at Stoke Newington's Dissenting Academy. Aside from hymn writing, he studied theology and philosophy. Watts wrote significant volumes which powerfully influenced English thinking.

One of the hymns Watts wrote was *Joy to the World*. Are you as surprised as I was to learn he never intended it as a Christmas song? If you look closely, you'll notice it never mentions the baby Jesus, shepherds, wise men, angels, or any of the typical trappings associated with the nativity story.

So, what's it about then?

Watts based his lyrics on Psalm 98, which is not about Messiah's first coming, but about his second, when he comes to judge the earth. The psalm tells us all of nature will join in the singing when that great day comes. Christmas may not always be a joyful time, but when Jesus comes back to set everything right, even the rocks will sing!

And what about the musical portion of this song? Adapted and arranged by the American composer Lowell Mason, *Joy to the World* sounds suspiciously like portions of Handel's Messiah in a number of places. Apparently, Mason felt plagued by the similarities all his life and paid homage to Handel by calling the melody *Antioch, from Handel*.

While it's hard for us to imagine singing *Joy to the World* all year round, I hope we can let the lyrics point us to the reason Jesus came: to save the world. And to be ready, because He is coming again.

When you hear or sing it this year, think of it in that light and see what happens in your heart. May you find it preparing him a little more room.

The Dawn of Redeeming Grace
(Appeared December 12, 2013)

The story behind *Silent Night* is familiar to many of us, but I needed to brush up on my facts. Turns out, it started in 1816 in a small Austrian village called Oberndorf when a pastor named Joseph Mohr wrote the simple words as a poem. Of course, the words were in German, and the poem was entitled *Stille Nacht*.

Two years later on Christmas Eve, the organ in St. Nicholas Church (Pastor Mohr's church) broke down just before the Christmas Mass. A tragedy! Determined that the Mass should not be without music, Mohr gave the two-year-old poem he had written to his organist and friend, Franz Xaver Gruber. Gruber must have been one speedy composer. He immediately wrote the melody and arranged it for two voices, choir and guitar – just in time for the midnight service.

The two writers of the carol thought they were simply doing something to get through a difficult situation. But almost 200 years later, *Silent Night* is still the most performed and recorded Christmas song in history.

A wonderful story about the song comes out of World War I. On Christmas Eve, fighting was actually suspended on many of the European fronts while people turned on their radios to hear an Austrian opera star, Ernestine Schumann Heink, sing *Stille Nacht*. Ms. Heink was not only an international celebrity, but the mother of one son fighting for the Germans and another son fighting for the Allies. Parents, can you imagine the turmoil in her heart or her longing for peace?

Her beautiful rendition of this song had the power to bring a few moments of peace to a very troubled world.

The song itself represents an event orchestrated by God himself to bring heavenly peace to earth. Was that Bethlehem stable truly silent? It's doubtful, what with the crowds, the animals, the shepherds and the angel choirs. But a larger sentiment rings true, that of the little baby who came to bring freedom to human hearts.

When that baby grew up, he said a most curious thing to his disciples. "Do not suppose that I have come to bring peace to the earth. I did not come to bring peace, but a sword. For I have come to turn 'a man against his father, a daughter against her mother, a daughter-in-law against her mother-in-law — a man's enemies will be the members of his own household." (Matthew 10)

Whatever did he mean? Was Jesus advocating violence?

When you look at the larger context, you see that he was quoting from the Old Testament prophet Micah. He wanted his disciples to understand that Jesus divides the world into two camps: those who follow him, and those who do not. Following Jesus in his original Jewish society would not bring peace to a family, but might even split it up, and they needed to be prepared. However, he never tells his followers to wage war on everyone else, and certainly not on one's family. If anything, this split would provide further opportunities for his grace to be demonstrated through us.

Silent or not, nighttime or not, it truly was a new day – with the dawn of redeeming grace.

A Thrill of Hope in an Evil World
(Appeared December 19, 2013)

Raise your hand if you can name the first song ever sent over the air via radio waves.

Here's a hint: it happened Christmas Eve 1906. Reginald Fessenden picked up his violin and played its melody after reading the Christmas story from the gospel of Luke. Radio operators aboard ships must have been shocked, for neither the human voice nor music had ever been transmitted this way.

Need another clue? The song's lyrics were originally written in 1847 by a French poet named Placide Cappeau (who, incidentally, had his right hand amputated following a shooting accident at the age of eight).

Adolphe Charles Adams composed the melody. To Adams, a man of Jewish descent, the poem represented a day he didn't celebrate and a man he did not view as the son of God. But he wrote the music anyway, at his friend's request, and at first the song was embraced by the Catholic church.

But then the original poet, Cappeau, left the church to join the Socialist movement and the church learned the composer was a Jew. They banned the song, declaring it unfit.

About 10 years later, American abolitionist John Sullivan Dwight was so moved by the words of the third verse, he translated the entire song into English and published it in his magazine. If you know your Civil War history, you can see why it quickly caught on in the northern United States during that time:

> *Truly He taught us to love one another,*
> *His law is love and His gospel is peace.*
> *Chains shall he break, for the slave is our brother.*
> *And in his name all oppression shall cease.*

And if you hadn't already guessed, now you know. *O Holy Night*, originally called *Cantique de Noel*, has remained one of the most loved and most recorded Christmas carols.

Did you see the Lincoln movie that came out last year or this year's *Twelve Years a Slave*? Abraham Lincoln remains a hero to many for taking the lead in abolishing slavery in America, but I can't help thinking Lincoln would weep if he knew it has not been abolished at all. Oppression has not ceased. According to numerous reports, there are more people in slavery today than at any other time in history. Human trafficking runs rampant.

This is probably not what you wanted to read in my Christmas column. The good news is we can make a difference and we don't have to fight this battle alone. Numerous organizations work hard to expose and abolish human trafficking. By buying fair trade, learning more about modern slavery, spreading the word, and joining a movement such as Free the Slaves, International Justice Mission, Defend Dignity or Servants Anonymous (among others), you as an individual can help.

Isaiah 58:6 says this: "I'll tell you what it really means to worship the Lord. Remove the chains of prisoners who are chained unjustly. Free those who are abused!"

OUT OF MY MIND

Their Old Familiar Carols Play
(Appeared December 26, 2013)

I'm going to assume you've heard of Henry Wadsworth Longfellow and take you back to 1861. That was the year the poet lost his wife in a horrible fire. She was 44 years old. The New York Times, on July 12, reported the following:

"While seated at her library table, making seals for the entertainment of her two youngest children, a match or piece of lighted paper caught her dress, and she was in a moment enveloped in flames. Prof. Longfellow, who was in his study, ran to her assistance, and succeeded in extinguishing the flames, with considerable injury to himself, but too late for the rescue of her life .... She leaves five children to mourn, with their father, their common loss."

Longfellow had already buried his first wife, Mary, after just four years of marriage when she was only 22. He was no stranger to loss.

The first Christmas after Fanny's death, Longfellow wrote, "How inexpressibly sad are all holidays."

A year after the incident, he wrote, "I can make no record of these days. Better leave them wrapped in silence. Perhaps someday God will give me peace."

It's not hard to understand why his journal entry for December 25, 1862 reads: "'A merry Christmas' say the children, but that is no more for me."

The next Christmas, 1863, was silent in Longfellow's journal. The American Civil War raged on.

On Christmas Day 1864, the beloved poet received word that his oldest son Charles, a lieutenant in the Army of the Potomac, had been severely wounded with a bullet passing under his shoulder blades and taking off one of the spinal processes.

Not knowing whether his son would live or die, Longfellow did the only thing a poet knows to do: poured out his heart on paper. As he sat alone with his grief, he penned words to challenge his own despair and called the composition *Christmas Bells*, little knowing how many people his work might eventually reach.

Eight years later, composer John Baptiste Calkin set Longfellow's words to music and it became the somewhat mournful carol you and I know as *I Heard the Bells on Christmas Day*.

If you have suffered loss and wounds, you know how Christmas and other holidays can heighten your pain. You can easily relate to Longfellow's fourth stanza:

> *And in despair I bowed my head*
> *'There is no peace on earth,' I said,*
> *'For hate is strong and mocks the song*
> *Of peace on earth, good will to men.'*

But somewhere in his outpouring of honest grief, hope came to Longfellow and he wrote words he chose to believe, despite all the evidence to the contrary:

> *Then pealed the bells more loud and deep:*
> *'God is not dead, nor doth He sleep;*
> *The wrong shall fail, the right prevail*
> *With peace on earth, good will to men.'*

Lt. Charles Longfellow did not die that Christmas, but lived. I can only surmise that his father's prayers were heard and God did indeed give him peace.

Faith is choosing to believe things contrary to evidence. It defies explanation. But it remains the very basis for peace on earth, goodwill to men. If 2013 has been a year of pain and despair for you, it may mean the bells of faith will peel more loudly and deeply for you than ever before in 2014.

Let's pray for it.

The Annual Newsletter: Jots from Joseph
(Appeared December 4, 2014)

What's more fun than the annual family newsletter, just in time for Christmas? For my December series this year, I bring you the newsletters of four characters from the Christmas story. May they inspire you to write your own!

Dear Family & Friends,

I may have said this other years, but this time it's really true: this has been the most amazing year of my life! Should you find the personal nature of this year's letter too much information, I apologize in advance. It is too intriguing not to share. But if you conclude that I have lost all sense, for that I do not apologize. I know what is true.

If you received last year's update, you know that I became engaged to be married. My fiancée, Mary, is a descendant of King David, like me. She's a sweet girl and I hope you get to meet her one day. For a few months last summer, however, I felt certain it would all be called off and I would be looking for another bride.

Mary went to visit her cousin Elizabeth and it felt like the longest three months of my life. You can imagine my joy when my future father-in-law arrived at my door early one morning to tell me Mary had returned the night before. But I doubt you can comprehend the devastation I felt when he told me the rest of the news. Mary was pregnant. Furthermore, she was already pregnant before she left Nazareth to visit Elizabeth. He looked sick with shame.

Naturally, he assumed I was the father and urged me to move up the wedding date. But how could I? The child was not mine! He did not believe me, and I am not certain he believes me yet, in spite of both Mary's and my insistence that I have not touched her. I only know the days that followed were the most difficult of my life. Sleep deprivation and distraction rendered me useless in my carpentry shop, so I went for a long walk while I begged God for direction. Tortured, I waffled between breaking off the engagement (how could I marry a woman who had proven so untrustworthy?) and playing the hero by marrying as quickly as possible and raising Mary's child as my own, no questions asked.

But who was the real father, and would thoughts of him haunt me all my days? Whose face would I see reflected in my child? Would I be able to love and care for him or her? Would I grow to resent Mary more with every passing year? I was already vexed with her for bringing this upon me. Yet, my wish to protect her from disgrace tormented me. She may never find another husband, given these circumstances. Her child would be despised and rejected. I've seen it before.

During this tortuous time, I experienced the most incredible — yet also the most real — encounter of my life. An angel of God came to me in a vision! I know no words with which to accurately describe him, but magnificent comes to mind. I'm a big guy and have faced tough men, but this visit had me feeling as fragile as wood shavings on my shop floor. Until he gently spoke my name and delivered his message.

"Joseph, son of David," he said. "Don't hesitate to get married. Mary's pregnancy is Spirit-conceived. God's Holy Spirit has made her pregnant. She will bring a son to birth, and when she does, you, Joseph, will name him Jesus — 'God saves' — because he will save his people from their sins."

You might think it would be easy to shrug off such an encounter as a weird dream. A little too much kosher wine the night before, perhaps. But I knew it was so much more. The relief brought by the angel's words was immediate and complete. I knew what I must do. Mary and I will go ahead with our plans and I will raise this miracle child.

Shortly afterwards, the Romans announced their upcoming census which, for us, will require a trip to Bethlehem. Mary assures me we have plenty of time to make the trip and return home before she delivers. I know many of you face similar trips for the same reason, so I won't complain. I have not visited Bethlehem since childhood and who knows what we may discover there?

So, rejoice with me, friends. I will soon have a wife and a son! Next year's letter will no doubt make you roll your eyes with my stories of little Jesus and how clever and handsome he is. Now I know it is my heavenly Father's face I will see reflected in his.

Until then, God bless you.
Joseph of Nazareth

TERRIE TODD

The Annual Newsletter: Notes from Nessa
(Appeared December 11, 2014)

What's better than the annual family newsletter, just in time for Christmas? For my December series this year, I bring you the newsletters of four characters from the Christmas story. May they inspire you to write your own!

Shalom, Family & Friends.
Oy vey! When I wrote last year's letter I was all fermisht about the announcement of the Roman census and the crowds it would bring to Bethlehem.
"It will be good for business," Hirshel insisted.
"It will be bad for business," I told him. "We'll wear ourselves ragged and still we'll be turning good people away."
He has more in his head than in his pocket, my husband. He spent the summer adding two rooms above the inn and hired his brother Feivel's girl to help me with the extra cooking and cleaning. Hirchel even had the chutzpah to suggest we expand our business by offering laundry services to the travelers. But I put down my foot. You can't sit on two horses with one behind, I told him.
When the travelers started shlepping into Bethlehem, oy such a racket like you've never heard. Such a stink with the sweating and the dirt and the animals. The inn filled up in no time and I have been run off my feet ever since.
"Sleep faster, we need the pillows," I told our guests. "You think this is a resort we are running?"
You older ones may remember that my father, rest his soul, named me "Nessa" because he said I would experience a wondrous miracle in my lifetime. It is a blessing my poor father is not around to see my life is nothing but drudgery and hard work. No miracles here.

Hirshel even rented out our bed while he and I take turns sleeping next door at Feivel and Yentl's house. That is, Hirshel takes his turn. I haven't slept since all this started.

I was mixing dough for the next day's challah when yet more travelers came to our door. A man with a very young wife. I was about to turn them away when I noticed the girl was very pregnant. Oy gevalt. The poor little thing had been travelling for days. She looked at me with big brown eyes and I had to look the other way. I called Hirshel to deal with it. He could turn them away without remorse. Men. They have no compassion.

But as I turned back to the kitchen, I could hear Hirshel offering them space in the stable. Anything for a shekel! I shlepped back to the door.

"Excuse me," I said to the young couple. "My husband is not right in the head."

I yanked Hirshel aside. "Hirshel, don't be meshugenah," I said. "There is no other place in all of Bethlehem? Can't you see this girl is about to give birth? You can't put them in the stable."

"I'm sorry, you will have to find somewhere else," I told the couple as I closed the door in their faces.

Men. They have no backbone.

I went back to my bread, but I could not put those big brown eyes and that big round boych from my head. I knew everybody in town was full.

"Hirshel," I said. "Go track them down and bring them back. We will make a bed for them in the stable. One night only, tell them! We can only hope they are gone before the little one comes."

But the Holy One works in strange ways, nu? When I went to check on them in the morning, the two had become three. I took them a bowl of hot kubbeh with fresh baked challah and wished them Mazel Tov. While they ate, I held the baby.

"This is something for the newsletter," I told Hirshel. Imagine, a baby born in our stable! And such a baby he is.

Smart. I could see it in his eyes. Maybe even a genius. But hardly a miracle. Certainly not enough to put Bethlehem on the map. They will be moving elsewhere later today. Maybe tomorrow. Now if you'll excuse me, I must cut this letter short. Hirshel is kvetching about a bunch of shepherds crowding into our stable. I must go see what all the ruckus is about.

From all of us here at Hirshel's Hideaway,
Nessa

The Annual Newsletter: Greetings from Gavish
(Appeared December 18, 2014))

A nd now, the third in our series of Christmas newsletters. How is your own coming along?

Howdy Ya'll,
I s'pose by the time you get this here letter, it will be old news. But I don't care. It's still the biggest thing what ever happened to me and I'll keep telling the story as long as folks keep listenin'. There ain't no need to embellish it, neither, because the truth is hard enough to believe even if I stick to the basic facts.

Now that I am 13, this is the year Pa picked me to go with him and the other shepherds on flock duty. Until this year, no matter how hard I tried, the sheep wouldn't come when I called. Pa taught me the right words and I tried to mimic his voice, but they would only come for him. Now that my voice is deeper, I am startin' to sound like my father and the sheep will come runnin' for me too. The first time that happened, Pa's chest popped out and he had a big grin on his face. I want to be as good a shepherd as Pa someday. It's the life for me!

We had been campin' in that pasture west of Bethlehem for about a week and the men were talkin' about movin' on in another day or two. We had the sheep settled for the night and those of us who weren't on guard duty was chillin' around the fire. This is my favourite time, listenin' to the men tellin' stories, every once in a while the gentle sound of the sheep. I was wrapped in my blanket and just about to doze off.

All of sudden, I thought I musta fell fast asleep and the sun was up. Everything was lit up like daylight, but it weren't the sun. I flipped over in my bedroll and saw where the light was comin' from — heard it, too. I ain't never seen nothin' like it in all my life and I don't mind tellin' ya I was shakin' like the tails on them little newborn lambs.

"What is that, Pa?" It looked like a giant, shiny person just kinda floatin' in the sky.

But Pa just stood there with his mouth hangin' open. My big, brave father was shakin' too. Then the angel or whatever it was started talkin'.

"Don't be afraid. I'm here to announce a great and joyful event that is meant for everybody, worldwide: a Saviour has just been born in David's town, a Saviour who is Messiah and Master. This is what you're to look for: a baby wrapped in a blanket and lying in a manger."

Before we even had a chance to soak this in, we saw thousands and thousands more angels, all singin' the most beautiful music I ever heard. They was singin' praise to God one minute and then, just like that, they was gone.

The men all started talkin' at once. What just happened? I was proud of Pa when he got everyone to quiet down for an orderly discussion. It didn't take long for them to decide we was runnin' off to Bethlehem (David's town, don't ya know) as fast we could go. I had never in all my life seen my father leave sheep untended, but this night I did. But then, this was a night of lots of strange things.

I don't know how the men figured out which stable to go to when we got to town. I was just followin' along. But wouldn't ya know it? We found a young couple named Joseph and Mary and a brand new little baby. He was lyin' in a manger, just like the angel said.

Well, we stayed awhile and then we run off, tellin' everybody we met about it and we're tellin' everybody still. I 'spect I'll still be tellin' about it when I'm an old, old shepherd.

Anyway, that was the highlight of my year, and Pa's too. Highlight of our lives, actually. We don't understand it all, but we know that must be one special baby to have angels announcing him. Cute little guy. He will likely grow up to be a carpenter like his pa. But if I had a chance, I'd teach him about *bein' a shepherd. A really good shepherd. The kind whose sheep know his voice and follow him everywhere.*

Kindest regards,
Gavish

TERRIE TODD

The Annual Newsletter: Musings from Melchior
(Appeared December 24, 2014)

Dearest and Most Esteemed Friends:
It has indeed been an outstanding year. I hardly know where to begin.

As you know from your perusal of last year's newsletter, my respected colleagues and I have studied the Hebrew Scriptures and found there a clear transcript of truth. In particular, the Messianic prophecies of Moses claimed our attention, and among these the words of Balaam: "A Star shall come out of Jacob; a Scepter shall rise out of Israel."

We also became well acquainted with the prophecy of Micah: "But you, Bethlehem, though you are little among the thousands of Judah, yet out of you shall come forth to Me the One to be Ruler in Israel."

We also knew the prophecy of Daniel regarding the appearance of Messiah, and came to the conclusion that His coming was near.

Then things became urgent. A mysterious light appeared in the sky which became a luminous star persisting in the western heavens. Impressed with its import, my colleagues and I turned once more to the sacred scrolls. As we tried to understand the meaning of the revered writings, we determined to go in search of Messiah. I confess to you, I was not entirely convinced. Judea was a long and arduous journey, particularly if, in the end, it proved unfruitful. My friends, however, were determined. I knew that if I stayed behind and they were proven correct, I would regret it all my days.

Prior to our departure, we meticulously chose suitable gifts for Messiah. We settled on three: Gold, a gift for a king; Frankincense, the burning of which represents prayer. As it is used by priests, we decided it would indicate the priestly nature of Messiah. Myrrh, a fragrant perfume, used in embalming bodies. We discussed this particular gift at length. Would we offend the recipient? In the end, knowing its great value, we agreed anyone would feel honoured to receive such a precious, costly gift. Everyone, after all, will die some time. Few will receive a royal burial.

The journey took months and I won't burden you with the details of it except to say that the light continued to guide our path in the most remarkable manner. I knew then that I would not regret the sojourn.

As protocol dictated, we sought out King Herod upon our arrival in Jerusalem. We were gravely disappointed that he did not already know of Messiah's coming. How could he not be aware of such a monumental occurrence? He did, however, appear most interested in what we had to say. His scholars confirmed their ancient prophecies pointed to Bethlehem as the place from which Messiah would come, so we continued on in that direction until the star reappeared.

This time, it led us directly to a house where it stopped and stayed. We did not know what to expect and I admit I felt more nervous than I had when approaching the king's court. But to our delight, inside we discovered an ordinary Hebrew couple with a very young son. The man assured us that it was the boy, not he, whom we sought. We looked at one another in wonder. When we asked the time of the child's birth, we knew the star had appeared to us the very night he was born.

My colleagues and I presented our gifts with deepest reverence, gratitude and awe. This child would forever change our planet, our calendar and our hearts. I feel so privileged to be alive at this time in human history and to see him with my own eyes. If I live to be a very old man, I will not encounter such an experience again. I am content. I can move into the future with renewed hope in my heart for all mankind, and I wish the same for you. I know that wise men and women will continue to seek him long after I am gone.

A wiser man than I was last year,
Melchoir

Christmas Presents I Remember
Part One: The Mix Master
(Appeared December 3, 2015)

I must have been around five the Christmas my parents gave me a little pink mechanical mixer. I loved that thing. It came with a yellow plastic mixing bowl, and when you pushed the spring-loaded button on the side (and kept pressing it), the mixers whirred round and round. Once you developed a good rhythm, those beaters could really pick up speed. In retrospect, the racket probably made Mom and Dad second-guess their choice.

I also received a bake set complete with tiny round pans and cake mixes. No Easy-Bake oven for me, though. Mom let me use her real one, with supervision. My little mixer stirred up the cake batter which filled the pans to create cakes the size of large cookies — which, if memory serves, my big brothers could devour in two bites. But that's okay. They tasted like cardboard.

Many months after Christmas, one of my mother's friends came to call, bringing her two daughters with her. I dreaded any visit by these particular girls because they had a tendency to rummage through everything in my room, break things, and leave it all in shambles without so much as a word from their mother. Sometimes my mom would take pity and help me clean up afterwards, but she insisted I be kind to these kids and share my toys.

On this particular day, one of the girls decided it would be great fun to take my mixer outside and use it to stir up a sand cake. Of course, the sand got inside the workings of the toy and completely halted its action. We cleaned the dirt out of it as best we could, but my little mixer never worked the same again. And of course, it was useless for real food.

I found it highly unfair that I was expected to extend grace to these destructive kids. At that age, I could not understand the challenges of a single-parent family or the enormous stress the mother of these two faced. I couldn't fully appreciate the many ways I had been blessed.

I wish I could say this childhood experience made me a more generous adult. I have a long way to go. But one thing I know. We all cause messes. We hurt, disappoint and take advantage of one another. Too often, we do so in oblivion and go on our merry way. Other times, we're aware of what we've done and try to make amends. But even our best efforts frequently fall short, for some things can never be repaired by human hands.

At Christmas time more than any other, we are given the ultimate example of sacrificial grace: the King of kings gives up his throne in Heaven to come to earth as a helpless infant. In scripture, we see Jesus moving toward the messes others made and miraculously coming through for them. He isn't afraid of our messes, either. He cleans them up and invites us to join him in his work and to pass that same grace to others.

"You must have the same attitude that Christ Jesus had. Though he was God, he did not think of equality with God as something to cling to. Instead, he gave up his divine privileges, he took the humble position of a slave, and was born as a human being." (Philippians 2:4-7 NLT)

May your mixer keep working, may your Christmas goodies turn out heavenly, and may your messes be saturated with God's grace.

Christmas Presents I Remember
Part Two: The Charm Bracelet
(Appeared December 10, 2015)

When I was in high school about 150 years ago, sterling silver charm bracelets were all the rage. Unlike the Pandora bracelets and their knock-offs that are so popular today, these bracelets were loose and clunky and noisy. But they were the thing to wear.

I didn't own one, but there was this boy. He and I were sort of an item, and I guess he wanted to impress me with an abundance of Christmas gifts that year. One of those gifts was the coveted charm bracelet, and he had chosen one charm to go with it. It featured two red hearts and the word "Sweetheart." Naturally, I loved it. At first, I was determined to not collect more charms but to keep only that one, making for a daintier piece of jewelry.

Then the unthinkable happened. I looked down at my bracelet one day and the charm was missing! I back-tracked everywhere I'd been that day, to no avail. My sweetheart charm was gone.

When my dad returned from a trip to Texas with a charm for me that looked like a little map of the state, I put that on my bracelet and had it soldered on so as not to lose it. Between then and graduation, I received nine more charms: a tiny typewriter for finishing first in a typing contest (an especially meaningful keepsake now that I'm a writer), a lobster from a friend in Nova Scotia, a graduation cap, a miniature diploma, a birthday charm, and another with my initial. Each time I received a new charm, I'd make sure to pay the extra to have a jeweler solder it in place. I'd learned my lesson!

Then one day, when my brother-in-law was cleaning out his car, what did he find but my Sweetheart charm between the seats. I couldn't believe it! If you've ever rediscovered something precious you thought was hopelessly lost, you understand how I felt.

Too clunky to wear, my charm bracelet has spent most of the last four decades in a jewelry box on my dresser. When our kids were little, they were sometimes curious enough for me to pull it out, tell them the stories behind each charm and about the sweet boy who gave me the bracelet.

Jesus told three stories about lost items — a coin, a sheep and a son. In each story, the lost thing is highly valued and missed. No stone is left unturned. The search does not end until the lost is found, safe and secure. Then a celebratory party breaks out!

He told these stories to help us understand we are precious to him. When we wander off, he pursues us relentlessly and lovingly. And when we return to him, he rejoices. Isn't it sweet to know someone feels that way about you? He made it pretty clear that this was his main purpose when he said, "For the Son of Man came to seek and save those who are lost." (Luke 19:10).

Of all the gifts I received that particular Christmas, the charm bracelet is the only one I still have. That boy who wanted to impress me with presents? It must have worked. Forty Christmases, three children and four grandchildren later, we are still an item.

Christmas Presents I Remember
Part Three: The Typewriter
(Appeared December 17, 2015)

In Grade 10, I took first year Typing. Our classroom held about 15 desks that came in two adjustable halves: on one side of each desk sat a grey steel manual typewriter, and on the other half we placed a copy of our typing textbook, looped over a stand so it stood upright. Our teacher, Mrs. Wangsness, was kind but firm. I did well enough that year to qualify for Typing II, which I took in Grade 12. By Christmas break of that year, I could type 80 words a minute on those clunky old manuals.

My parents must have decided it would be worth the investment and surprised me with a brand new, brown and tan Sears Selectric typewriter in its own carrying case for Christmas. I was floored! It cost more than $200, a ridiculous sum for a Christmas present in 1976. It came with ribbon cartridges that you simply slid into the side and discarded after use. A secondary cartridge held a correction ribbon whereby you could type over your errors with white and, voila! Your mistakes magically disappeared. Provided you typed on white paper, of course.

I lugged that thing to typing class every day for the remainder of the school year while the rest of the class lumbered away on the manuals. It probably weighed more than five of today's laptops, and all it could do was type!

That spring, a nearby business college sponsored a contest for high school students and I represented my little school in typing. They allowed us to bring our own typewriters, so I carted along my trusty Selectric, plugged 'er in, and went to work. I found it challenging and more than a little stressful. At lunch time when Mr. Myers asked how I thought I'd done, I told him I felt satisfied that I had done my best. He agreed that was the main thing.

At the awards ceremony later, they called out the winners' names starting with third place. I hoped it might be me, but no. As they prepared to announce the second-place winner, my hopes lay somewhere down around my feet. And I was right; someone else's name was called.

Then they called the first-place winner and I nearly fell off my platform shoes. I won! The prize was a $400 scholarship to the college which I never took advantage of, and a medal which lies tarnishing somewhere in our storage room. I made my parents proud, though, and landed a job right out of high school working in the offices of the Portage Co-op store.

I carried that old typewriter with me into married life and used it to type my husband's college papers, crank out letters home, and create newsletters for the student wives' club. I even earned a few bucks typing papers for other students. Later, I wrote annual family Christmas newsletters and drama scripts for church.

Sometime after we obtained our first computer in 1996 and I learned how to use it, I donated the 20-year-old typewriter to MCC and I have no idea whether it still exists.

And no, I don't miss it.

But I'll always feel grateful for that beautiful gift. Did my parents suspect that I would one day make my living as an administrative assistant or that I would become a published writer? I don't know, but I shudder to think what a challenge either of these would be without those typing classes and my good old personal typewriter to practice on. It was a gift that kept on giving.

Good investment, indeed!

Christmas Presents I Remember
Part Four: The Doll House
(Appeared December 24, 2015)

The Christmas I was seven, I had my heart set on the most beautiful tin doll house in the Simpsons-Sears catalogue. It wasn't one of those old-fashioned two-storey houses open in the front, either. Mine was a ranch style, with a roof that lifted off so you played with it from above. The curtains and carpets were lithographed on; the plastic fireplace, doors and window frames snapped into place; and it came with a complete set of trendy plastic furniture. Pictured beside the house stood a doll family consisting of dad, mom, sister and baby brother. For weeks I stared at the page, planning how I would arrange the furniture and which dolls would sleep in which room.

I thought I'd never survive the wait. Christmas morning, it seemed my little heart would beat right out of my body when I opened that dollhouse. I can't remember which parent or sibling helped me put together the "some assembly required" house, but what a joy it was to behold when at last it looked just like the picture on the box. I artfully placed the furniture, and it was finally ready for my doll family to move in.

But alas. The sold-separately doll family did not exactly fit their new home, even though they posed so optimistically beside the house on the same catalog page. Not only were they too large to walk through the doorways, sit on the chairs, or sleep on the beds, they came with a piece of paper telling us how to order a family that *would* fit the house. The correct sized family was not to be found in the catalog at all. What a rip-off. My sense of injustice and my tendency toward impatience both kicked in. I figured I'd show them a thing or two by playing with the oversized dolls anyway. I crammed their bodies into the chairs and allowed them to vault over the door frames. Poor things probably didn't sleep much with their feet hanging off the ends of the beds like that, but then how much sleep could they get anyway with their shoes permanently on? I managed to put in many happy hours over the next couple of years, but somehow my magnificent gift always felt a little tainted. I guess it was one of my first lessons in the greedy world of retail.

Although my beloved house eventually rusted and ended up in the trash, I recently saw the same model on a collector's web site in all its glorious detail. I studied the photos of each room and let the memories sweep over me. The chart said this house sold for $6.99 in 1965 and would sell for $130 today. They made no mention of dolls, proportionate or otherwise.

Years later I would find it a little ironic that I spent 26 years of my adult life living in a tin house. I appreciated our mobile home most of the time, but it certainly did not increase in value and I often longed for a "real" house, with a foundation beneath and a garage nearby. Now I have that, and I love it. But even if I did not, it would be okay. You see, the baby in the manger grew to be a saviour who would seal my eternal destiny. The most talented carpenter who ever walked the planet is preparing a home for me. The One who paints the sunset is choosing the colours. I don't know what it will be made of, how large it will be, or how it will be furnished. But I do know this: I am going to *fit*! It's going to be absolutely, completely, 100 per cent custom-designed for me by the One who made me and knows me better than I know myself. And best of all, He will be there too! Now *that's* a Christmas present worth waiting for.

OUT OF MY MIND

Christmas Presents I Remember
Part Five: The Radio and the Cassette Tape Recorder
(Appeared December 31, 2015)

In 1972, if you wanted to hear your favourite song, you had to wait until it played on the radio. Unless, of course, you were rich enough to buy it on a forty-five or the entire album on a vinyl record or cassette. Cassettes were pointless, because chances are you didn't have anything to play them on anyway. And even if you were so lucky, if you wanted various hits from various artists, you needed to make your own mix tape.

Lucky for me, I owned a little avocado green, RCA transistor radio. My parents had given it to me the previous Christmas and throughout the year I dutifully listened to CKRC for all my favourite songs, wearing out untold nine-volt batteries in the process. So many of the hits from that year have become classics: Don McLean's *American Pie*, Robert John's *The Lion Sleeps Tonight,* and *Puppy Love* by my boyfriend, Donny Osmond, who I was certain would fall madly in love with me if only we could meet.

After a year of listening to my radio, my parent surprised me with my own cassette recorder for Christmas of '72! Hallelujah! I knew precisely how I would spend New Year's Day. When the radio station counted down the top hits of the year, I'd be ready. I stocked up on long-play cassettes — 45 minutes each side, for a total of 90. Six or so of these puppies should be enough for me to capture the day's offerings. I set up my recorder next to my little radio, placed the microphone right in front of the radio's speaker, and hit record as soon as they began the Top 100 countdown. I would have a hundred greatest hits available at my fingertips to listen to any time I wanted! Life was good.

It required discipline. In order to get the most out of my tapes, I had to change them when they were getting too full to hold one more song without missing the start of the next. I refused to stop the tapes and listen to what I was capturing, because I didn't want to risk missing a single song. These amazing tapes would surely carry me through my teen years and beyond!

After the Number One song was played and recorded (*The First Time Ever I Saw Your Face* by Roberta Flack), I finally allowed myself the luxury of listening to my tapes.

Talk about disappointing.

While the radio itself fell a few smooth tones short of a state-of-the-art sound system, placing the microphone right in front of the radio's little speaker was the straw that broke the camel's ear. What I had captured was mind-numbing static with an occasional recognizable tune in the background. Hours and hours of it.

But you know what? I'm glad the tapes didn't turn out. Why? Because I would have obtained them without contributing anything. I wasn't buying a record or a concert ticket, I wasn't even listening to commercials. Copyright piracy may not have been a familiar term back then, but it's what I was trying to do. I was freely taking the hard work of composers and musicians, most of whom take years to reach the place where they can earn anything, not to mention the people who produce, engineer and promote the work. I was stealing, plain and simple.

Now that I'm a writer, I have a better understanding and a higher regard for copyright laws. They exist for a good reason. If you wouldn't approve of someone absconding with your paycheque, wouldn't you think twice before copying someone's work without their permission? Besides, it's against the law.

If you're listening to pirated music or watching pirated movies, I invite you to start fresh and resolve to discontinue the habit in 2016. A clean conscious is a gift you give yourself.

Happy New Year.

OUT OF MY MIND

Christmas Ornaments I Love - Part 1
The Glass Nativity Ball
(Appeared December 7, 2017)

*E*ach year, I purge a few more Christmas decorations. The few I'll never part with and the stories behind them are the subject of this year's December series.

In the spring of 1999, I hatched a brilliant idea. I would write a play for Y2K!

The working title was *God is Under the Weather*. A church drama team gathers on the afternoon of New Year's Eve to strike the set and put away all the props from their Christmas play. A blizzard materializes so quickly and fiercely, they become stranded at the church. Along comes a traveler seeking refuge from the storm and assistance with car problems. To pass the time, the team performs its short Christmas piece for their out-of-town guest, thus creating a play-within-a-play.

The team includes Jessica, a teenager who shares a special bond with their Shakespeare-quoting team leader, Oscar, even though neither of them knows she is his biological daughter. Her widowed mother, Gail, comes along to help but has no intention of rekindling a long-dead romance with Oscar. (Are you still with me?)

Another teammate has brought along his pregnant wife who goes into labour. The power goes out. The church phone is dead. And it's 1999, so the few who might own cell phones find them dead, too.

As the story unfolds, secrets are revealed, hearts are laid bare, souls are inspired, and a baby is born on the stroke of Y2K.

I sent this dazzling work of genius off to the top publishers of church drama scripts, certain they'd clamour for it. I wondered whether Sandra Bullock or Julia Roberts would play the lead when the movie came out.

In the play-within-the-play, one character receives a gift of a delicate glass nativity scene inside a glass ball. I didn't know if such a thing existed. When I found the exact ornament while browsing a fundraising catalog from our kids' school, I knew it was a sign. I practically heard the Hallelujah chorus while cherubs danced above the catalog. I ordered the ornament immediately, so I'd be ready when my play hit the big time.

In my naivety, (funny how similar to "nativity" that sounds), there were so many things I did not understand. Such as:

- Churches do not want to put on plays between Christmas and New Years, and even if they did...
- Publishers don't want scripts for plays that have never been produced, and even if they did...
- Publishers do not want to publish a script that would only be useful for a once-in-a-lifetime event, and even if they did...
- Publishers would have needed to see this script in 1996. By the time I mailed the script, directors should have been handing out parts!

Naturally, the play was rejected. Naturally, I felt crushed. Though the full play was never produced, I did sell the shorter play-within-a-play years later to a publisher who included it in a Christmas collection. I have no idea whether it's ever been staged.

But the little glass nativity scene hangs on our tree every year. You might think this monument to my humiliation would not be worth hanging on to, but I still like it. It's a reminder of so many things, like surviving life's disappointments, and all I've learned in the intervening years. It reminds me what's truly important: the baby in the manger who loves me anyway and who understands rejection to a depth I'll never experience.

Not even my family knows the significance of that ornament, since I've never shared the story behind it. Until now.

What's your favourite ornament?

Christmas Ornaments I Love – Part 2
The Pageant Bears
(Appeared December 14, 2017)

Long-time residents of Portage la Prairie remember the energetic Christmas banquets put on by Portage (now Prairie) Alliance Church through the 1990s and into the 2000s. At its peak, our banquet ran for eight nights over two weekends, just to accommodate all the guests who lined up outside our doors early on an October Saturday to purchase tickets. Contrary to popular assumption, the event was never a fundraiser, but a labour of love by dozens of volunteers over hundreds of hours and months of rehearsals. The banquets became known for magnificent music and drama, marvelous meals and delightful decorating throughout the building. For many guests, the ambience of Christmas sights, smells and sounds provided their kickoff of the season.

Although usually involved on some level, I'd never had to lead the whole production. Until 2003. Previous leadership had moved away, and it fell on my shoulders to steer the team in gifting our community with another creative Christmas experience. We chose a 1950s theme called *Christmas at Velma's Diner*. It turned out to be our biggest undertaking and probably the most fun one yet.

I was scared stupid.

One of the smartest things we did, though, was recruit prayer partners. We asked members of our congregation to "adopt" one person who would be serving all the nights of the banquet —musicians, actors, technicians, etc. They agreed to pray for that person every day for a month leading up to and throughout the banquet nights, and find ways to encourage them. Each "adoptee" knew they had someone to call if they needed prayer for their health or anything else.

I hit the jackpot when my friend Susan Beauchamp adopted me as her prayer partner. I knew she would faithfully talk to God about me. What I didn't know was:

a) how challenging the event would become;

b) that during that busy season, my husband would take a fall on the ice while working hundreds of miles from home and fracture a bone, putting him off work for a month and increasing the stress to a whole new level; or

c) that Susan would bring me a gift each week leading up to the banquets. By the end of the stint, I had collected a set of four adorable Christmas Pageant Bears. How appropriate!

Lined up together, the little bears were reminiscent of children presenting the Christmas story on stage. Each day when I saw them, they reminded me someone was praying specifically for me and for each of my teammates.

Eventually, PAC's Christmas banquets ran their course and we moved on to other ways of blessing our community. But I still delight in unwrapping my pageant bears every December and displaying them — a wonderful reminder of the power of prayer, of God's sustaining grace through a stressful time, and of the loving care of a sweet friend.

Christmas Ornaments I Love – Part 3
The Ugliest Little Stocking
(Appeared December 21, 2017)

As a stay-at-home mom of two preschoolers, I eagerly anticipated a morning out each week where women were free to connect, learn together, and relax while their children were lovingly cared for. It was a program at my church cleverly called LIFT ("Ladies in Fellowship Together") and it probably saved my sanity in those early years of parenting. The program continues today in a little different format and name (MOPS – "Mothers of Preschoolers"), but still acknowledges the deep need for this kind of break for busy young parents.

The kids enjoyed going to LIFT, and they loved the volunteers who cared for them so well. Naturally, we young moms appreciated them too! Most weeks, the kids came home with a little craft they'd made. One year as Christmas neared, the volunteers helped the kids make tiny Christmas stockings from green felt with their names in gold glitter. Could anything be more beautiful?

By the time our third child, Reuben, came along, our family had invented a strange little game with those stockings. The game became a tradition. The kids hid their little stockings somewhere in the branches of the Christmas tree. Then, while they were asleep or otherwise occupied, their dad and I hunted for those stockings, tucked a mini candy cane into each one, and hid them in a different branch for the kids to find on Christmas morning. No one ever talked about it. Somehow it just evolved, and remaining silent was part of the fun.

There was only one problem. Reuben didn't have one of those little stockings. He didn't mind, because he was still too little to care. But his sister cared. Mindy took it upon herself to make her baby brother his own little stocking. She cut one of her own well-used, every-day socks down to size and glued gold garland around the top. Now Reuben could participate, too. It may have been the saddest looking little stocking ever, but it was made with love. I felt touched by Mindy's compassion. Like most siblings, our kids fought and drove each other crazy through their years under our roof, and I guess that's what makes this memory so precious.

The game grew increasingly challenging every year as the kids became more clever at hiding the stockings. Nobody even liked candy canes much anymore, but tradition is tradition and it continued through their teens.

One by one, the kids grew up and left. The little stockings eventually went with their owners to their new homes. But somehow, Reuben's funny little misfit stocking is still at our house. And every time I see it, I smile. My heart is warmed by the memory of a silly family Christmas tradition and of the priceless love of a (mostly) devoted sister.

Christmas Ornaments I Love – Part 4
The Little Wooden Ornaments
(Appeared December 28, 2017)

"This is just wrong," I mumbled as I stepped out of the store's festive holiday glitter and into the lukewarm humidity of East Texas in mid-December. The Chipmunks chirped *We Wish You a Merry Christmas* over loudspeakers in the parking lot where teenagers in yellow rain slickers sold evergreen trees. Small bunches of live mistletoe could be purchased for a quarter apiece, and I decided to splurge. It grows wild in the south, a parasitic plant clinging high atop trees some entrepreneurial soul had mustered enough courage to climb.

It was 1980 and my first Christmas away from home in Manitoba where Christmas sounds, looks, and feels like it's supposed to: the sharp crunch of snow underfoot, little kids bundled into snowsuits like overstuffed teddy bears, and wisps of white frost clinging to mustaches. Hubby was in university and we were expecting our first baby. With money tight, we'd agreed a trip home was not feasible. We would create our own holiday memories instead. We found a little artificial tree for three dollars at a garage sale and decorated it with one small strand of multicolored lights and a set of tiny wooden ornaments. Painted red and gold, the set included bells, Santas, skaters, rocking horses, angels, toy trains, and my favourite, a wee nativity scene. Made in China, the characters' painted-on faces were Asian in appearance, reminding us of the universal nature of the holiday and how it didn't really matter where we celebrated.

But as Christmas Day approached, I grew melancholy. Thoughts turned to my siblings gathering at home, the coats piling up on Grandma's bed, the homemade cabbage rolls and perogies being consumed, and the wild pandemonium of nieces and nephews tearing into their gifts. I pictured them enjoying it all while we sat in our dreary apartment with our Charlie Brown tree, exchanging practical gifts like socks and pencils. Though longing to set up a nursery, my nesting instinct was trumped by our empty bank account. I yearned for a little snow. Surely all of this was rationale for a pity party, and I zealously indulged.

Then, as Hubby read aloud the familiar words from Luke 2, I looked at my round tummy and thought of our coming child. I felt him move and I identified with Mary. She, too, found herself far from the familiar faces of home. The climate in Mary's homeland of Israel was far more comparable to Texas than what felt like "proper Christmas weather" to me. The stable where she gave birth was anything but cozy and inviting. Not only did Mary have no nursery to decorate, she barely had a roof over her head! Yet her humble obedience resulted in the greatest gift ever given — the birth of Messiah. I'd been making it all about my own traditions and memories. Perhaps it was time to focus on the one whose arrival we celebrated, wherever we found ourselves and whatever the circumstances.

Each year, when I pull out those tiny wooden ornaments, I'm reminded of that lonely, long-ago Christmas and of the lessons learned. I recall how little we had, but how rich we were.

Let every heart prepare him room.

The Marvelous Human Christmas Tree
(Appeared December 6, 2018)

One of the highlights of my preschool Christmases was the annual concert put on by the students of the Amaranth Elementary School. The entire community came out, packing into the local hall, bundled in our boots and parkas. We'd watch the kids perform and at the end of the night, Santa Claus showed up with a gift for every kid — even those of us too little to go to school. Even at that age, I knew Santa was pretend. It didn't matter. I was all about the present.

Oddly enough, the concert I remember best was the one I had to miss. I'd come down with a dreadful cold and sore throat and tried to convince my parents I was well enough to attend. They weren't buying it. Dad stayed home with me, if I remember right. My deep disappointment at having to stay behind was reduced when Mom and my siblings returned, bringing my still wrapped gift from Santa. It was a jigsaw puzzle.

By the time I hit Grade 1 (we had no Kindergarten), I felt more than ready to perform in my first Christmas concert. Our teacher, Mrs. Cooper, organized her class into a living tree. Dressed in green crepe paper and gold tinsel, we were somehow stacked in layers to form a glorious living Christmas tree. Some kids were sparkly ornaments. Others, decked out in wrapping paper, represented the gifts underneath. Each had a line to say.

If anyone thought to take a picture, I have never seen it — which is probably just as well. No photograph, especially in black and white, could ever reproduce the magnificence of that tree in my memory bank.

Of course, somebody had to play the star at the top. I always figured I was chosen for this distinction because I was the tallest in the class. Whatever the reason, I was thrilled. But how would I ever memorize all those lines?

Big sister helped, and I went over and over them. And over them. The night of the event, I remember our principal lifting me to the top of the step ladder or whatever they'd rigged up, decked out in shining gold tinsel and feeling like a star indeed. More than a half century later, I still remember my lines:

*I am the star, see its bright Christmas light
That shone on the manger that first Christmas night!*

Although I have since memorized many lines, none have stuck like the ones I learned as a six-year-old.

Did that first taste of the spotlight kindle inside me a flame which would lead to a lifelong interest in the stage and all things theatrical? Could be. I do know that when God places a dream in your heart, it does not easily die. And if it does, it wasn't God who killed it.

I see three lessons here for parents of young children. One, if you want your children to believe you about God (or anything else), don't lie to them about Santa Claus. Two, whatever you want your kids to remember forever, get it into their heads early! And third, pay attention to their engagement level at concerts. You might just see a noteworthy glimpse into their future — a passion which you can play an important role in nurturing.

That Time I Played Scrooge
(Appeared December 13, 2018)

I was about nine years old the year my Sunday School class had only two kids in it — another girl named Marlene and me. When it came time for the annual Christmas concert, our teacher, Mrs. Johnson, chose a two-character play for Marlene and me to perform. The premise of the play was that a sweet young girl would teach her crochety old grandfather (who said "bah humbug" a lot) the real meaning of Christmas. Mrs. Johnson allowed that the elderly character could just as easily be a crochety old grandmother, and assigned that role to me.

I was mortified.

I gave Mrs. Johnson half a dozen reasons why she had it backwards. Marlene should play the grouchy old grandmother and I should play the sweet young girl. Marlene had short hair, mine was long. Marlene was bigger than I, and a little older. I did not want to play a grouchy old woman who says, "Bah humbug." I had never heard of Charles Dickens or his spooky stories, so the expression made no sense. Who says "bah humbug" anyway? How was that even a thing? It was the dumbest play ever and I refused to approach it with even the slightest smidgeon of enthusiasm.

But Mrs. Johnson stuck to her guns. I would play the grouchy old woman, no questions asked. Oh, I was grouchy all right. I wanted to run away. I stubbornly decided to play my role so badly the audience would see I was actually a sweet young girl who had no business trying to portray an old grouch.

Mrs. Johnson suggested my character could be knitting.

I didn't know how to knit, I argued.

Sewing, then.

Oh, fine!

So I held this scrap of fabric in one hand and a needle in the other, which I kept stabbing through the material. Don't ask me what I was supposed to be making or mending. Convinced our audience would feel appalled by how poorly-cast this play was, I could already imagine the post-concert conversations that would take place in living rooms for miles around:

"What was Mrs. Johnson thinking, casting Terrie as that grouchy old lady?"

"I know, right? She clearly should have played the sweet young girl."

"What a shame. Ruined my whole night."

"Maybe even my whole life. So unfortunate."

The one unfortunate thing I see now is that Mrs. Johnson missed an opportunity to turn the whole scenario around with a little simple psychology. If she had appealed to my nine-year-old ego by explaining that she was giving me the more challenging role, the one demanding the best acting and the most stretching, I'm sure I'd have fallen for it and jumped in. I would have acted my socks off.

But she didn't.

And I didn't.

If the Ghost of Christmas Past could take me back to 1968 and show me my belligerent, nine-year-old self, I'd feed that stubborn kid the same line I drilled into my drama team years later until they grew sick of it: "It's not about ME!"

I didn't understand that then. Somewhere along the way, good mentors gave me a more mature perspective on teamwork. Thank God, Ebenezer Scrooge isn't the only character who can be reformed.

You'll Shoot Your Eye Out!
(Appeared November 21, 2019)

Do you ever find yourself 30 minutes into a movie before realizing you've already seen it? I almost never intentionally watch a movie more than once, with the exception of Christmas movies. So, for my Christmas column series this year, I'll tell you about the movies I and my family watch nearly every year.

A movie set in the 1940s was released in 1983 to little attention in theatres. Over the years, however, *A Christmas Story* starring Peter Billingsley as young Ralphie Parker has became one of the most played films on television. In 1997, Turner Network Television began airing a 24-hour marathon dubbed "24 Hours of *A Christmas Story.*" They ran the film 12 consecutive times beginning at 7 p.m. on Christmas Eve and ending Christmas Day. (We are not THAT fond of it.)

We were first introduced to this movie around 2005 by our adult children. It seemed odd that they loved it, given that the setting dated back to before even my birth. But to them, it's a classic. Its Canadian connections add to the appeal. While the story is set in the fictional town of Hohman, Indiana, many of the scenes were shot in Toronto. Watching my kids enjoy something usually pulls me in, too. Somewhere along the line we acquired the DVD with special features like interactive trivia quizzes about the show and interviews with the now adult child actors. Today, you can tour the house in Cleveland, Ohio that provided the home's exterior shots in the movie. Later, the owner remodeled it to look like the movie set's interior and opened it to the public.

The charm of the film is the narration provided by the adult Ralphie Parker, reminiscing about the Christmas he was nine. The narrator is Jean Shepherd, the author of the stories on which the movie is based. His 1966 book, *In God We Trust: All Others Pay Cash*, is a collection of semi-fictional anecdotes from his childhood.

In the movie, Ralphie wants only one gift for Christmas: a Red Ryder Carbine Action 200-shot Range Model air rifle. Ralphie's desire is shot down by his mother, his teacher and even Santa Claus at Higbee's department store, all giving him the same warning: "You'll shoot your eye out."

Riddled with hilarious and memorable scenes, I can see why this movie became such an icon. Who could ever forget the kid who sticks his tongue to a flagpole on a double-dog dare, the terrifying visit to Santa, Ralphie in the despised pink bunny suit, the secret decoder pin, the old man's major prize of a leg lamp, or the hilarious scene near the end in the Chinese restaurant?

The tenderness of this movie comes in the form of an unexpected present from Ralphie's father. We see Ralphie snuggled in bed on Christmas night with his gift by his side, while adult Ralphie says this was the best present he had ever or would ever receive.

Who among us doesn't long for an expression of love from a caring father?

Our heavenly Father gave us the best gift we have ever or will ever receive. The first Christmas present wasn't purchased at a store or placed under a tree. It was a little baby who grew to become our Saviour — a gift of love and life and peace and hope and restoration. He is the perfect gift. May you find him this Christmas.

How the Grinch (Almost) Stole Christmas
(Appeared November 28, 2019)

One movie in our DVD must-watch collection is the 2000 version of *How the Grinch Stole Christmas* with Jim Carrey in the title role. It's based on Theodore (Doctor Seuss) Geisel's 1957 book by the same name. Making a feature-length movie out of a children's storybook requires much expansion of the original. The writers of the screenplay created an entire past for the Grinch that makes him a somewhat sympathetic character and explains why he hated Christmas and the residents of Whoville. They also needed to add several extra scenes and plot points to the story, while staying true to Seuss's rhyming style.

You may or may not be a fan, but Jim Carrey could not have been a better choice. If ever a role called for his maniacal style, this one does. Carrey delivers. I think it's his performance and the brilliant makeup work that bring me back to this movie. My favourite lines do not appear in the book, like when the Grinch steps on the scale to discover his heart is down a size and he promises, "This time, I'm keeping it off!"

When the Grinch receives the invitation from Cindy Lou Who to their Whobilation festivities, Carrey adlibs. Flipping the pages of his calendar, the Grinch reads his tight schedule aloud:

"Four o'clock, wallow in self-pity; Four-thirty, stare into the abyss; Five o'clock, solve world hunger, tell no one; Five-thirty, jazzercize; Six-thirty, dinner with me — I can't cancel that again; Seven, wrestle with my self-loathing. I'm booked."

The part where the Grinch teases director Ron Howard by donning Howard's iconic ball cap and "directing" Max the dog on how to play a reindeer was all Jim Carrey's. Howard loved it and left it in.

Like most Christmas movies, this one makes no references to the real Christmas. Its redemption comes in the lessons on bullying and its long-range results, on the emptiness of consumerism, and on the value of community, love and goodwill.

But the real Christmas did include a grinch. His name was Herod the Great and he, too, had a past. Known for his architectural ambitions, this king of Judea was brutal. He executed members of his own family, banished at least one wife in order to "marry up" politically, and unfairly taxed the Judeans. Scholars agree Herod suffered throughout his lifetime from depression and paranoia. He was so concerned no one would mourn his death that he commanded several distinguished men to be killed at the time of his own death to ensure the displays of grief he craved would take place. Fortunately, this order was not carried out.

One equally horrific command was realized, however. King Herod felt so threatened when he learned about the birth of Jesus Christ, he determined to have the child murdered. When his initial plan was thwarted, he ordered all male children under the age of two in Bethlehem killed. While scholars tell us the total number of babies murdered would have been a dozen or so (not hundreds like is sometimes portrayed), I've sometimes wondered how I would have felt toward Jesus years later if I'd been one of those bereft mothers and if I understood why my child had died.

Jesus escaped this massacre, thanks to a warning given to Joseph in a dream. Like the Grinch's, Herod's attempt at stealing Christmas failed. Not long afterwards, Herod died an excruciating death.

Unlike the Grinch, Herod never experienced an epiphany. He never came to understand that, "Maybe Christmas doesn't come from a store. Maybe Christmas means a little bit more."

Elf: A Longing to Belong
(Appeared December 5, 2019)

First, a bit of trivia that "Elf" fans may not know. Remember Buddy's 13-second-long belch after guzzling a two-litre bottle of Coca-Cola? The burp was real, but dubbed in by Canadian voice actor Maurice LaMarche (who voiced Brain from "Pinky and the Brain," among many other cartoon characters). We should feel so proud.

This 2003 movie stars Will Farrell (who stands six-foot-three) as Buddy, a human raised by Santa's elves. It always makes me laugh, but be sure you're in the mood for extreme silliness when you decide to watch it.

Buddy has never been told he's not an elf, and he grows up feeling inferior. He's far too large for the elves' homes and furnishings. He can't make toys as quickly as they can. Though he feels loved by Papa Elf who adopted him, and accepted by the other elves who are too kind to hurt his feelings, Buddy knows he doesn't fit in.

When Buddy learns he's a human whose mother died and that he has a biological father unaware of his existence, he treks from the North Pole to New York City. His mission? To find his father and redeem him from Santa's naughty list. The people he encounters, including his father, assume he's completely dysfunctional and in need of serious help. All kinds of crazy scenes play out as Buddy gradually wins over his half-brother, his stepmother, a department store elf he's quickly falling in love with, and — finally, his father. The group must then save Santa's sleigh from certain destruction by raising NYC's level of Christmas cheer. Buddy ends up a hero.

The touching part of this story is the part to which our souls relate: the hunger for belonging. We yearn to understand our roots, find our people, know where we fit. We long for father, and when that longing is met with rejection, it becomes the harshest rejection of all.

Regardless of race, class, nationality or gender, our relationship with our father is deeply tied to our identity. That need is so strong in us, it can drive people into bad relationships, gangs and cults. Even those fortunate enough to enjoy a good relationship with their parents understand the need for more. We were designed to be loved perfectly, but no parent or partner can measure up.

Deep inside, we long to know who we truly are. Whose we are. Though we may not admit it, our souls desire a relationship with our Creator. The good news is our Creator desires one with us even more. Christmas made it possible. We don't need to make a long trek to him. He sent his son to us. Because of the sacrifice Jesus made, look at what the Bible tells us about who we are in him:

I am a child of God. (John 1:12)
I am a friend of Jesus. (John 15:15)
I will not be condemned by God. (Romans 8:1)
I am accepted by Christ. (Romans 15:7)
I have wisdom, righteousness, and redemption. (I Cor. 1:30)
I am a new creature. (II Corinthians 5:17)
I am set free. (Galatians 5:1)
I am blessed. (Ephesians 1:3)
I am chosen. (Ephesians 1:4)
I am forgiven. (Ephesians 1:7)
I am loved. (Ephesians 2:4-5)
I am provided for. (Philippians 4:19)

That's only a partial list, but it includes 12 verses for you to look up — one for each of the 12 days of Christmas. Google them if it's easier. I hope you'll take some time this Christmas season to remember — or perhaps to discover for the first time — the identity and belonging your Creator offers you because of Jesus.

Merry Christmas!

A Charlie Brown Christmas
(Appeared December 12, 2019)

Technically, I'm not sure you can call this brilliant piece of work a movie because it's only 25 minutes long — 30 with commercials inserted. Nowadays, you can watch it any time, in full colour, without commercials, simply by finding it on You Tube. But when I was a kid, it aired once a year with plenty of fanfare leading to the big event so you could be sure to catch it — provided the winter weather didn't mess with your antenna and turn your TV screen to snow. Even in black and white, it was worth waiting for.

A Charlie Brown Christmas was created in only six months in 1965, on a shoestring budget. The producers broke from common practice by hiring children to do the voice work, by using a jazz soundtrack (performed by pianist Vince Guaraldi), and by not using a laugh track. Experts predicted it would be a huge flop. Fifty-four years later, this classic remains a must-see in many homes every Christmas.

The story begins with a typically depressed Charlie Brown, who visits Lucy's Psychiatric Help booth to share his dismay over the commercialization of Christmas. His sister Sally writes to Santa saying she wants cash — particularly 10s and 20s. Lucy complains about always getting toys instead of what she wants: real estate. Even Charlie Brown's dog Snoopy succumbs, turning his doghouse into a gawdy display in hopes of winning a neighbourhood contest.

Upon receiving Lucy's five-cent advice, Charlie takes on the project of directing the Christmas play, which only leads to more frustration as the entire cast remains distracted by the glitz and glitter of Christmas. When Charlie picks out a Christmas tree, he chooses a spindly one — symbolically, the only real tree on the lot — recognizing that it just needs a little love. For this too, Charlie Brown becomes a laughingstock. In desperation, he cries out, "Can't anyone tell me what Christmas is all about?"

To which a tiny voice responds, "Sure, Charlie Brown. I can tell you what Christmas is all about."

Thus begins the pivotal moment when little Linus, blanket in hand, takes the spotlight. He quotes Luke 2:8-14 verbatim from the King James Bible. At the end, in his sweet little lisp, Linus says, "And that's what Christmas is all about, Charlie Brown."

The simple but brilliant message reflects the heart of Peanuts creator Charles Shultz. One subtle but important element of Linus's big scene goes unnoticed by most of us. At the exact moment when the angel says, "Fear not!", Linus drops his security blanket to the stage floor.

When our daughter and son-in-law named their son Linus, I knew I wanted to give him something significant for his first Christmas. I hunted down a little figurine of Linus van Pelt as he appears on stage for his recitation. When you press a button on the bottom, you hear the story from Luke in Linus's voice. I hope it keeps working until our Linus matures enough to appreciate the full meaning of it.

Are you enjoying freedom from security blankets because God's gift at Christmas taught us that perfect love casts out fear? I hope you'll take some time this season to watch *A Charlie Brown Christmas* with fresh eyes and an open heart. Enjoy the nostalgia. Reflect on Linus's recital. Notice the blanket drop. Read the passage for yourself. And join the children when they sing, "Peace on earth and mercy mild; God and sinners, reconciled."

The Nativity Story
(Appeared December 19, 2019)

Nearly every Christmas Eve, when we return home from the candlelight carol service at church, I pop in our DVD of the 2006 movie, *The Nativity Story*. Like any Hollywood production of a biblical story, this depiction of Christ's birth comes with plenty for critics to hiss at in terms of accuracy. Probably the most glaring is the visit of the wisemen to the stable, arriving at the same time as the shepherds almost immediately after his birth. Historians know the visit came many months later.

It doesn't bother me, because the key elements are all present (including Mary's virginity and the angelic visits.) I love the music and wasn't surprised to learn the score was made into an album and nominated for a Dove award. The way the wisemen are portrayed offers bits of comic relief. The plots of Herod and the Romans' taxation practices give a glimpse into history and the oppression under which the Judeans lived. Elizabeth's delivery of John the Baptist provides realistic insight into what life might have been like. The scenery, the costumes, the animals — all of it works together to bring you much more than your standard Sunday School lesson.

Though I know how it ends, I'm always brought to tears at the tender moment when Mary's baby arrives and the expressions on his parents' faces say it all. Which brings me to what I love best.

Instead of the impossibly sweet and serene Madonna usually portrayed when an actor is brave enough to tackle the role of Mary, we see someone more human. Keisha Castle-Hughes (a New Zealander who was 16 at the time) played Mary as a headstrong, thoughtful adolescent transformed by an unimaginable responsibility. I think she demonstrates a beautiful balance of surrender to God's plan, confident independence and strength of character.

On the arduous journey from Nazareth to Bethlehem, Mary comes to recognize and appreciate Joseph's integrity — and therein lies my second-favourite thing. We know little from the Bible about Joseph, other than that he was a "devout man." This rendition shows several examples of Joseph being generous, kind and considerate. In her positive review of the movie, Ann Hornaday of The Washington Post concluded "… [perhaps] Jesus became Who He was not only because He was the Son of God, but because He was raised by a good man."

The Bible tells us Joseph was a carpenter, and the assumption is Jesus learned this trade from him. My heart has a soft spot for carpenters because my grandfather was one. He always smelled of sawdust — one of the happiest smells I know, because it reminds me of him and because it generally means some sort of progress is in the works.

I wish we knew more about Joseph. Wouldn't he be a huge encouragement to fathers? Think about the self-sacrifice involved in accepting as your own a child you did not father and then giving him all the love, protection, guidance and care you'd give your own. Add the fact that this child was like no other before or since — the son of God himself. A little daunting, wouldn't you say?

Watch the movie if you can. Reflect on the good example set by Joseph. And if you have men of real integrity in your life, men with servants' hearts and courageous spirits, be grateful. Let them know they're appreciated.

Merry Christmas!

New and Glorious Morn
(Appeared January 2, 2020)

It's 6:30 in the morning and we've just said goodbye to our Calgary kids who came for a whirlwind week of Christmas chaos. Toddlers lacking in routine but rich in sugar. Sweet moments of opening gifts, playing with toys, cuddling up to read stories, laughing at their cute expressions. Biting our tongues over temper tantrums and whining and the house turned upside down. They've become reacquainted with cousins, aunts and uncles—and even a great-grandmother the little one had never met. They've been taken to church, to the playground, and around the block.

Now it's time to say goodbye. We squeeze the stuffing out of them and send them on their way, grateful for good travelling weather and praying for safety.

I take my coffee into the living room and sit staring at the tree, only partially lit due to a failed string of lights since some time Christmas Eve. In the stillness, I reflect on our time together. *What just happened here?* I'd entered into it determined not to entertain impossible expectations—or any expectations at all. A group photo would have been nice, since it was our first time together in two years. But I knew better than to bank on it. We managed to collect all thirteen of us under the same roof for only two hours, during which the little ones slept.

I'd asked God to help me adopt a servant's heart, to gladly make each day as good, each meal as tasty, each bed as comfortable, each event as convenient for others as it lay within me to do.

How did I do, God?

He doesn't answer. All I know for sure is I'm exhausted. I drift off for a bit, wondering how to spend this day. Should I kick it into high gear, restore the house to order? Or should I lie around in my pajamas watching Christmas movies, polishing off the eggnog, fudge, and hot apple cider? I could take advantage of the quiet, buckle down at my computer and hammer out some new columns or maybe even the first chapter of a new novel. Or perhaps I should give my sluggish ol' body a head start on 2020 by going for a brisk walk and drinking a gallon of water.

For now, I doze.

When I open my eyes again, the sun—which we have not seen for days—streams through my living room window. It laser-beams its radiance across the top of our mantel, brilliantly illuminating the nativity scene. In his creativity, kindness, and gentleness, God reminds me once again of what all the fuss was about. Or what it was *supposed* to be about.

In the end, I spend the day in moderation. Some laundry and puttering, a bit of writing, a short nap, a little fresh air and healthy food along with the leftover treats. My heart is at peace, because I know that whatever post-holiday feelings I might be sorting, the joys and disappointments, the not nearly enoughs and the much-too-much, God is always sufficient. The goals or dreams or worries I might have for the new year pale in light of the one true gift that is mine every day: God's love, sent to us through a baby in a manger.

Made in the USA
Columbia, SC
22 November 2020